PRAISE FOR *"Mom, everyone else does!"*

"Real issues, true stories, and wise advice by a counselor and mom who's 'been there.' If you have a teenage daughter, RUN and buy *'Mom, Everyone Else Does!'* The mother-daughter questions throughout each chapter are worth the price of the whole book!"

—SUSAN ALEXANDER YATES, author of *And Then I Had Teenagers: Encouragement for Parents of Teens and Preteens*

"My wife and I have been raised by two daughters and one son, and each struggled with the power of peer pressure. For that matter, we do too. The perspective of one's community is a powerful force for good or ill, and this book is an honest and wise walk through the minefield of adolescent temptation. Sharon Hersh is the guide I'd most want to help me name the war and encourage me to live well in the face of the struggle. She has walked the same miles with her own children, and as a brilliant therapist, she has guided others like us with bold love and fierce compassion. If you have daughters or sons, this is wisdom you cannot afford to miss."

—DAN B. ALLENDER PhD, president of Mars Hill Graduate School and author of *The Wounded Heart, Bold Love, How Children Raise Parents,* and *To Be Told*

"Sharon Hersh, a trusted counselor, author, and mother, offers a wise, courageous, and practical guide for connecting and shaping the hearts of mothers and their daughters. If you are a mother of a teenage girl, this book will change you and your relationship."

—SCOTT COUPLAND, associate professor of counseling at Reformed Theological Seminary

"I read everything Sharon Hersh writes. As the director of a large Christian counseling agency, I make her books a standard resource. In *'Mom, Everyone Else Does!'* Hersh dispels the myth of protection that Christian parents cling to and helps us confront the realities of today's addiction-prone world. By speaking to both moms and daughters, Sharon seeks to build a strong relationship in sound, practical ways that work. When it comes to teenage peer pressure, this book will help you become your daughter's strongest ally!"

    —GREGORY L. JANTZ, PHD, certified eating disorder specialist and
      founder of The Center for Counseling & Health Resources, Inc.

"Mom, *everyone else does!*"

a hand-in-hand book

"Mom, *everyone else does!*"

Becoming your daughter's ally in responding
to peer pressure to drink, smoke, and use drugs

sharon a. hersh

SHAW BOOKS
an imprint of WATERBROOK PRESS

"Mom, Everyone Else Does!"
A SHAW BOOK
PUBLISHED BY WATERBROOK PRESS
2375 Telstar Drive, Suite 160
Colorado Springs, Colorado 80920
A division of Random House, Inc.

All Scripture quotations, unless otherwise indicated, are taken from the *Holy Bible, New International Version®*. NIV®. Copyright © 1973, 1978, 1984 by International Bible Society. Used by permission of Zondervan Publishing House. All rights reserved. Scripture quotations marked (BAR) are taken from the *New Testament: A New Translation,* copyright © 1969 by William Barclay. Used by permission. Scripture quotations marked (KJV) are taken from the *King James Version.* Scripture quotations marked (MSG) are taken from *The Message.* Copyright © 1993, 1994, 1995, 1996, 2000, 2001, 2002. Used by permission of NavPress Publishing Group.

Names and details in some anecdotes and stories have been changed to protect the identities of the persons involved.

ISBN 0-87788-025-5

Library of Congress Cataloging-in-Publication Data
Hersh, Sharon A.
    Mom, everyone else does! : becoming your daughter's ally in responding to peer pressure to drink, smoke, and use drugs / Sharon A. Hersh.—1st ed.
        p. cm.
    Includes bibliographical references.
    ISBN 0-87788-025-5 (alk. paper)
    1. Teenage girls—Family relationships. 2. Mothers and daughters. 3. Teenage girls—Health and hygiene. 4. Teenage girls—Conduct of life. 5. Communication in the family. I. Title.
HQ798.H48 2005
248.8'629—dc22   2004026883

Printed in Canada
2005—First Edition

10 9 8 7 6 5 4 3 2 1

To Graham—My son, my hero

CONTENTS

FOREWORD

Why didn't this child come with an instruction manual? Just give us the directions and we'll follow them, and we'll get the desired results—unless something goes wrong. But then there should be a trouble-shooting section, too… As the mothers of daughters, how many of us haven't had these sentiments?

Sharon Hersh doesn't give us that longed-for operating manual in this book. She gives us something better: a guide to working hand-in-hand with God to create our own instruction manual—the only one that will work with *our* daughters, each one unique and precious and mystifying (and did I mention infuriating?). We are the *only* ones equipped to take the basics that Hersh, a mother and therapist, gives us and then build on them in the *only* way that will "work" with our one-of-a-kind girls.

For those of us who would prefer a ready-made plan, a checklist, and a certificate of successful completion when our daughters turn twenty-one, the thought of making up our own rules *could* start us quaking in our pumps. And it probably would, if Sharon Hersh were not who she is, and hadn't been where she's been, and was not willing to share it all. There is no "This is how I've done it, ladies. Now watch, and learn." No "Okay, you've really fouled this up, and you'd better get with it before society swallows up your kid completely." And definitely no "Get tough, take control, and show that young'un who's boss!" Hersh does none of that in this book, because that is not who she is. Who she is informs and infuses a far more healing guide—healing for us as well as for our daughters.

Sharon Hersh's professional experience has taught her that the effects that alcohol, illegal drugs, and tobacco products have on adolescent girls are specific to their gender, as are their emotional, mental, and spiritual responses to just about everything (or hadn't you noticed?!). Her life's work has been centered on mothers and daughters, and the result is a deep knowledge that there is no one-size-fits-all model for parenting or dealing with substance abuse. (Oh, that we could all take our girl-children to *her* office!) The Just Say No campaign was only the beginning of awareness. Hersh's work in the field takes us far deeper—into the thoroughly feminine world where the need to belong and to be loved outcries the "no" we tell our young women they should "just say." The good news is that as mothers of daughters, we *have* that female expertise, that woman's touch, as we confront the statistics and the harsh realities we and our daughters must face.

Coupled with the author's vast knowledge and keen understanding is her honesty. I know how many times in the raising of my now twenty-five-year-old daughter, I shriveled like a raisin when "learned" women and "successful" mothers treated me to stories from their bottomless reserve of maternal wisdom. I felt as though I either ought to turn Marijean directly over to them and allow them to finish the parenting I had obviously botched from the delivery room on, or smack those Super Moms soundly on the mouth just for being so perfect. There is none of that condescension in the pages of *"Mom, Everyone Else Does!"* Sharon Hersh reveals the personal struggles that have taken place not only with her children but within herself. With courageous transparency she takes us into her world, where the professional training and the countless hours of research and one-on-one experience with girls and moms were stripped away, leaving only the pain and the fear and the heartbreak of kids in trouble—of herself in trouble. She writes vividly of mothering styles that aren't effective and shows us how to mother according to our personalities and those of our daughters. She speaks from hard-won experience, having made the mistakes and learned from them.

With her professional expertise and her agonizing personal experience firmly at the foundation of everything she writes, Hersh provides the two elements that are essential in dealing with the "Everyone else does!" cry. Those elements are the practical and the spiritual—the concrete as well as the power of God that passes understanding. We must have the answers to both kinds of questions: *What does God say?* and *What does that look like in this particular situation?* Because the cry of teenage girls is no longer, "Everyone else wears their hair hanging down over their eyebrows!" or "Everyone else's mom lets them stay out past eleven!" Now it's "Everyone else gets high at lunchtime!" "Everyone else parties all weekend!" and "Everyone else is smashing their hopes drink by drink and puff by puff!"

When we're anguished over the sound of our daughter's sobs or the piercing shout of "I hate you!" when we're terrified by the sight of our daughter's bloodshot eyes and flattened emotions and abandoned dreams, we want to know *what to do*—and yet we're not sure we *can* do it, whatever it is. Sharon Hersh stretches out her hand—one scarred and strong from the journey—and says, "Come on. I'll show you how to get to God. I'll show you how to get to yourself. And then you'll know how to get to your daughter, whatever that looks like."

Fellow moms, you are about to experience some peace in the midst of your pain and fear as you read this book. You will find out that you're facing responsibility, not blame, and that you are equipped to recognize what that responsibility is and handle it very effectively. All the things that impede you in your relationship with your daughter will be kicked to the curb as you read. You are going to find out how to go beyond your normal reaction to an abnormal situation and into true wisdom, which, let's face it, is not "normal" in the world our daughters move in. You will be empowered as you discover the influence you *do* have on your daughter and find out what you're doing right and what you can change. Have faith that you can do as Jesus does—not simply saying, "You're bad!" but finding out what is at the root of that "badness" and helping it heal.

I love the way Sharon Hersh uses the word *ally*. She encourages each of us to be the person who unites with our woman-child for the purpose of finding a rich, God-filled, hope-drenched life. I wonder if Sharon realizes that she is our ally in that same way. She comes alongside *us* just as she is teaching us to walk hand-in-hand with our girls. If you take her up on her offer, hang on, because what you are going to learn from her book will not only change your daughter's life, it will change yours.

—NANCY RUE

ACKNOWLEDGMENTS

With heartfelt gratitude to:

Kristin and Graham—Thank you for giving me access to your lives. For being honest about your struggles. For learning from my mistakes. For charting a course to be wholly who God created you to be.

My parents, John and Kathleen Baker—Thank you for modeling how to love a prodigal, how to wait for a prodigal, and how to welcome a prodigal home.

Josie and Joan—mothers of fierce compassion, bold courage, and unconditional love.

My editor, Traci Mullins—You are, by far, the best at developing a manuscript. But I also know you to be relentless in developing a life of recovery and service to others.

Don Pape and all the supportive staff at WaterBrook Press and Shaw Books—Your commitment to teenagers and their parents is a shining light in an often dark and stormy world.

Every Mother's Battle

The truth is, raising teenagers is neither as simple nor as complex as the threat-mongers make it seem. You can do everything "right" with your child and have him grow up terribly wrong. You can make terrible mistakes with your child and have her grow up just right. Not every kid who smokes pot will suffer lifelong addiction. Not every kid who seems to be able to drink "responsibly" can. It's up to parents to know the difference, to know when there's a problem—even when everyone else says there isn't, even when everyone else says there is. It's up to us to find solutions when solutions are what's needed.

—MEREDITH MARAN, *Dirty*

Smoking. Drinking. Drugs. No other aspects of teenage culture are more threatening to parents. When our daughters inevitably act out "typical teen" problems and behaviors such as skipping school, using profanity, or shirking chores and family responsibilities, we sigh, "Well, at least it wasn't drugs." When we hear of some other poor family with an out-of-control teenager, we shake our heads and conclude, "They'd better send her away to some place that can get her head screwed on right." When the problem of drinking or drug use hits home, we may respond in paralyzing shame, "Don't tell anyone about this."

The irony of teenagers and substance use is this: We fear this problem more than almost any other, and we feel less equipped to help our daughters with it than with any other. And yet we blame ourselves for this problem more than we do for any other adolescent struggle. What a setup for disconnection from our daughters as well as for debilitating contempt for ourselves!

When my now college-age daughter, Kristin, was a freshman in high school, I came face to face during the first week of school with the epidemic drug and alcohol problem among teenagers. Kristin told me about a "party" for the new cheerleaders at one of the girls' homes. I envisioned popcorn, pizza, and Cokes as the fare for the evening as these pimply-faced new high schoolers launched their adolescence. I have since learned that a "party" for teenagers almost always means alcohol, and sometimes drugs, and seldom means a gathering hosted by someone's parents. When I dropped Kristin off at 7:00 p.m., she was one of a few girls at the party. The evening ahead still appeared fun and harmless to me. But when I picked up Kristin at 10:00 p.m., I knew immediately that this evening had not been about making memories and eating pizza.

After I rang the doorbell, Kristin came to the door looking like a deer caught in the headlights. The house was in total chaos, and I smelled alcohol. I saw no parents. When Kristin got into the car, my voice became shrill as I asked accusatorily, "So, how was the party?" I immediately blamed Kristin for this out-of-control teenage world.

She answered quietly, "It was a little different than I thought it would be."

I immediately shot back, "I smelled the beer. What were you thinking? Why didn't you call me? You had no business being in that house, and you know it!"

Once again Kristin answered quietly, "I'm sorry, Mom."

I didn't know what she was thinking, and I really didn't care. I was terri-fied. If my daughter's first high-school party was a "beer bash," then what was ahead? Kristin and I approached—or avoided—each other warily all week-end. I was thinking about her carelessness and the perils of high school. I didn't know it, but she was thinking about her overwhelming task of navigat-ing a world splashed with booze and immersed in substance use.

First thing Monday morning, I called a family counselor. I was thrashing around blindly in fear's dark dungeon, envisioning days ahead of eavesdrop-ping on my daughter's conversations, searching her purse and backpack, and keeping her away from her partying classmates. When Kristin and I met with the counselor and I told him about the weekend's events, he asked a question that poured more fuel on my fear but allowed my daughter to breathe a sigh of relief. "Sharon, do you think you're going to be able to keep Kristin away from drugs and alcohol?"

I immediately answered, "Yes." I was an informed and persistent parent. I could keep this threatening foe at bay.

He looked at Kristin when he said, "Then you'll need to take her out of school. Alcohol and drugs are everywhere—even in the classroom." Kristin was nodding her head. A tear trickled down her cheek.

All of a sudden I knew that this was an opponent much bigger than I was. I didn't know the statistics yet, didn't have a heart full of stories of teenagers caught in the grip of drugs and alcohol abuse, but somehow I knew at the core of my mother's heart that substance use and abuse was a powerful reality in my daughter's world, whether or not I was ready to face it. My daughter didn't need to say it, and the counselor didn't say it in so many words, but I knew the answer to his question about whether I thought I could prevent Kristin from being exposed to the dangers of smoking, drinking, and drugs: "Of course not." As I considered that my daughter might or might not refrain from experimenting with and abusing substances in her adolescent and early-adult years, I had to face the fact that Kristin was now living daily in a world where "everyone else does." Or so it seemed to her—as it does to most every teenager in twenty-first-century America.

Statistics and stories alike confirm that today's girls are growing up in a world in which it seems as though *everyone* is using some type of substance. The statistics are sobering. If you were to stand in the hallways of your daughter's high school and look at the teenagers clad in today's fashions yelling to one another about the game on Friday night or the assignment in algebra, you would see teens with substance-abuse problems. The reality is that one in every four of those teenagers has a problem with substance abuse.[1] Further statistics reveal what happens along the way as teenagers experiment with and become dependent upon drugs and alcohol. According to a compilation of statistics from researchers Katherine Ketcham and Nicholas A. Pace,[2]

- Four out of every five girls in your daughter's high school will use or try some type of drug or alcohol this weekend. If you drive over to the middle school, the statistics are equally alarming: Three out of every

five girls ages twelve to fourteen will use or try some type of substance
this weekend!

- Five percent of all deaths of kids between the ages of fifteen and
  twenty-nine are attributable to alcohol.
- Eighty percent of young women in high school reported having at
  least one drink. Fifty percent reported current alcohol use. By the time
  these young women are high-school seniors, 33 percent will be heavy
  drinkers. (Heavy drinking is defined by the *Diagnostic and Statistical
  Manual of Mental Disorders* as having four or more alcoholic drinks
  per day.)
- Teens who drink are *seven times* more likely to have sex and twice as
  likely to have sex with four or more partners.
- Almost 50 percent of adolescent victims of crime said they were drinking and/or using a substance at the time they were victimized.

Even if your daughter is not using drugs or alcohol, she is still affected by
substance use because her culture is permeated with it. This book will help
you understand your daughter's world and will educate you about the realities of substance use among adolescent girls. If your daughter has ever come
home with beer on her breath, or if her eyes sometimes look a little "funny,"
this book will help you recognize symptoms of possible substance use or
abuse. And if your daughter has already plunged deeply into alcohol or drug
abuse, this book will give you hope that you can still enter her world and
powerfully influence her—even if she is under the influence of a destructive,
mood-altering substance.

I hope this book not only shatters naiveté about this subject but also
diminishes the fear and shame parents often feel when their children smoke,
drink, or use drugs. The most important question for you to ask is not "What
did I do wrong?" but "How can I help?" I fear that many well-meaning parents, especially Christian parents, often hide the truth from themselves and
each other that their children are not immune from the overwhelming pressure to "Take a few sips," "Smoke a few puffs," or "Try a little of this." This book
will educate you about the battle and will offer encouragement that although
it is a battle none of us can avoid, it is one in which all of us can have a positive influence.

This book will tell you the truth about teenagers and substance use, but it contains good news as well: You *can* face the truth about your daughter's world and the peer pressure she feels to drink, smoke, and use drugs, and you *can* connect with your daughter to become her ally in helping her resist negative peer pressure while developing her own positive identity. You can even develop a new identity of your own as well—that of a savvy, strong, compassionate mother-guide able to effectively help your daughter in the midst of this overwhelming battle. The kind of mothering needed to help your daughter stand up to substance use and abuse is *hand-in-hand mothering,* a willingness to learn as many ways as you can of responding to your daughter out of a heart filled with limitless love for her.

- When your daughter asks to go to a party on Friday night, you are the ally she needs.
- When your daughter sneaks a few beers up to her bedroom, you are the ally she needs.
- When you find cigarettes in your daughter's purse, and she answers your questions with a shrug, "Mom, *everyone* smokes. It's no big deal," you are the ally she needs.
- When the principal calls to report that your daughter is "high" at school, you are the ally she needs.
- When your daughter returns from a movie, and her slurred speech tips you off that she probably wasn't where she said she was, you are the ally she needs.

Becoming allies. It sounds good, doesn't it? It is invigorating to discover that amid the statistics and stories of teenage substance use and abuse, you can become your daughter's ally. An ally is one who knows the enemy, understands the battle, and is always ready to lend a hand.

As you educate yourself about adolescent drinking, tobacco use, and drug use, equip yourself with strategies for helping your daughter. Encourage your daughter—and yourself—that you can be women of resolve and resilience, strength and vision. In the midst of the battle, you will have the opportunity to experience the reality of the biblical promise: "Two are better than one, because they have a good return for their work" (Ecclesiastes 4:9).

Alcohol and drugs may be a powerful presence in a teenager's world, but parents can be a powerful presence as well. In the chapters that follow, we will look at four areas that will help you build a framework for becoming your daughter's ally. First, we will examine mothering styles and consider options for developing a powerfully positive presence that your daughter cannot deny in the midst of overwhelming temptation and confusion. To do this, you need to understand your own fears and beliefs about alcohol and drug use. Second, we will look with unflinching honesty at your daughter's world—the temptations she faces, the consequences she experiences when she makes bad or foolish choices, and the ways in which you can connect with her when everything in her world is pressuring her to disconnect from you. Third, we'll look at practical ways to establish, or reestablish, connection as we answer some tough teenage questions, such as "What's the big deal about smoking?" or "Mom, did you ever drink or use drugs?" Finally, we'll look at the realities of overly influential and destructive peers and teen substance addiction, and we'll explore treatment options for teens who have developed addictions. Teenagers who are using drugs and alcohol inevitably induce panic in their parents. But this panic can actually become a gift because it shows us—and our daughters—how much we care, and it compels us to take positive and effective action. This book will help guide you through some of the difficult decisions you will be faced with if your child develops a problem with cigarettes, alcohol, or drugs.

Included throughout this book are interactive sections titled Just for You and Just for the Two of You. These sections contain questions, ideas, and exercises that can help you and your daughter formulate your own core values regarding substance use as well as strengthen your relationship with each other. You will gain insight into your particular mothering style and learn what is and is not effective in helping your daughter as she faces the inevitable peer pressure to drink, use drugs, and smoke. As you become equipped to be an effective ally for your daughter, you will learn to *use* the very challenges your daughter faces to influence her personally and spiritually.

I realize that sounds like a lofty promise. But my sincere hope and passion for your daughter—and mine—is that in the midst of countless opportunities to experiment with substances, she will not only "just say no," but she will also be equipped to respond to negative peer pressure in ways that are in keeping with her developing sense of personal integrity. She will know who she is and have a vision for her continuing development as a young woman of strength, compassion, courage, and core values.

Once your daughter enters the teenage world, the drug war comes home—whether or not you're ready. If your daughter is still a preteen, you would be wise to take time now to educate and prepare yourself. If she is already a teenager, remember that it's never too late to become informed. Even if your teenage daughter doesn't experiment with or use alcohol or drugs herself, she *will* be impacted by a world that laughs at getting high and considers weekend parties a convenient opportunity to get drunk. I learned very early on during my daughter's high-school years that the temptations she faced to use drugs and alcohol were bigger than I was and were out of my control. But I also learned that these temptations were opportunities to connect with my daughter with wisdom and compassion as well as invitations to me to surrender to the One who is bigger than anything we may face.

I left the counselor's office that day holding on to the words of the apostle John, "For the Spirit in you is far stronger than anything in the world" (1 John 4:4, MSG). I wondered how that Spirit manifests Himself during beer "keggers" and among all the paraphernalia of drug and alcohol use. I came home and picked up my Bible. The pages literally fell open to the answer: "Greater love has no one than this, that he lay down his life for his friends" (John 15:13). This book is my answer to how we can lay down our lives for our daughters and love them with a love more powerful than anything their world has to offer.

Part 1

Understanding Your Worlds

Our kids' teen years constitute the most-feared period of a parent's life. From the time they're babies, we're warned about the horrors to come. "Just you wait," we're told. As if our new-parent culture shock and suddenly sleepless nights are nothing compared to What Will Come.

We fear adolescence for a lot of reasons. We worry about our kids' safety. We don't want to lose control. We don't want our kids to experience pain—and we remember too much pain from those years in our own lives. We're warned that the parent-teen relationship, for its part, is intrinsically adversarial. Our kids will be raging wild against us and hating everything about us down to the way we brush our teeth. They'll be making life choices so far from anything we ever would have chosen for them that we'll be hating them, too.

It's true our kids will not be us. But the real and lived separation of our worlds, it turns out, is far from anything that…conventional wisdom ever taught us. Teenage kids are complex, fragile, feisty. The life phase they're going through is full of optimism, curiosity, tribulation, and unexpected twists. Becoming the parent of a teenager is just as myth-shattering, mind-blowing, heartbreaking, and awesome as becoming a parent in the first place.…

This is a trip that is worthwhile. Through the stereotypes and fears. Through the grief and magic. Into adolescence. But this time, as a parent. As a mother. Into her world. And back to my own.

—ARIEL GORE, *Whatever, Mom*

Chapter 1

A Call to Courage

And look at what she was doing to my image as a mother. It's not that I thought I would win a perfect mother award, but I had done all the right things in raising her, and now she was single-handedly taking my name out of the running. If she was doing drugs, what was that saying to all my friends about my parenting skills? We became like two pieces on a chessboard, moving warily around each other. What she wore, where she went, who her friends were all became bloody battlefields. But we were both losing. I was afraid I couldn't trust her, so I didn't. She certainly didn't trust me, and she avoided me at all costs.

—NICOLE JOHNSON, *Raising the Sail*

M om, please don't be mad at me." I heard Kristin's panicked whisper when I answered my cell phone. I was eating dinner at a friend's house. Kristin and her neighborhood girlfriend were having a "few friends" over to both of their homes for an informal house-to-house party. The plan was for the group to gather at our neighbor's home for dinner and then migrate over to our home for the rest of the evening. I planned to be home from my dinner engagement in time to pop the popcorn and help the gang settle in to watch a few movies.

"What's wrong? I'll be home in a few minutes. I'm just finishing dessert."

"Mom, there are a lot of kids here. I don't even know some of them, and the house is kind of a mess. I promise I'll clean it up. I don't know how things got so out of control. *Please* don't be mad," Kristin pleaded.

Being a conscientious, concerned parent, I first thought of...*my house!* "Did someone spill on the carpet?" My voice became shrill. "Are there kids in my bedroom?"

I knew this involved more than a case of potato chips ground into the carpet and Coke spilled on the love seat when Kristin replied, "Mom, just hurry!"

I quickly excused myself from my friend's lovely dinner. I didn't know exactly what to say. *I gave my daughter permission to have an unsupervised party, and my home has turned into* Animal House? I couldn't say that. After all, I write books on parenting. This couldn't be happening to me, in *my* home.

"I need to get home." I offered a lame and false excuse. "Kristin needs my help working the DVD player."

As I drove home I really didn't know what to expect. Kristin was in the ninth grade—that transition year between the pimples and orthodontia of middle school and the increasing independence of high school, driver's license and all. She occasionally attended parties, but I was pretty sure she never drank or used drugs, and she expressed a lot of anger at and concern for friends who did. I trusted Kristin, and yet as I watched the kids file out of her high school, lighting cigarettes as soon as they reached the parking lot, I wondered how she would withstand the peer pressure to smoke, drink, or use drugs.

I remembered a Friday night a few weeks earlier when Kristin had come home from a party at a friend's home and seemed distant. She wouldn't look me in the eyes and said she was too tired to talk. Had I missed something? Would I know if Kristin was using drugs? I knew Kristin had a lot of friends who "partied." I'd smelled cigarette smoke on Kristin's friends' clothes more than once. Kristin had received telephone calls in the middle of the night from drunk friends, and she had confided in me pretty openly about some of the scenarios of high-school social life. Was I naive to think that Kristin was so different from her friends?

On that short drive home, I went from fully trusting my fourteen-year-old daughter to carefully planning how I would take her to a drug treatment facility first thing the following morning. I was incredulous that Kristin—my strong, wonderful daughter—could have let this happen, and I was feeling the grip of shame. How could *I* have let this happen? When Kristin asked to have a group of friends over to our home, I trusted my daughter. But I underestimated the power of her peers and was naive about the powerful influence teenagers have on one another.

In adolescent sociology, there is a word for what happened at our home: *herding.* "Herding" is a phenomenon that evolves as groups of teenagers look for a place to hang out, an unsupervised haven. One kid got the word that Kristin was having a party and alerted another kid, and before we knew it, our house was filled with a herd of miscellaneous kids.

When I drove into our neighborhood, I could not believe the scene before me. The streets were lined with unfamiliar cars, and groups of kids were gathered in tight circles in front of my neighbors' houses. Most of the kids were smoking. Kristin had sounded the alarm, "My mom is on her way home," and the herd had moved out into the streets. I saw a few empty cans of Keystone beer discarded along my neighbor's driveway. (I later learned that the presence of Keystone—one of the cheaper brands of beer—is almost always a tip-off to teenage mischief.) I knew my respectable, elderly neighbor would not have carelessly thrown the empties out into his yard.

When I walked into my home, I felt a bit disoriented. The furniture was out of place, and the rooms were littered with candy wrappers, pop cans, and other trash. Kristin looked as if she was on the verge of tears. "Mom, I'm so sorry!" I sank into the sofa only to discover a bag of partially eaten McDonald's burgers crammed under the pillow. Then I noticed a large area of discoloration in the middle of my round, cherry-wood coffee table. I tried to wipe it off. "What's this?" I asked. "The table is stained or something."

"Mom, I'm so sorry. Travis spilled his flask on the table, and I guess the alcohol did that," Kristin explained.

My head was spinning. *Flask.* Who had been in my home? I pictured middle-aged men swilling a drink from their sterling silver flasks as they played a hand of poker. *Flask.* Teenage boys and girls had been in my home drinking from *flasks* while they ate their McDonald's cheeseburgers and listened to pop music?

Suddenly I knew what that smell was that had assaulted me when I walked in the front door. I went into the kitchen and sniffed as I opened cupboards and looked under the sink. "Where's the beer? I can smell it," I snapped at my daughter.

"I tried to clean it up," Kristin answered. "When I told everyone you were coming home, a few kids knocked over their beers trying to get out of here."

My feet were sticking to the floor as I wandered through the kitchen, sniffing the odor of cheap beer and imagining teenagers sitting around my kitchen table playing drinking games. The collage of sights, smells, and images mobilized me. I walked outside and starting marching up and down the street. One look at me, and the "herd" disbanded. I prayed that everyone would get home safely and be "found out" by observant parents. I also prayed that the kids wouldn't say they had been at my house.

Kristin and I picked up the Keystone cans and cigarette butts from our neighbors' driveways and headed into our house. We filled trash cans, mopped floors, and sprayed Lysol, hoping to cover the foul odors of the night. Finally, we sat down to debrief.

"Kristin, what happened tonight?"

"Mom, I'm not sure. This is what kids do. This happens *all the time.* I thought I could control it."

"Well, if this is what happens all the time, you're not going out again or having anyone over. No more parties!" I was putting my foot down. I might have been naive before this night, but I had a permanent mark on my coffee table to remind me that teenagers don't pop popcorn and watch movies anymore.

Kristin looked me right in the eyes, and with tears streaming down her face, she said, "Mom, if you want me to stay away from drugs and drinking, then I can't go anywhere—not even to school. It's what everyone does—all the time."

It was taking me some time, but Kristin's out-of-the-chute experiences with the realities of her high-school adolescent culture were revealing to me that my strong, Christian daughter was not going to be immune from the presence and pressures of drugs, alcohol, and cigarettes.

WHEN THE WAR ON DRUGS HITS HOME

I went to bed that night with snapshots of my daughter's sweet friends flashing through my mind. Abby holding a Keystone beer. Travis sipping from a silver flask, acne sprinkled across his chin. Dana, Whitney, Joel, and Darius sitting around my kitchen table drinking beer while glancing at a plaque of the Lord's Prayer on the wall in front of them. And then even more frightening images came to mind of boys and girls I didn't know drinking, possibly smoking pot, and making out in the upstairs bedrooms.

My heart filled with fear at the thought of a world in which my teenage children and their friends lived already soaked with booze and permeated with mind-altering experiences. As I learned the statistics, I was shocked to discover that 50 percent of high-school girls use alcohol, and by the time these young women are seniors, 33 percent will be heavy drinkers.[1] In fact, a three-year study underwritten by Bristol-Myers Squibb found that "despite recent declines in overall youth substance abuse, more than a quarter of high-school girls smoke or binge drink, and a fifth of them use marijuana."[2] But the statistics on substance use in the adolescent world were leading me to an even scarier conclusion: Not only does one in every four teenagers use drugs or alcohol but girls may actually be using substances more frequently and in greater quantities than boys.[3]

I had heard the stories in my counseling office—from a fourteen-year-old girl who drank a six-pack and had sex with a boy she didn't even know; a girl who started smoking pot at lunchtime every day during her freshman year of high school and was flunking most of her classes; and a seventeen-year-old

JUST FOR YOU

1. How have you viewed the war on drugs? Have you seen it as something that happens in other cities or in "society" or in other families? or as something that would destroy you if it came into your home?

2. If you believe that drugs and alcohol affect *other* people's kids, how does this belief shape your attitudes about their effect on you and your daughter?

3. If you believe that drugs and alcohol would threaten you and your family if your daughter started abusing them, what impact does that belief have on you and your parenting?

4. What is your immediate reaction to the statement "Everyone does it"?

5. List any personality traits and personal experiences that might increase your effectiveness in helping your daughter deal with the pressure to use drugs and alcohol.

girl who'd been smoking cigarettes since she was fourteen and wanted to stop. I also knew that, according to researchers, girls' substance use can descend into abuse more quickly than it can for boys, and in many cases, the health consequences are more severe for girls.[4]

But suddenly all the statistics and stories came home—literally. I realized that even if Kristin did not smoke, drink, or use drugs, many of her friends did, and she was often directly impacted by their substance use. Even if she "just said no" for now, she was still at risk. My naiveté was quickly evaporating. If Kristin was already being pressured to smoke, drink, and use drugs at fourteen, how could she resist for the next four or five years? That night the war on drugs became much more personal for me.

EVERYONE IS DOING IT

The number one health problem in America is substance abuse. It causes more death and illness than any other preventable condition. Four times as many women die from addiction-related illness as die from breast cancer.[5] Children who start to drink or use drugs before the age of fifteen are *four times* more likely to become addicted than those who start after age twenty-one.[6] All of a sudden, in the aftermath of what I had expected to be a harmless get-together of Kristin's friends, the girls represented in these statistics had faces.

Binge drinking, huffing (inhaling vapors from a rag soaked in hairspray, gasoline, or paint thinner), weed, cocaine—certainly these are subjects for drug-education experts. Aren't they? We mothers are willing to attend PTA meetings, bake cookies, and help our daughters with their science projects, but we hope to avoid the world of drinking and drugging—especially when it comes to our little girls. And that's part of the problem.

Girls today are using drugs and alcohol in record numbers. Again, researchers are not sure why, despite all the drug-education and prevention efforts, *girls* appear to be using substances more frequently and in greater quantities than boys. One theory is that girls have complied with the push for "girl power" over the past fifteen years by enrolling not only in more math and science classes but also in high-risk behaviors. One thing is certain: Help for girls who abuse substances is to be found among women who understand the unique female vulnerability to drugs and alcohol and who live authentically powerful lives that model how to say no to the overwhelming peer pressure teens face. A report from the National Center on Addiction and Substance Abuse at Columbia University suggests that prevention and treatment "tailored to the needs of girls" is essential to reducing substance abuse. This study suggests that treatment directed specifically to girls might save "1.1 million women from becoming alcoholics, 500,000 from drug abuse, and 8 million from smoking"![7] What better woman to lead the charge than *you*, her mother, who knows your daughter and her needs and can guide her through the overwhelming peer pressure.

WALKING HAND IN HAND WITH YOUR DAUGHTER

I mean it when I say that this book started close to home. It actually started before my daughter's party-gone-awry. It started with my own substance-abuse problem. I am a recovering alcoholic. I know firsthand the danger of substance use and the ensuing damage. In this book we will look at the origins of addiction—when the occasional substance use becomes abuse and eventually obsession. But don't think that because I am intimately acquainted with this subject, I felt qualified to take on this battle in my daughter's world. There have been many times when I wanted to either hide under the covers or hand my daughter over to an "expert" and come back and get her when she was all fixed.

In fact, that drive home to my daughter's party-gone-wild was a moment of truth for me. At that moment, I knew I needed to decide that I was going to mother with my eyes wide open. I needed to arm myself with every available resource to help my daughter and develop a mothering strategy that would give me a place of influence in my daughter's life in the midst of all the other overwhelming influences that surrounded her. Many times I have had to remind myself that God gave Kristin to *me*, not to drug-abuse prevention experts. He also entrusted your daughter to you, intending that you guide her through the inevitable struggles of adolescence.

We will look at some scary subjects in the pages that follow, but my hope is that you will experience "moments of truth" as you learn to respond in ways that will enable you to become your daughter's ally in saying no to negative

peer pressure and yes to developing her own positive identity. I suspect that
you picked up this book because something is going on with your teenager,
and you want to know or feel compelled to know about these subjects. You
might not feel very brave, but you are already acting courageously.

Sometimes we need "hard evidence" to shake us from denial. Look at a
recent picture of your daughter and think about any evidence you've gathered
(like the stain on my coffee table) that indicates she is already confronting
peer pressure to drink, smoke, or use drugs. Maybe you found a pack of cigarettes in her purse. Or you're staring at a drinking ticket she got from the
police while attending a party. Or her report card reflects that something is
going on.

You have all the evidence you need to convince you that your daughter
could get caught up in a life-and-death battle that will put her at risk, erode
her self-confidence, take away her choices, and mark her world with sights
and sounds that she should not have to experience. You are the one to take
her hand and prayerfully and hopefully walk forward. I love the words of the
old jazz pianist Hazel Scott: "Who ever walked behind anyone to freedom? If
we can't go hand in hand, I don't want to go."

And as you walk hand in hand with your daughter, know that there is
Another who takes *your* hand and walks beside you. Before entering an overwhelming battle, the great Old Testament warrior Joshua spoke the following
words as a reminder to himself and his tattered and teetering people:
"Strength! Courage! Don't be timid; don't get discouraged. GOD, your God,
is with you every step you take" (Joshua 1:9, MSG).

Now is the time for you to begin interacting courageously with your
daughter. One of the best bits of advice I've received over the years came from
a dear older woman in my church. During a time of prayer, she must have
sensed my fear and "overwhelm-ment" in the midst of parenting teenagers.
She whispered to me, "If you don't feel courageous, be determined. In the
end, they look the same." Even if you're feeling a little shaky as you try to deal
with your daughter's substance-use issues, be determined to keep your eyes
open, your heart tender, and your purposes clear.

One of my most prized possessions is a postcard from my daughter that I
keep on my desk. After her party-gone-awry we had a long talk, and I told
her that we would have to trust each other, learn together, and begin to for-

mulate a plan for her to live well in the midst of the inevitable challenges and temptations of substance abuse. On Monday morning I found the postcard on my desk. On the front of the card in bold letters on a lime green background was the word *begin.* On the back of the card, Kristin thanked me for being in her life, for not freaking out, and for believing in her.

To this day, when I am feeling overwhelmed and afraid, I heed this postcard's advice. Take it from me. Just *begin.*

JUST FOR THE TWO OF YOU

The following questions will help you begin to enter your daughter's world and get a sense of what would convey to her that you are a powerful presence in her life. Tell your daughter that you will listen to her responses with an open mind and that you won't use anything she discloses against her. If you have blown it in this regard in the past—we mothers are experts at begging our daughters to tell us things and then turning around and hitting them over the head with their disclosures—ask her to risk trusting the "new you," who wants to be present in her world in a compassionate and confident way.

1. Do you think "everyone" in your world is using drugs and alcohol? What tells you this is the case?
2. How do everyone else's choices affect you?
3. Have you ever been with one of your friends when she or he was drunk or high? How did it make you feel?
4. What do you think I believe about drug, alcohol, and tobacco use?
5. What are you most afraid of in my response to this reality in your world?
6. What kind of response do you want most from me?

Chapter 2

Becoming Your Daughter's Ally

*"Moses! Moses!"... God said,..."Remove your sandals from your feet.
You're standing on holy ground."...*

*GOD said, "I've taken a good, long look at the affliction of my
people.... I've heard their cries for deliverance...; I know all about their
pain.... I'm sending you...to bring my people...out of Egypt."*

*Moses answered God, "But why me? What makes you think that I
could ever [do this]?... They won't trust me. They won't listen to a word I
say.... I don't talk well. I've never been good with words.... I stutter and
stammer.... Oh...please! Send somebody else!"*

—EXODUS 3:4,5,7,10,11; 4:1,10,13, *The Message*

Mothers understand Moses's fears, excuses, and doubts. When our daughters are afflicted by the ever-present temptations to drink, smoke, and use drugs, we're not sure we are the ones to help them make different choices. When our little girl stumbles in from a Friday night with friends with beer on her breath and disequilibrium in her eyes, our thoughts go to finding an expert to "save" her or to locking her in her room until she turns twenty-one. We watch the commercials that proclaim that parents are the "antidrug" and suggest that if we just talk to our kids, they'll steer clear of drugs and alcohol. But in our hearts we fear that we don't know the magic words these commercials suggest will automatically come forth when we talk to our daughters about these tricky topics. Like Moses, we stutter and stammer.

The Office of National Drug Control Policy knows about our fears and failures. It reported in 2000 that despite the fact that federal spending on the drug war is increasing every year, the number of students experimenting with and using drugs is also increasing every year. The report goes on to say that "one of the behavioral issues facing many parents with adolescents today is the high rate of drug and alcohol experimentation. Parents tend to avoid this behavioral and health issue *more than any other* when it comes to their teenagers" (emphasis added).[1]

IN THE TRENCHES

Janet was a mom in the trenches of the drug war. She had experienced reluctant but rapid induction into the world of teenagers and substance use when she discovered that her daughter, Alex, was regularly smoking marijuana and drinking. Janet learned about weed and dealers, bongs and nickel bags, forty-ounce bottles of beer, and Saturday-morning hangovers. She also learned about the apathy and steady overall decline of substance abusers as she watched her daughter's grades fall and her interests flatten.

"How do *I* help her?" Janet asked me after learning her daughter had received a ticket for being a "minor in possession (of alcohol)" at a weekend party. "I can ground her. I can lecture her. I can pretend this isn't happening. I can cry, rant, and rave. Believe me, I've even thought about running away myself. But I can't help her. I don't know how."

Janet didn't know it, but she had just outlined the mothering roles we are most comfortable with. Depending on our personality types and the models of mothering we've observed and experienced, we tend to fall into predictable styles of mothering, especially when the going gets tough. We do what we've always done, what our mothers did, or what we think the mothers around us are doing. The problem is that our daughters' substance use is out-of-the-ordinary behavior. We are right to be shocked when our daughters are drunk, our middle-school girls smoke pot, or our sweet children begin smoking cigarettes and reek of tobacco. Our daughters' out-of-the-ordinary behavior is a plea for out-of-the-ordinary mothering. Lectures won't work. Crying will not solve this problem. Denial could be deadly. And detaching ourselves from our daughters will sever them from a lifeline when they need us most.

In this chapter we are going to look at four different styles of mothering. These styles are simply *postures* in parenting. Posture is what makes certain activities possible. When I stand, I can walk or run. When I sit, I can lean back or relax. When I lie down, I can rest or sleep. Likewise, the "posture" you take in response to your daughter's substance use or experimentation has specific results for both of you. There is no one right posture in parenting. However, your posture during the trials and tests of adolescence determines whether you become your daughter's sergeant, victim, observer, enemy—or ally. Remember that your daughter desperately needs an ally.

And I believe *you* are the ally your daughter needs. Why you? Because *you* are the one God gave to your daughter. You know her. You know what foods she likes and how she likes the pillows arranged on her bed. You watched her discover ladybugs and chocolate pudding. You read her *Goodnight Moon* and took her to buy her first bra. You've prayed about her grade in algebra and reminded her to wear her retainer. You told her about Jesus. Your mother's intuition nudged you to encourage her to take piano lessons and to be careful with the new girl who moved in down the street. You know your daughter. You've taught her. You've loved her. And deep in your heart, you believe that ought to count for something. *It does.* All of your knowledge, teaching, and love have been leading to this moment in time when your daughter needs *you* more than ever.

Your daughter may not think she needs you, but she does. You need to believe—heart and soul—that you are the one to help your daughter confront the temptations of teenage life and make choices that will define who she is now and who she is becoming.

As we explore four common mothering styles, we will uncover roadblocks that can keep you from being the most powerful ally possible to your daughter. We will also look together at some ways to begin to form an effective alliance with your daughter.

When Janet first asked me for help, her parenting posture, metaphorically and literally, was flat on her face. Perhaps you've been there. You've tried swooping in on your daughter from above and lecturing her, only to get a stone-faced response. Or maybe you've been on your knees at your daughter's feet, begging her to stay away from drugs, and she's simply sneaked out and smoked pot anyway. We all can empathize with Janet's desire to run as far away from her daughter's world as possible. But I knew Janet couldn't really run away. Neither could I. Neither can you. Like it or not, this God-given bond between mother and daughter has us hooked. I wanted to tell you Janet's story because she is an inspiring example of a mom who responded to the crisis in her daughter's life by transforming the way she mothered. She became her daughter's powerful ally in the battle with drugs and alcohol.

As you prepare to become your daughter's ally, remember that you are on holy ground. I could promise Janet that she would discover gifts in the midst of her scary upheaval. And I can assure you that as you commit to becoming your daughter's ally, you can also become a woman of wisdom, resilience, strength, and compassion, able to use the challenges in your daughter's life to help her develop those same qualities.

MOTHERING FROM ABOVE

MOM: I want to talk to you about what happened at school today. What were you thinking—smoking pot at school? Don't you know what that does to you? It destroys brain cells. It impairs memory. You'll end up flunking out of school. You are already failing in three classes. Don't you realize that smoking pot is against the law? Do you want to end up with a criminal record? I want to know where you got the drugs.

DAUGHTER: I just got them from some kid at the park. I don't know who it was. It's not that big a deal. Everyone was doing it. I promise I won't do it again.

MOM: You're right you won't do it again! You're grounded until further notice, and I'm calling the school to put a halt to your going off-campus at lunch.

DAUGHTER: Great. Now I won't have a social life at all.

MOM: Good. I don't want you to have a social life if it's going to get you into this kind of trouble. Why did you do it?

DAUGHTER: I don't know.

MOM: I want you to go to your room and think about an answer so you're ready to talk about this later.

The mother in this scenario is right. Her daughter made a foolish, destructive, illegal choice. The mother is right to impose consequences. She is right to be suspicious of her daughter's social life. This mother used her knowledge and parental authority to talk to her daughter, dispense discipline, and demand answers. The end result is predictable. These two will be in a standoff—possibly even further apart than before the drug-use incident. Mom may feel an immediate sense of control, but sooner or later she will be frustrated because she doesn't understand *why* her daughter is using drugs. Neither mother nor daughter will trust each other. Mom won't trust her daughter to avoid temptation without tight controls in place, and the daughter won't trust her mom or tell her mom what's happening in her life for fear that even tighter controls will be imposed.

As we discussed in the last chapter, parents need to be armed with information about drug and alcohol use. However, information used for the sole purpose of "catching" and controlling our daughters will put us in the role of "police" mothers. And information garnered primarily to "educate" our daughters—rather than ourselves—will just fall on deaf ears. No matter how much you know about drugs and alcohol, your daughter will believe she knows more.

What is missing from this scenario is not the mother's lack of knowledge about drugs, but her lack of knowledge about her daughter. A mother using both knowledge and understanding when talking with her daughter might say, "It makes sense to me that you would smoke pot right now. I know that you are going through a lot and are feeling a lot of stress, and marijuana takes away the pressure for a little while. But we have to find another way to help you deal with the pressure. Pot is illegal and potentially damaging."

Write this at the top of your list: Get Understanding!
Throw your arms around her—believe me, you won't regret it;
never let her go.

—PROVERBS 4:8, MSG

Acknowledging your daughter's challenging world may open the door to further discussions about what is really going on and how you might help. A mom who tends to mother from above must temper her knowledge with understanding.

Consequences are necessary when our daughters make bad choices. However, they will seldom walk through the doorway of consequences to open-hearted connection with us. Throughout the rest of this book, we will look at many possible, appropriate consequences for our daughters' substance use and discuss how to use them to teach our daughters. For example, a mom committed to creating logical consequences might say, "I don't want to be your policeman, but I can't ignore what has happened. It's serious. Tomorrow we will talk about putting some random drug tests in place to help you say no to this temptation and to help me begin to trust you again." Consequences that are implemented for the sole purpose of shutting down or punishing our daughters can crush the relationship. But consequences that spring out of strength and hope for the future can be life giving to the relationship.

The mom who has a tendency to mother from above must temper her consequences with creativity and vision. While it is understandable for a mom to resort to lecturing and controlling when her daughter's behavior is foolish and scary, she will not forge an effective, and possibly life-saving, alliance by relying on this mothering style alone. Perhaps you wonder what the alternative is to control, especially if your daughter is in the midst of dangerous and destructive behavior.

It may be helpful to remind yourself that, ultimately, you can't control your daughter. You've observed her defiant attitude while she's grounded. You're not in control. You've caught her hanging out with forbidden friends. You're not in control. You've found empty alcohol bottles hidden under her bed after you removed all the alcohol from your home. You're not in control. Really, all you can do is creatively and wisely structure logical consequences as you pray and wait for a change of heart. What doesn't make sense is for you to let your own heart become hard and angry as you wait for your daughter's heart to soften. A mother committed to being a hand-in-hand ally uses her knowledge to understand her daughter, creates logical consequences, and waits for her daughter *while she works on herself* to become wiser, more resilient, more compassionate, and to clarify her vision for her daughter and herself. If you're not sure of your vision for your daughter in the midst of your present difficulties, read on. This book will help you regain a vision of who your daughter was meant to be.

Janet had tried lecturing and controlling her daughter, only to be dismissed and disobeyed. But one conversation became a turning point in her relationship with her daughter. Janet told me that she had started the conversation by saying, "Alex, I'm tempted to focus only on what you did, but I'm not going to do that. I suspect that there are some things going on in your life that make smoking pot and drinking seem like reasonable choices to you. Tell me what you like about what you're doing."

Alex's response was predictable: "I don't know, Mom. It just feels good."

Janet's response was not predictable: "Okay. Tell me about the things in your life that don't feel good right now."

The door to connection opened a crack because Janet sat down *with* her daughter rather than looming above her.

THE ABOVE MOTHER

Goal: To tell what she knows. To get things under control.

Role: Instructor, police officer.

Fear: "If I don't get my daughter under control, there's no hope for us."

Response to Substance Use: "You will not do that again!" "You will do exactly as I say!"

Favorite Motherisms: "If you want a war, you've got one!" "You're grounded!"

Daughter's Response: "I can't let my mom know what is going on in my life." "I don't care if I get caught, I'm going to do what I want."

MOTHERING FROM BENEATH

MOM: I don't know what's gotten into you. I never thought you would use drugs. What am I going to do? Maybe you should talk to someone. Is there a counselor at school? Oh, honey, please tell me you won't do this again.

DAUGHTER: Mom, it's not that big of a deal. Everyone tries it. I won't do it again. I promise.

MOM: Oh, honey, please don't. When I was your age, I smoked pot. I'm so sorry I did. It's probably the reason I didn't do very well in school. I don't want you to make the same mistakes I did.

DAUGHTER: Okay, Mom. I promise.

The mother in this scenario is right too. She is right to think that her daughter might need help from a counselor. However, her suggestion that her daughter get help because she, as a mom, is feeling helpless will only erode the mother/daughter relationship. When we suggest counseling for our teenagers, it should not be a compensation for our own inadequacies. So often a girl who comes to see me for counseling because her mother feels helpless will go in one of two less-than-desirable directions. She may heed my advice and grow to respect me, but she may feel increasingly disconnected and more disrespectful of her mother. Or she will justify invalidating our work together because I am "just her therapist," not her mother.

Mary Pipher, in her wonderful book *The Shelter of Each Other*, writes, "Clients must learn to trust in their relationships with their therapists. But therapists should be transition relationships for them. At best, a therapist is a consultant who helps people process life thoroughly. In terms of priorities for loyalty and attachment, therapists should come after family, friends, and co-workers. We care about clients, but we are hired to help them."[2]

A mom committed to becoming her daughter's ally might say, "A lot is going on here that I don't understand. I think we need to find someone to talk to together, someone who can hear and help you, and someone who can hear and help me." A mom who thrusts her daughter into the arms of an expert without being involved herself sends a message that she is less than God intended her to be and that her relationship with her daughter is not important. The mother who has a tendency to mother from beneath must not only be an informed catalyst for her daughter's getting help, she must also include herself in the process.

The mother in this scenario is also right in realizing that her own history of drug use is important in relating to her daughter. However, announcing her own failure is not a wise or powerful way of helping her daughter make different choices. When it comes to disclosing to our daughters our history with drug and alcohol use, we must be careful. It is essential that we first understand why we used drugs or alcohol, how it harmed us, and how and why we stopped. If we are still drinking socially or smoking cigarettes, we must know why we are choosing to do so. In chapter 8 we will explore more fully the question of our own alcohol and drug history, what to disclose to our daughters, and when and how to disclose it.

It is never appropriate to disclose your history by saying, "Don't make the same mistake I did." A teenager hears these words and thinks, *Why not? You seem to have turned out okay.* A declaration of failure that is not connected to a story of growth and a resolve to change is impotent. The mom who tends to mother from beneath needs to do some personal work on understanding her past and seeing how it has shaped her. She also needs to examine her current values and attitudes toward alcohol and drug use. An intentional life that grows out of our past mistakes and is rooted in core values speaks most powerfully to our daughters.

---

*Knowing how another human being lives and functions
on the inside—how he or she handles the vicissitudes of
life, copes with its joys and frustrations, faces critical
choices, meets failure and defeat as well as challenge and
success—is what enables us to feel prepared for life.*

—GERSHEN KAUFMAN, *Shame: The Power of Caring*

Janet told me how this topic of disclosure came up in her conversation with Alex. "I don't get what the big deal about this is. Everyone at school smokes or drinks. Didn't you when you were in high school?"

Janet answered wisely and kept the door to communication open: "You bet I was tempted to smoke and drink. It might not have been as prevalent when I was in high school as it is now, but it was still around a lot. I want to tell you what I learned from my mistakes and my successes, but not right now. I have the feeling you want to know about me to justify making the choice to smoke or drink again. I think we can have a great conversation about both of our experiences when we are ready."

A mother committed to being a hand-in-hand ally is ready to use everything, including good counsel and her story, for the sake of her daughter. She wields these tools most powerfully as she stands *beside* her daughter rather than cowering beneath her.

THE BENEATH MOTHER

Goal: To keep her daughter out of trouble by pleading her own helplessness.

Role: Victim of her daughter's helplessness and her own.

Fear: "If I don't find someone else to help my daughter, she will be lost."

Response to Substance Use: "I feel so afraid and helpless."

Favorite Motherism: "I am in over my head."

Daughter's Response: "I am too dangerous and too much for my mother to handle!" "My mom is so weak! I can get away with anything."

MOTHERING FROM A DISTANCE

MOM: I don't know what you're thinking—smoking marijuana! You had better get your act together now, or you are going to live with your father.

DAUGHTER: Fine. I'll pack my bags and leave right now.

MOTHER: You do whatever you want. You always do anyway.

DAUGHTER: Maybe that's because you don't really care what I do, as long as I don't inconvenience you. You're ready to ship me away whenever there's trouble. You make such a big deal out of everything. Everyone I know smokes pot.

MOTHER: Of course I care about what you do. But you are old enough to take responsibility for your own choices. And the truth is, if you continue to make bad choices, I'm not going to enable you. You'll have to move in with your dad.

This mother is also right. She recognizes that her daughter needs to take responsibility for her own choices, and she doesn't fall into the mothering trap of taking her daughter's bad behavior personally. When our daughters are in trouble, it is essential for us to remember that we are separate beings. However, when our daughters are in trouble, even though it may be uncomfortable for both of us, what they need most is our presence. The mother who tends to mother from a distance risks losing her daughter completely when she disconnects in times of trouble. Mothers who share custody arrangements, like the mother in this scenario, know how easy it is to threaten shipping our daughters off to the other parent when times get tough. This is part of the tragedy of divorce. We send a destructive message to our daughters when we suggest that we will be with them only when they are good, happy, and respectable.

God offers a different parenting perspective in Psalm 46:1 when He promises to be present *in times of trouble.* One of my most treasured possessions is a questionnaire my son filled out in Bible class when he was in the sixth grade. Two weeks before the questionnaire was distributed, Graham got into trouble. I knew he was in trouble by the look on his face when he came home from school. After a few questions he confessed his misdeeds. During lunch he had written some inappropriate sentiments about the school on some playground equipment. He hadn't been caught, but he feared his actions would eventually catch up with him, and he knew he had done wrong.

We talked about the error of his ways, and then I went to the cleaning closet for supplies. We drove to the playground (after dark) and erased the mischievous markings together. Of course we can't always undo our children's mistakes, and more often than not, they have to face the consequences. In this instance, however, I thought that Graham's guilty conscience and anxious heart, as well as the fifteen minutes he spent scrubbing the playground equipment, was punishment enough. My response to Graham was less about punishment and more about presence.

I knew Graham had gotten the message when I read his answer to the question on the Bible-class questionnaire: "How do you experience the love of God?" He wrote: "When you do something stupid, and your mom is still nice to you and helps you fix your mistake."

We can remain present with our daughters in the midst of their most terrible mistakes by expressing our unconditional commitment to them and by asking how we can help. They may need to experience the consequences of their choices. They may need to get outside help and counsel. But they still need us.

Janet began to practice out-of-the-ordinary mothering during her daughter's out-of-the-ordinary crisis when she made an out-of-the-ordinary decision two days after Alex got her drinking ticket. She called me from her cell phone: "I just picked Alex up from school. Our bags are packed, and we're leaving in a few minutes for my sister's house. We're going to stay there for a while to see if we can connect and come up with some options for Alex."

"What about school?" I asked.

"I don't know. I'm not sure Alex is going back there. If she misses a few weeks, the school will help us get her caught up. I just know we need to do something different." Janet sounded calm and confident. Her extreme actions were the calculated actions of committed presence in her daughter's life.

"How is Alex taking this?" I asked.

We are born helpless and dependent, and after birth our brains
continue to grow. Unlike monkeys, who can run
around within hours of birth and are self-sufficient
within a few months, it takes humans in even the simplest
of environments more than a decade to be independent of parents.
Homo sapiens need families to survive.

—MARY PIPHER, *The Shelter of Each Other*

"Oh, she's mad at me and a little surprised—maybe a little intrigued. She asked if we were running away from home. I told her, 'No, but we are running away to a place where we can talk about what you want for your life and figure out the right way for you to get it.'"

"Pray for us," Janet concluded, "and I'll call you from the road."

I bowed my head right then and prayed for this mother who was willing to go to any lengths for her daughter who was in trouble. A mother who is willing to become a hand-in-hand ally with her daughter resists the urge to run in fear or disconnect from the swirling chaos. She may not have all the answers, but she knows the answers can only be found *with* her daughter, not at a distance from her.

THE DISTANT MOTHER

Goal: To make her daughter take responsibility for her life.

Role: Observer

Fear: "If I get too close, I'll make things worse or get sucked into the chaos."

Response to Substance Use: "This is your problem."

Favorite Motherism: "You have to work this out yourself."

Daughter's Response: "My failures result in losing love. I am on my own."
"My mom doesn't care about me."

MOTHERING FROM TOO CLOSE

MOM: Honey, you can't keep making these bad decisions. We have to figure out what we are going to do.

DAUGHTER: Mom, this is not your problem.

MOM: Oh yes it is. I am responsible for you, and what you do is a reflection on me.

DAUGHTER: Mom, don't worry. I won't do it again. Everyone tries pot once.

MOM: I know you won't, because I'm going to help you. I'm going to start picking you up from school every day during lunch. We'll go out to lunch together. I want us to start having Bible studies together. You have to get close to God again.

DAUGHTER: Mom, don't do that. Please! Don't embarrass me.

MOM: Honey, I don't want to embarrass you. I just want to be with you and keep you from getting into trouble. I'll do anything. I can't stand the thought of you smoking pot.

DAUGHTER: Mom, this isn't about you.

This mother is also right. She knows that her daughter needs her. Her instinct to be with her daughter is wonderful, but her motivation is flawed. The mother in this scenario is hovering, not necessarily for her daughter's sake but for her own. She wants to be with her daughter to ease her own anxiety, to live her daughter's life for her, and to keep her daughter from being a bad reflection on her. The hover mother can *look* really good. She is involved, informed, and interested in her daughter's life. But the strength of our connection with our daughters is weakened when we perceive our daughters failures and struggles as *our* failures and struggles. When I take over my daughter's life, I lose the capacity to mother from a wise and centered reality, and I send the message to my daughter that she is not capable of living her own life.

The hover mother not only confuses her responsibility with her daughter's, but she also confuses her responsibility with God's. We hover mothers tend to be "better" to our daughters than God is! We want to wipe away the consequences of our daughters' behavior, do their work, and make it all okay. We teach our daughters to rely on us rather than on themselves or God. The mother in this scenario might say, "You have let yourself down. I hope we can have some conversations about why you are sabotaging your grades and your future. I want you to have the life that you want. I want to help you figure out what's keeping you from that life and what you can do to attain it." And then this mother prays. Prays for guidance and for God's intervention in her daughter's life. She knows that she can't superimpose a spiritual life on her daughter. She can only model a relationship with God built on trust. The hover mother needs to stay close to God, trusting in His care for her and her daughter. The mom who mothers from too close risks turning her positive bond with her daughter into a yoke that can keep both mother and daughter from becoming their individual bests.

Janet called me often during her two-week hiatus with Alex. They had good conversations as well as some knock-down-drag-out arguments. They agreed on a new school for Alex as well as weekly random drug tests. The new school would allow Alex to take cosmetology classes at the local community college, something she had been wanting to do. The drug tests would allow Janet to relax her grip on Alex a bit. "We have a long way to go," Janet told me when she returned from the getaway. "I wake up every day asking for God's wisdom and protection. I wish I knew how everything is going to turn out. I just know what we are supposed to do *today*." Janet was in the best posture possible for mothering. She was close to her daughter, but closer still to God.

THE HOVER MOTHER

Goal: To make her daughter's life easier.

Role: Caretaker.

Fear: "If I don't take care of this, my daughter will fail, and I will be a bad mother."

Response to Substance Use: "This is my problem."

Favorite Motherism: "Let me make it all better."

Daughter's Response: "I am helpless." "My life is not my own."

JUST FOR YOU

Your answers to the following questions will help you further identify your primary mothering style. Remember that the goal of this exercise is not to find out everything you're doing "wrong," but to discover your primary posture in mothering so you can adjust it to best meet your daughter's needs.

1. When my daughter gets into trouble, I
   a. lecture/punish.
   b. feel anxious.
   c. walk away.
   d. try to fix it.

2. When my daughter is sad, I
   a. lecture/punish.
   b. feel afraid.
   c. walk away.
   d. become tearful.

3. When my daughter's friends make me uneasy, I
   a. condemn/criticize them.
   b. feel afraid.
   c. don't comment.
   d. encourage her to find different friends.

4. When my daughter is happy, I
   a. feel successful.
   b. feel happy.
   c. feel distant.
   d. feel responsible.

5. If my daughter smokes, I
   a. forbid her from ever doing it again.
   b. wonder what I did wrong.
   c. let her make her own choices.
   d. remind her of what our friends and family will think of her.

6. When my daughter feels lonely and as if she doesn't belong, I
   a. tell her that to have friends she has to be a friend.
   b. worry about what's wrong with her.

   c. tell her that having friends is not the most important thing in the world.

   d. feel responsible.

7. When my daughter withdraws from me, I
   a. suspect she is doing something she shouldn't be doing, punish her, and make her spend time with me.
   b. feel as if I've done something wrong.
   c. let her be by herself.
   d. try to do all her favorite things so she'll want to be with me.

8. If my daughter comes home with alcohol on her breath, I
   a. ground her immediately and lecture her on the dangers of drinking.
   b. don't say anything because I don't want her to get mad at me.
   c. tell her how stupid drinking is.
   d. stay with her and devise a plan to keep her from drinking again.

9. When my daughter won't talk about her feelings, I
   a. scold her.
   b. am intimidated by her silence.
   c. leave her alone.
   d. try to articulate her feelings for her.

10. When my daughter's grades start slipping, I
   a. lecture/punish/structure new rules.
   b. feel like a bad mother.
   c. let her work it out.
   d. start doing her work for her.

11. If my daughter tries drugs, I
   a. take away all privileges/punish.
   b. am completely panicked and don't know what to do.
   c. send her to a home for troubled girls.
   d. keep her with me at all times.

If most of your answers were "a," your mothering style is from above. If most of your answers were "b," your mothering style is from beneath. If you mostly answered "c," your mothering style is from a distance. If most of your answers were "d," you tend to be a hover mother.

YOU DON'T HAVE TO BE
A SUPERMOM TO BE AN ALLY

The hand-in-hand mom uses knowledge for the purpose of understanding her daughter. She creates logical consequences that give her daughter hope that she can survive her present troubles and have a chance to begin again in the future. She helps her daughter find the right help and is involved in the process. She uses her past mistakes and growth to help her daughter feel less alone and to give her a model for learning from her own mistakes. She perpetually offers her unconditional presence to her daughter while allowing her daughter to take responsibility for her own actions. She prayerfully distinguishes between her responsibility, her daughter's responsibility, and God's responsibility.

If you're feeling overwhelmed by all of this, don't close the book yet. In the pages that follow, we will flesh out the concept of hand-in-hand mothering as it relates to your daughter's temptation to smoke, drink, or use drugs. But don't forget the final resting place for the hand-in-hand mom is in your relationship with God. You can forge a strong alliance with your daughter only to the degree that you have an alliance with God that is even stronger. He promises to be "a very present help" in times of trouble (Psalm 46:1, KJV). The word *help* in the Hebrew language of the Old Testament means "to come alongside" and reveals God's posture in relationship with us, His beloved children. He doesn't stand above us, judging or condemning us for not doing it right. He is not beneath us, surprised or overwhelmed by the troubles in our lives. He is not at a distance, unmoved or untouched by our problems. And He is not hovering to immediately undo our misdeeds or take over our wills. He is *with* us, committed to our growth and good in the midst of the most unthinkable problems or overwhelming circumstances.

I hope it comes as good news that you are not responsible to banish drugs and alcohol from the adolescent world, to make everything better for your daughter, or to erase her temptations and struggles. You are responsible to be with her, and it is possible to be present with grace, courage, creativity, hope, and vision, even in the scary context of substance use.

Just for the Two of You

This exercise will help you understand what type of relationship your daughter perceives that you have with her. Prayerfully consider asking your daughter the following questions. Use your daughter's answers to evaluate where she perceives you place yourself in relationship to her. These bold questions and her honest answers can help open the door to a different and better relationship.

1. Do you think I listen when you tell me what's going on in your life?
2. Do I quickly move into a lecture or my own agenda when you describe your struggles?
3. Do you feel as if I think you're a problem that needs to be fixed?
4. Are you afraid to tell me your struggles because I'll freak out or cry?
5. How does my fear make you feel?
6. Do you feel as though I care too much or not enough about your struggles?
7. How do you wish I would respond when you talk about temptations or struggles involving cigarettes, alcohol, or drugs?
8. What do you wish I wouldn't say or do when you talk about temptations or struggles with substances?
9. Do you think I trust you? If not, why do you think that?
10. Do you think I trust your friends? If not, why do you think that?
11. What do you think you need to do to build my trust in you? Do you think my desires and expectations are reasonable or unreasonable? Why?

Chapter 3

You, Your Daughter, and the Peer-Pressure Cooker

Peer pressure today is…more subtle and internalized…it's much more sophisticated. Drugs and alcohol are so much a part of teen culture that the motivation to drink and do drugs comes from an internal pressure to belong, not someone standing over you with a joint forcing you to smoke.

—ROSALIND WISEMAN, *Queen Bees and Wannabes*

I read the above description of today's sophisticated teenage peer pressure months ago when I first began the research for this book. I *observed* this sophisticated peer pressure last spring when I took my daughter to Cancun, Mexico, for spring break.

We had planned this trip as a graduation present, and I anticipated white beaches, balmy breezes, and afternoon siestas. What I did not anticipate were streets lined with kids clad in beachwear, scoping one another out in hopes of "hooking up." I saw hundreds of tan, attractive, fun-loving teenagers—all with drinks in their hands. I learned that in Mexico it is legal to drink at age eighteen, and even then an ID is seldom required. During our first hour at the hotel pool, four handsome boys from Chicago bought drinks for my seventeen-year-old daughter and me. When the waiter brought us the drinks, I watched Kristin flip back her hair and look in the direction of the charitable boys from the Windy City. I asked the waiter if he could exchange the drinks for Diet Cokes, and then I told Kristin that we would be spending the rest of our vacation in our room!

"It must be hard to resist all of the temptations to drink," I said to Kristin during one of our conversations that week. As I observed the teenagers along the beach, I knew that I was getting a firsthand look at the recreational life of many of today's teenagers. All of the kids looked like nice kids, and as Kristin observed, "It looks like they're having so much fun. They seem more relaxed and not intimidated about meeting new people." Kristin told me that the Cancun party scene was exactly what it was like on Friday and Saturday nights with her friends. "The only difference is that drinking is not legal, so the drinks don't come from waiters or bartenders. They come from parents' liquor cabinets or are purchased with fake IDs."

We also had occasion to observe the darker side of the Cancun party life. Later in the week, one of the boys at the pool confessed that he had awakened that morning with a tattoo he had somehow, somewhere gotten the night before. He had been so drunk he didn't remember the experience. He winced when he looked at me and said, "My mom is going to kill me."

Kristin and I got up each morning to jog along the beach while most of the teenage partiers were trying to sleep off the night before. Sadness flooded my observations of this world under the influence of hormones and alcohol when we saw one girl passed out at the bus stop at 8:00 a.m. She was lying on the sidewalk, oblivious to the city waking up around her. Kristin and I looked at her and then looked at each other. "It's not all carefree fun, is it?" I asked. It was a rhetorical question.

The week before our vacation, one of Kristin's friends crashed his car on the way home from a party. He broke his neck and almost died. His blood alcohol level was 302 mg/dl, a severely toxic level. What disturbed Kristin most was that the night after the accident, many of the boy's friends gathered for yet another party. And almost everyone was drinking.

THE POWER OF FEMALE BONDING

Peer pressure today may be more subtle than the stereotypical taunt, "If you don't party, you can't be our friend." But its power is undeniable. It is a power that overrides family values, disregards legal consequences, and pulls at every teenager in America. Girls are especially susceptible to peer pressure. An important study released by the National Institutes of Health in 2001 concluded that "peer pressure was positively associated with drinking for girls and not boys."[1] The study reported that girls are more likely than boys to drink to fit in with their friends.

The disturbing findings of this study actually point the way to helping our daughters resist negative peer pressure. It should not surprise us that girls are more influenced by relationships. Females are by nature more relational than males. We bond over diets, marriage problems, and the latest guest on *Oprah*. Considering that the world our daughters live in a great deal of the time is saturated with drugs and alcohol, we should not be surprised that our girls are bonding over drinking and using drugs. Rosalind Wiseman, co-founder of the Empower Program (a nonprofit violence-prevention organization that works to empower girls), writes a description of this bond, which might be troubling to many parents:

> Alcohol and drugs are a fact of life in adolescent culture. Chances are good your daughter has tried or will try alcohol and/or drugs. If she does them regularly, another bonding experience she'll have with her friends is taking care of each other when they're drunk or high. It isn't an absolute certainty that your daughter will get drunk or high when she goes to a party. It just shouldn't come as a surprise to you if she does.[2]

The good news is this: If relationships have the potential to harm, they also have the potential to heal. You cannot choose and control your daughter's friends, but you can significantly influence *your* relationship with your daughter. Waging war against your daughter's peers will most certainly end in defeat. Teenagers are intensely loyal, and if your daughter senses that you are on a crusade against her friends, she may join her friends to fight you. You are indeed in a war, but it's a war *for* your daughter—to help her make healthy decisions about drugs and alcohol, protect her body, soul, and spirit from the potential ravages of substance use, and develop a growing awareness and confidence in who God has uniquely made her to be.

The peer-pressure cooker can be a powerful context in which to develop a hand-in-hand alliance with your daughter. In this chapter we will look at the pressures your daughter feels to be cool, to belong, and to be "okay" with herself. We will also look at how we can use the peer-pressure cooker to help our daughters discover their significance, find their place in the world, and develop self-esteem.

In learning to deal with this culture of their peers, teenagers take their first major steps away from their parents' houses and out into the wider experience of the world. It isn't easy. It isn't always fun. It happens too fast. To hear teens talk about dealing with new moral challenges is to sense, sometimes, wistfulness beneath the bravado.

—Peter Grier, "Peers as Collective Parent"

The Currency of "Cool"

During the 2003 school year, I surveyed the junior and senior classes of one of the largest high schools in the Denver area and received more than five hundred responses. Although I was not conducting a scientific study, I think the survey findings accurately reflect the consensus of most teenagers today. I asked just one question: What makes someone "cool"? Listed below are the eight most frequent answers.

- Being "hot" (In case you're not fluent in "teenspeak," being "hot" means being exceptionally attractive.)
- Being able to "party"
- Having an outgoing or funny personality
- Being good in sports
- Having nice clothes
- Having cool friends
- Having a lot of money
- Being nice or kind

We could spend a great deal of time dissecting these responses to examine different aspects of teen culture, but for purposes of this book, we need to note that the second most popular response was "being able to 'party.'" On the first day of school, most teenagers quickly look around, not to get an idea of their classes and academic requirements, but to see how everyone else looks. What follows is a tremendous rush to make any necessary corrections in order to fit in. Only a small percentage of girls will satisfy the primary requirement for being cool and join the elite ranks of the "hot" girls. The rest will compensate by acquiring the right accoutrements to ensure they fit into the social scene.

Perhaps we should back up and ask why it's important for teenagers to be cool. Adolescence is a time of powerful transition. No other time of human development, except the first years of life, can compare to adolescence and all the changes that occur during this stage of life. As your daughter navigates this time, she is trying to find what makes her valuable and unique. And the most valuable commodity in the teenage world is the "currency of cool."[3]

A mother of one of my counseling clients expressed her contempt for the concept of cool. She told me, "I pray every day that my daughter won't be popular. I don't want her to be cool." I understand this mother's desire that her daughter experience more than the superficial realities of high school. However, her disdain for the realities of her daughter's world is akin to a missionary living in a foreign country with complete disregard for the language, customs, and rituals of that country. Dean Borgman, professor of youth ministries at Gordon-Conwell Theological Seminary, writes, "The elements of youth culture are as precious to them as the language and rituals, music and dances are to tribal societies."[4] If we want to influence our daughters to be young women of substance and values, we must not underestimate or dismiss the elements of their culture.

THE NEED TO BE SPECIAL

I believe that every negative teenage behavior reveals a positive, legitimate need. The longing to be cool and the willingness to drink or use drugs to obtain cool status reveal a need to be special. We all experience a deep longing to be really good at something, to be recognized and pursued by someone, and to be known for our unique gifts and talents. Adolescent girls who want to be cool want so much more than the superficial.

Krista's parents sent her to see me for counseling because she had come home drunk on two consecutive Friday nights. Her parents were understandably afraid, and they were confused about Krista's behavior. "She has everything," her mother told me. "She's pretty and popular. We have a nice life-style. Why would she need to drink?"

I didn't know the exact answer to that question for Krista, but I suspected it had something to do with her needing more than external things. I knew she was looking for something to satisfy her internal thirst for significance. But identifying a teenager's longing for something deep and spiritual is not always easy. Teenagers are conditioned to live on the surface and focus on external realities. I have learned that the fastest way to get to a teenager's heart is to talk about her peer relationships. This is where many parents miss the boat. They tell me, "I don't care about her friends.... I know this boyfriend won't last.... Her friends don't really care about her and aren't a good influence." But understanding the peer-pressure cooker and helping your daughter develop strategies to survive peer pressure *require* that you acknowledge and accept the importance of her peer relationships.

So I asked Krista what was happening in her social life. She told me that she had just broken up with a boyfriend. I asked, "Did you really care about him?" I saw a flicker of pain in her eyes.

"We went out for six months." (That's a long time in a teenager's life.) "I guess I really liked him."

"What happened?" I asked.

With a flat tone she told me, "He 'got on' my best friend." ("Got on" in teenspeak means that they kissed and probably more.)

I waited a moment, looked at Krista, and spoke with compassion, "Wow, you have been through a lot. You've lost your boyfriend, and your best friend has horribly betrayed you. I don't know how you're handling it all."

"Yeah," she hurried past my tenderness, "and they were at the first party I got drunk at."

"Oh, I am so sorry," I said. "That must have been awful."

"I don't know. Once I started drinking, I had fun. I flirted with some other guys..." Krista faltered for a minute.

I continued, "The alcohol numbed the sting of unfaithfulness and betrayal, and..." I looked at Krista, hoping that she would fill in the rest of the sentence.

"And it made me feel pretty and special."

I was not surprised by Krista's story or the place of alcohol in it. Drinking not only temporarily released her from the pain and rejection of her friend and boyfriend, but it created a false sense of significance. It bolstered her courage to flirt, talk to others, and find a place at the party. Because so much of a teenager's significance comes from her peers, anything that makes her feel good about herself in a social setting is going to be a powerful temptation.

Although I was not surprised by the impact of Krista's peer relationships and their influence on her choice to drink, her mother was. I spoke with Krista's mom and asked if she was aware of Krista's situation. She said she knew about the boyfriend and best friend, and then said, "But frankly, I haven't given it that much thought."

"Krista has been through so much," I replied. "She has been lied to, cheated on, and humiliated in front of her friends. She's lost a boyfriend she really cared about and lost her best friend. She needs lots of tender loving care."

"Oh, Krista," her mom's terrified heart softened. "I didn't even think of all you've been through. I was just mad and afraid."

A tear trickled down Krista's cheek.

"Go home," I told mother and daughter, "and treat your daughter like she has been in a terrible accident. Pamper her. Be kind. Make her feel special. We'll talk more about the alcohol next week."

Christ's love for the church is "marked by giving, not getting. Christ's love makes the church whole. His words evoke her beauty. Everything He does and says is designed to bring the best out of her."

—EPHESIANS 5:25-26, MSG

Perhaps you're like Krista's mom right now. In your mind, your daughter's behavior has eclipsed anything else that might be going on in her heart and life. Your fear and anger have extinguished your curiosity and compassion. At times like these, remember the following principles and use them to begin building an alliance with your daughter:

- Be interested in your daughter's friends.
- Affirm, empathize, congratulate, commiserate.
- Acknowledge your daughter's strengths, gifts, and unique personality

traits, especially on days when you have to look really hard for them.

Offering your daughter this affirmation and support, even when she is not living at her best and is not the easiest to love, might keep her from looking for love and a sense of significance in a can of beer or a puff of drugs.

I would also encourage you to use the following Just for the Two of You exercise to get to know what's going on in your daughter's world. Then you will be in a much better position to influence and guide her with power and compassion.

Just for the Two of You

1. Schedule time with your daughter to take a walk, go out for ice cream, or window shop. Use the time to ask about her peer relationships.
   - Ask about specific friends: "What's Karen involved in these days?" "Who is Jessie dating?" "What kind of car is Brian driving?"
   - Resist the temptation to pass judgment on anything she might tell you. If she tells you about the shocking or scandalous behavior of a friend, say, "That sounds scary" or "I wonder what's going on with her."
   - Ask about her social life: "Who do you like right now?" "Have you and Katie talked recently?"

   If you have a history of asking about your daughter's friends in order to make judgments, give lectures, or create rules, you may have to try asking these kinds of questions *several* times before your daughter believes you are genuinely interested in her social life. When your daughter believes that you sincerely care about her friends and friendships, she will begin to trust you with her true longings, emotions, fears, insecurities, and hopes.

2. Consider what makes you feel special and become intentional about offering the same to your daughter. (Some ideas might come to you if you start by making a list of things that others have said or done for you that have affirmed your significance.) Even if your daughter is acting out or pulling away from you, you can still offer gifts of

affirmation, kindness, care, and love to her. Release your mother's heart to love your daughter, even if she is wayward and difficult right now. Here are some suggestions to get you started:

- "You have always been so funny. I don't know where you get your sense of humor, but I love it!"
- "I am so sorry no one has called you to go out this weekend. I know how much you want to be included. I hurt for you."
- "I was just thinking about all the stresses in your life. I don't know how you manage. I want to do something to help you. Is there anything you want from me?"
- "I overheard you talking on the phone. You are such a great friend. You listen and have good things to say. Your friends are lucky to have you."

THE CRAVING TO BELONG

Adolescents use drugs and alcohol for a number of complex reasons, but there is one reason that permeates them all: Teenagers want to belong. They desperately want to fit in, be a part of a group, to identify with someone. Adolescent girls drink and use drugs because it makes them feel like they belong, links them to other teenagers, and gives them an identity as someone who is cool, who can party, who does what everyone else is doing.

When Krista and her mom came back for their second session, I could tell that Krista's mom was still angry.

"She's got another boyfriend," she explained. "Why can't she just be alone for a while? Why does everything have to be about her friends?"

"How good are you at being alone?" I gently asked Krista's mom.

She stopped and looked surprised. We forget that our teenagers are human. That our daughters are really no different from us. We want to belong, have friends, and feel "a part of." In fact, these are some of the underlying motivations we have for getting married, joining book clubs, and going to church. Likewise, our daughters have boyfriends, go to parties, and sometimes drink or use drugs because these things give them a sense of belonging.

The importance of peer acceptance intensifies if our daughters feel disconnected from us. If we are critical, demanding, or distant and immersed in our own problems or work, our daughters will feel even more desperate to find acceptance among their peers. Dr. Ron Taffel, family therapist and author of *The Second Family,* explains:

> So what's the constant in [teenagers'] lives? Certainly not parents or grandparents, nor the parade of transient adults that marched through their childhood. No, these kids look to their *peers* for guidance and support—peers who don't criticize or correct but merely accept them for who they are.[5]

I asked Krista's mom to leave the office so that Krista and I could talk. I asked Krista, "What makes you feel like you fit in with your friends?"
She answered without hesitation. "Having a boyfriend."

JUST FOR YOU

Ask yourself the following questions to help you better identify with the importance of relationships in your daughter's life as well as the effects of peer pressure on her.

1. Did you ever drink or use drugs when you were a teenager? If so, do you remember substance use giving you a sense of belonging?
2. What effect did peer pressure have on your use of drugs or alcohol?
3. Did you use drugs and alcohol as an escape? From what?
4. Remember a time when you felt like you didn't fit in? How did you respond?
5. How do you feel when your relationships are being threatened?
6. Identify all the places you "belong" right now—marriage, family, work, church, book club, and so on. How important are these places of belonging to you? What difference would it make in your life if you did not have them?

(*Remember:* Your daughter is no different from you in her need to belong, identify with a group, and experience connection.)

"And if you don't have a boyfriend?" I asked.

"Then doing what everyone else is doing."

"Does that mean drinking?" I asked.

"Sometimes. Not everyone drinks. But it's the easiest thing to do. It immediately makes you a cool person in the group."

Krista had quickly identified two of the primary factors that make teens susceptible to peer pressure: the need to be special and the need to belong. And she had explained the role of drugs and alcohol: They are the *easiest* means of feeling cool and accepted. Once again, the answer to our daughters' struggles with peer pressure is found in understanding the struggle. Of course they want to belong. Don't you? We were created with the longing to connect at the core of our identity. When connection is threatened or lost, it is our natural instinct to look for a way to reconnect.

Adolescence is the time to strengthen our connection with our daughters. This can be hard because it is also the time when teenagers develop outside interests and friends and generally spend more time away from home. You cannot keep your daughter from seeking a sense of belonging among her peers. If you try to, you are setting yourself and your daughter up for disaster. You can, however, provide an environment of acceptance and security at home that will help her feel less desperate for peer relationships. Three parenting postures, in particular, will help you give your daughter a sense of belonging as she tries to find her place within her world.

AN OPEN HEART

Acknowledge, accept, and affirm that your daughter's peers are important to her. If she reports on the bad behavior of a friend, she is probably testing you. Will you accept her friends? Will you accept her when she behaves badly? Being tolerant of your daughter's friends, welcoming them into your home, and encouraging your daughter to be a good friend will open the door to your daughter's heart. *Your open heart will open her heart.*

If your daughter tells you about the bad behavior of her friends because she subconsciously wants to alert you to her own bad behavior, you will be better equipped to address her behavior and guide her toward an alternative if you have an open heart. Ron Taffel explains the need for an open heart:

Adults and teens often find themselves caught in a "dance"—fruitless exchanges that lead to the same old arguments and cause kids to tune out. Changing the dance enables us to see both our children and ourselves more clearly. To do that, though, we have to learn how to listen instead of automatically losing it. Unfortunately, adolescents usually talk when it's hardest for adults to hear.[6]

AN OPEN MIND

So what if your daughter tells you that one of her friends got "trashed" last weekend at a party? Do you tell her that she'll never see that friend again? Do you say, "How could she be so stupid? I hope you realize what a bad friend she is"? or "If your friends are drinking, you're probably drinking too. You're grounded!"?

All of these responses are reasonable. But all of them will disconnect you from your daughter. And if she's disconnected from you, she will feel more desperate and justified in connecting with her friends. Your connection with her is strengthened when you are curious, compassionate, and creative. You might ask, "What was she drinking? How did it make her act? What did you feel for her when she was drunk?"

You can express empathy and expectations creatively: "I'm sorry she put herself in that position. I bet she felt horrible the next day." "If you made those choices, I would feel awful about the consequences you would experience." This assumes that you've had conversations about the consequences of drinking in your family—the physical consequences (feeling sick and tired), the emotional consequences (feeling guilty), the spiritual consequences (feeling distant from God for a time), and the family consequences (loss of driving privileges, social privileges, etc). We will talk more about setting up consequences in a later chapter.

You can also support your daughter's social life with creative, positive input. "It sounds like your friend could use a friend right now. Do you want to do something with her next weekend?" A mind that is open to more than fear and control, judgment and condemnation will have room for ideas that show your daughter you acknowledge the importance of her peers and want to see her develop positive peer relationships.

AN OPEN HOME

I'm sad that teenagers don't often get together with their families anymore to bake cookies and watch old movies. They wait for parents to leave and then swarm in for some unsupervised activities. When you open your heart and mind to your daughter's friends, you will want to open your home as well. If you and your daughter have a good relationship, your home might even become a gathering place for teenagers. I hope that happens for many of you, but it is rare. You are more likely to succeed in creating an open home for your own child where she can talk about her peers, complain about her friends, and feel your love and support.

I'm also afraid that, all too often, teenagers feel trapped between their two worlds of family and friends—much like a child in the midst of a custody dispute in a bitter divorce. Don't force your daughter to choose sides. Acknowledge her need to belong in the world of her peers, support her as she tries to find her place, and provide her with as many opportunities as possible—youth-group activities, volunteer work, sports, and hobbies—to find a place of acceptance.

I asked Krista's mom to spend two weeks repeating one sentence to herself whenever she heard about or observed Krista with her peers: *This is really important to her.* I hoped this would help her keep an open heart and mind to her daughter's need for peer acceptance. She came back with a good question that introduces the third factor that makes teens susceptible to peer pressure.

JUST FOR YOU

Parenting a teenager is the perfect time for you to think about your own peer group. We parents of adolescents need one another. We need to talk about our parenting dilemmas, complain about the teen culture, and brainstorm together about positive parenting strategies.

1. Create your own parenting support group. The following guidelines will help get you started. You will want to develop additional guidelines to meet the unique needs of your group.
   - Start small. Get together with a few friends who have teenagers in the same age range as yours.

- Commit to being honest with one another. This is not the place to pretend that you have it all together. (We parents are not immune from peer pressure!)
- Make a list of books, speakers, and other resources that might be of help to the mothers in your group.
- Commit to pray for one another.
- Honor confidentiality.

2. Although a group can provide a foundation of support, you will need one or two close friends to be your allies in the trenches of parenting. Pray about and look for a friend with whom you can be transparently honest, pray openly, and "let your hair down" throughout the ups and downs of parenting a teenager. You might seek out someone whose kids are grown or someone who is in the same stage of parenting that you are in. When you meet together, commit to the following:

   - *We will be honest.* Talk about the need for confidentiality, the things that might keep you from disclosing the realities of your life, and the benefits of being vulnerable and transparent with each other.
   - *We will not just focus on problems; we will look for solutions.* If you meet together just to complain about your daughters and gripe about the teen culture, you will leave feeling dissatisfied and guilty. Perhaps you will want to use this book as a guide for addressing struggles by finding solutions. The value of accepting another person's perspective is that you will be shaken loose from the paralysis of seeing only your point of view, which inevitably keeps you stuck in your circumstances.
   - *We will remember that we (and our daughters) are in God's hands.* Use this time to pray for each other and remind each other that God is present and "far stronger than anything in the world" (1 John 4:4, MSG).

THE HUNGER FOR SELF-ESTEEM

"I understand that Krista needs friends. I understand that they make her feel special and like she belongs. I just don't understand why she picks the friends she does. She's such a special girl, but she picks bad friends. Why?"

"That's a great question," I said. "What kind of friends would you like Krista to pick?"

Krista's mom looked at her daughter and plowed ahead, "How about friends who have goals and do well in school? I want her to choose friends who say no to drugs and alcohol and who are involved in good things." Krista's mom started talking faster. "I want Krista to have friends who are Christians, who are confident and outgoing, and who are great leaders."

Krista was staring out my office window. I got her attention. "Krista, do you feel like you are confident, outgoing, a leader, and sure of your goals and values?"

"No," she answered without hesitation.

"Why not?" her mother asked immediately. "You're such a great girl."

The problem was that Krista didn't *feel* like a great girl.

Of all the factors related to peer pressure, the most powerful one is the hunger to feel okay with oneself. Often the difference between a teen's experimental use of drugs and alcohol and her chronic, even addictive, use of these substances is rooted in how she feels about herself. If an adolescent girl believes that she will never feel special or find her place in the world because she is somehow flawed, then alcohol and drugs can become the perfect escape from the pain and a dangerous opportunity to feel okay, even if just for a little while.

Krista told me that she never felt pretty enough or skinny enough. She was in the trap that our media-saturated culture often puts girls in. Krista explained to me that she was somewhat shy and didn't feel confident enough in herself to meet new people and be fun while she was with them. Her personality type did not allow her to be naturally outgoing, bubbly, and fun. And Krista told me that she felt inferior to a lot of her friends.

We explored these self-esteem issues for several weeks before we uncovered one of the roots of her sense of inferiority. When Krista was nine years old, she had been sexually abused by an older cousin. She'd told her parents about the abuse, and there had been appropriate ramifications for the cousin. But Krista had never fully explored the damage of this experience on her heart and soul.

If you take Krista's personality, experiences, and the sometimes hard and harsh world of growing up female, and then merge them with the inevitable ups and downs of adolescent life, you have the perfect setup for a girl to become vulnerable to substance abuse. Drugs and alcohol empower shy personalities, numb painful experiences, and give the user a sense of "okayness." Krista had already explained that drinking was the easiest way into The Group, and she had begun to experience alcohol as the easiest way to feel okay about herself.

How can we help our teenagers to not take the easy way out, especially when that way can be destructive? We have to model for them how we ourselves are developing self-esteem and continually create a context in which they can do the same.

I asked Krista if she was willing to learn some ways to cope with her personality type, life experiences, and the inevitable difficulties of teenage life that might not be "easy." I told her that she seemed like a girl who might want to rebel a little and do something radical and hard. She sat up a little straighter at the idea that rebellion could be okay, and she liked the idea that I saw her as someone who might take risks and do something a bit extreme. She was uncharacteristically eager to hear what I had to say next.

Just for You

Ask yourself the following questions to help you better identify with your daughter's struggles with self-esteem and her personality type.

1. What is your personality type (e.g., shy, outgoing, sensitive, efficient, scattered)? What adjustments have you made in your life on the basis of your personality? Have you ever taken a class to learn skills to deal with your vulnerabilities?

2. What experiences (such as past abuse, painful relationships, personal failures, and so on) have eroded your self-esteem? How have you dealt with these experiences?

3. What gives you self-esteem (e.g., affirmation from others, personal accomplishments, spiritual growth)?

4. What have you taught your daughter about healthy self-esteem, and how have you modeled this for her? If you haven't, what is holding you back?

ACCEPT YOUR UNIQUE PERSONALITY

One of the primary reasons mothers bring their daughters to see me for counseling is that they hope "we" can change their daughter's personality—change her from being shy to outgoing, from sensitive to not caring what others think, from messy to organized. I immediately let them know that not only can "we" *not* change their daughter's personality, but it would be a tragedy to try. Our goal is to get both mother and daughter to accept how God has made the daughter and to help her learn to live her best life with her personality type, not against it.

I asked Krista to identify the good things about her more introverted personality. She had trouble at first, but eventually she could identify that she was a good listener, a loyal friend, and didn't always have to be the center of attention.

Her mother inserted, "Oh, Krista, you're not that shy. You always have friends."

I didn't doubt her mother's external observations, but I knew that she was missing Krista's internal reality. "It's not easy, is it, Krista?" I remarked. "I bet you have to work really hard to be with your friends, and I'm sure that gets exhausting."

Krista looked relieved to know that somebody understood her. Her mom looked a bit perplexed. For us parents there are times when our own problems, turmoil with our children, or the inevitable chaotic gyrations of adolescence paralyze us and prevent us from really seeing our daughters—which is why we would be wise to consult a counselor or ask friends we trust to help us gain a more accurate perspective. Acknowledging Krista's personality type helped both her and her mom understand Krista's particular vulnerability to drugs and alcohol. "Of course you want to drink, Krista," I said. "It makes everything feel easier. But another option might be doing some 'self-talk' during a social setting to help you feel okay with yourself."

Krista and I talked about social anxiety and ways to address it. She was curious about the techniques, but she acknowledged that just having a beer would be easier. (See the resource section at the end of this book for information about techniques to help with social anxiety.)

If, in a nonjudgmental way, you can help an adolescent understand that she is taking the easy way out and challenge her to try something harder, you will create a context for her to develop self-esteem. A little short-term motivation might help as well. I told Krista that if she would try the exercises we discussed for one month and report back to me—whether or not they helped—we would celebrate with a session at Starbucks.

EXAMINE YOUR EXPERIENCES

I told Krista that the sexual abuse she'd experienced not only made her more vulnerable to drugs and alcohol but also increased her likelihood of becoming addicted. More than one-third of the women who struggle with drug or alcohol dependencies are trying to cope with past abuse. Studies have confirmed that sexual abuse during childhood is "a strong predictor of later problem drinking."[7] Teenagers are often desperate to talk to someone about what has happened to them. As parents we sometimes shut down our daughters when they want to talk about painful past experiences because we feel guilty or powerless. Sometimes involving a counselor in talking about hurtful experiences can help both parent and child find healing.

Krista told me her story of sexual abuse. We identified her lingering confusion that she was at fault for the experience and her lingering anger that her parents had not protected her from it. Neither her guilt nor her anger was rational, but Krista still needed to hear from someone she trusted that it wasn't her fault and that her parents can't protect her from everything. This second realization was particularly important because it helped Krista understand that she was living with a sense of terrible anxiety, fearing that something bad was going to happen at any minute and that she was powerless to keep it from happening. Every social interaction was fraught with fear and suspicion. Using alcohol helped her relax and stop being hypervigilant.

Once again, the problem revealed a solution for Krista. We began to talk about personal power. We looked at the differences between Krista now and when she was nine years old. Now, she has an accumulation of experiences, she has an uncanny sense of danger, and she has an ability to articulate her thoughts and feelings in a way she couldn't when she was sexually abused. We talked about Krista's power to say no, her wisdom in sensing unsafe situations, and her "spunk" in taking care of herself or asking for help. Krista liked identifying these positive things about herself. We then looked at how alcohol erodes her personal power, diluting her wisdom, taking away her ability to speak clearly and convincingly, and undermining her commitment to self-care.

The unthinkable experience Krista had at age nine became a vehicle for discussing and acknowledging her growing strengths. I watched Krista's resolve to be sober increase as she realized that she didn't want to abuse herself and lose her positive and powerful attributes.

TAKE RESPONSIBILITY FOR YOUR SELF-ESTEEM

We often believe that self-esteem is something others give us. If we transition from adolescence into adulthood without believing we've been given the appropriate self-esteem, we will either feel like victims or will continue on a quest to find someone or something that will make us feel okay about ourselves. But self-esteem is something we give *ourselves* as we live well, develop our unique gifts and talents, and understand who we are in God's eyes.

I challenged Krista to live well, which for her meant to abstain from drinking. I encouraged her to see the payoff from making the choice not to drink. She would be in control of what she did. She would avoid conflict with her parents. She would feel better physically. (I always remind adolescent girls that drinking can make them gain weight.) And she wouldn't put herself at risk for getting into trouble. I told her I'd make a deal with her: "If you don't feel better about yourself after a month of saying no, you can fire me and find another counselor. If you do feel better about yourself, you owe *me* a trip to Starbucks!" (Starbucks is a very important part of my counseling practice!)

Sometimes our daughters don't find self-esteem because they don't know where to look for it. Our task as mothers is to create a context in which our daughters can *discover* self-esteem rather than to just lecture, instruct, and threaten them about it. Krista and I talked about finding something she was good at. She believed that she was really good at hair and makeup, but she immediately discounted this talent. She was afraid that it wasn't really important. So I asked her to teach a mini-seminar to some of my younger adolescent clients on makeup and hair. Krista's self-esteem soared as she discovered she was able to use a talent she enjoyed and was good at to help others.

Perhaps you're thinking it was easy for me to challenge Krista because she wasn't my daughter and was therefore more open to suggestions from me.

I agree with you. Now is the time to find someone—a good counselor, a youth worker, or a family friend—who will be a positive influence on your daughter. If you have to pay someone to fill this role, it will be money well invested. But don't discount the power *you* have to encourage your daughter to develop self-esteem. You can accept and affirm her personality type while helping her find tools that will enable her to stretch beyond her comfort zone. You can help her deal with past hurts by talking about them, offering your empathy, and providing resources such as counseling. You can create

JUST FOR THE TWO OF YOU

1. Make a list of the things that make you feel good about yourself. Here are a few ideas to get you started:
   - exercise
   - doing something for others
   - doing what I say or promise I will do
   - laughing
   - giving special thought or consideration to my family

2. Ask your daughter to list what makes her feel good about herself. Talk about the differences in your personalities that these lists reveal.

3. What are some feel-good experiences you could share? Once again, here are some ideas to get you started:
   - Ask your daughter if she wants to train with you for a 5K race or a women's triathlon.
   - Listen for the needs of one of your daughter's friends. Ask your daughter if she wants to buy a card for her friend and leave it on the windshield of her car or leave a care package on her doorstep.
   - Buy your daughter a journal to chronicle her progress in a particularly hard subject or toward a specific goal.
   - Have a "laugh-in"—watch funny movies together.
   - Leave special notes or little gifts for your daughter. When she asks, "What's the occasion?" tell her that doing things for her makes you feel good about yourself. After I did this with my daughter, she began leaving me a little note every morning.

contexts in which she can discover, improve, and use her unique gifts and abilities.

Is any of this easy? No. But you can form a powerful alliance with your daughter as you both determine to find life-giving alternatives to the easy way out.

Krista was not out of the woods by any means. We were just beginning. I knew that there would be countless times ahead when Krista and her parents would need to reevaluate and renegotiate. But I hoped that they now had a few more tools to build a framework of mutual respect that would help them survive the peer-pressure cooker.

In the next chapter we will examine other ways you can use specific moments with your daughter to enter her world and help her avoid and/or confront the temptation to smoke, drink, and use drugs.

Chapter 4

Entering Your Daughter's World

Parents assume their daughters want to push them away—
when they simply need a different kind of closeness.

—TERRI APTER, *The Myth of Maturity*

M om, there's been a little problem. That's what she said: 'Mom, there's been a little problem.' And then she started giggling."

My friend Carol was telling me over the phone about her horrible day. Her daughter had called her shortly after lunch from the vice principal's office at school. Carol continued her tale of trouble. "I asked her, 'What's going on?' 'What do you mean by a "little problem"?'"

"Well, Mom. I went to English class high…"

"I didn't even wait for her to finish her sentence," Carol said. "I dropped the phone and ran for my car. I knew exactly what I was going to do."

Carol had been "shadowboxing" with her daughter's drug use since the beginning of the school year and had confided in me her concerns for Blair, who was in the tenth grade. Blair had been a fairly good student throughout middle school, but when she entered high school, her grades started dropping. Blair's parents had tried everything—tutors, bribes, punishment—to help her with her grades, but they continued to drop. More disturbing was her mood at home: She didn't seem to care about anything. Blair stopped engaging with the family and often retreated to her room. In desperation Carol searched Blair's room when she was at school and found what she thought was marijuana. She confronted Blair, and Blair told her it was the remnant of "someone else's joint."

Carol continued to watch Blair and observed some of the most common signs of drug use—consistently poor grades, loss of interest in normal teenage activities, lack of interaction at home—but she couldn't find any concrete evidence. Sometimes Blair would come home and seem exceptionally tired or a little "out of it," but Carol wasn't sure whether it was marijuana or teenage malaise. Carol talked to the school counselor and learned that a lot of kids bought drugs and sometimes used them in a park not too far from the school. Carol started "staking out" the park, looking for her daughter. A few weeks earlier she had seen Blair coming out of the park, but once again she could not find any evidence to confirm her suspicions about Blair's drug use.

When Carol got the telephone call from her daughter, the mounting tension of her fears and frustrations erupted. Carol told me about the rest of that afternoon of "mothering madness."

"I drove to the park by the school, parked my car, and ran to the area where the kids hang out. I started walking up and down the canal in the park where all these kids were sitting and talking, and I started shouting, 'My daughter's name is Blair, and if you sell her any marijuana, I will hunt you down and see that you are arrested. *Leave my daughter alone.*'"

I listened to my friend with a mixture of disbelief and respect. I understood her fierce heart for her daughter and her fears that Blair was being pulled into a world where Carol could lose her completely. "Then what did you do?" I asked a bit tentatively.

"I drove home. I wasn't ready to see Blair yet. I needed to calm down. When I got home I went out on our deck in the backyard. I started crying and praying out loud, 'God, how did this happen? We love Blair. We've tried to be good parents. *My daughter's on drugs,* and I don't know how this happened!'

"I started moving around the deck furniture," Carol continued. "The movement was kind of aimless at first, and then I just started throwing it over the railing. I'm not sure why, but piece by piece I picked it up and hurled it over the railing into the backyard. And then I was exhausted. I drove to the school, picked up Blair, and brought her home. She's in her room right now. I don't know what to say to her. I don't know what to say to myself or anybody else. *How did this happen?*"

MOMENTS OF TRUTH

Carol had experienced some pretty excruciating moments of truth: her daughter's dismal report cards, Blair's changing moods, evidence of drugs in her bedroom, and Blair's telephone call from school reporting that she was high. Moments of truth come when circumstances or our intuition forces us to face reality and compels us to make a choice about the newly revealed truth. Moments of truth come in all sizes and shapes and at all hours of the day or night. Moments of truth, no matter how dramatic or ordinary, can result in denial or understanding, in paralysis or empowerment.

And you forget how you stood in her room and how the center of your stomach felt so cold. When you found the cigarette. When you found the blue pipe. When you found the little bag she said was aspirin.... And then there was something and then something else and then you were on a crazy train ride rumbling through a night landscape that you didn't recognize and everything was different and everything normal was gone.

—MARTHA TOD DUDMAN, *Augusta Gone*

In this chapter we are going to confront the truth about teenage substance use and what it means for you and your daughter. We are going to look, with our eyes wide open, at the symptoms of drug and alcohol use. These are *moments of truth*. We will begin to look beneath the surface at *why* girls use drugs and alcohol. Only one thing is worse than coming face to face with the hard realities about our children, and that is dismissing or denying what has come to light. *Moments of meaning* come when we act on the truth. In the pages that follow, we are going to begin building a framework to help you intervene in these moments of truth and meaning so that you can help your daughter gain the resolve to say no to peer pressure and to develop her own identity as she makes choices. These are *moments that matter*. These moments confirm to your daughter that you are courageous enough and committed enough to hang in there with her no matter what she does.

SYMPTOMS AND STATISTICS

The statistics about girls and drinking and substance abuse cannot be ignored. Although we've looked at some statistics already, I will continue to present statistics about teens and drugs and alcohol. Why? Because I've noticed an interesting phenomenon in working with parents and adolescent girls. Parents are often forced to face the truth about their daughter's behavior in the midst of a crisis of some sort—bad grades, legal problems, confirmed suspicions. A storm erupts. There are threats and consequences. And then the storm calms. Understandably, parents want to forget these awful moments and move on. They sometimes avoid asking further questions or ignore new symptoms because they don't want to face another storm. Consequently, it takes another crisis or even several crises to precipitate change.

The most far-reaching study to date on teenage girls and alcohol, tobacco, and drug use was released by the National Institutes of Health in January 2001. One conclusion of the study stated, "Most teens who drink and smoke think their parents don't care."[1]

I am relentless in my efforts to keep statistics about teenage alcohol and substance use in parents' minds so we will be ever-vigilant and ready to enter our daughters' worlds with confidence and to engage with them about matters of life and death.

As I mentioned in the introduction, the most recent statistics suggest that one out of every five girls entering college *already* has a problem with drugs or alcohol. The next time you're at your daughter's high school, count out one in every five girls, and you will feel the enormity of this battle. Surveys also confirm that girls have matched boys in alcohol consumption, and that females twelve to seventeen years old surpass males in the use of cigarettes, cocaine, inhalants, and prescription drugs.[2] These statistics report chronic or heavy use of these substances. The statistics for recreational or infrequent use are even more alarming.

Whether or not your daughter uses drugs and alcohol, these statistics suggest that her peers are using drugs and alcohol. Many sociologists call a teenager's peers "the second family." Just as one family member's abuse of drugs or alcohol inevitably affects the whole family, so it is in your daughter's teenage world. She is influenced, impacted, and interacting with kids who have a drug and/or alcohol problem. I don't think it's a stretch to say that *every* teenager is impacted by drugs and alcohol. In his excellent book on teenage life, Dr. Ron Taffel explains:

> Drugs and alcohol are ubiquitous, too. Liquor flows at parties hosted by the best and the brightest. Most kids don't need to leave home to imbibe. In many cities and some suburban areas as well, teens tell me it's possible to "order in" pot. Some dealers hand out business cards, offer a menu of different varieties, and promise delivery in under thirty minutes—faster than Domino's. Kids also…tell me that nowadays pot is so prevalent in public venues—movies, theatres, arenas—that, "If routine drug tests were administered after concerts, we'd all fail, even kids who never took a toke [a marijuana cigarette]."[3]

In later chapters we will look at alcohol and drug use in more detail. It's a good idea to do some further reading on specific drugs and their symptoms. (See the resources section at the back of this book.) You need to know more about drugs and alcohol than your daughter does. Your knowledge will not only equip you to see warning signs and interact with your daughter but will also give your daughter a sense of safety. Our daughters need to know that we can handle them and anything that is part of their world.

JUST FOR YOU

Take the following quiz to determine how much you know about drugs and alcohol. The questions are intended not to make you feel stupid but to reveal your knowledge or lack of knowledge about a significant reality in your daughter's world.

1. Wetting the lips or excessive thirst (known as "cotton mouth") may indicate what type of drug use?
2. Periods of sleeplessness followed by long periods of "catch-up" sleep may indicate of what type of drug use?
3. The effects of smoking pot can last for two days. True or false?
4. What are the most dangerous drugs, which are also the drugs most often used by children under fourteen?

5. What is the most popular illegal drug in America now?

6. "Huffing" refers to what type of drug use?

7. If your daughter avoids eye contact when you question her, what type of drug might she be using?

8. What is a "Jell-O shot"?

9. A female who consumes the same amount of alcohol as a male may achieve a blood alcohol level 25 to 30 percent higher than a male. True or false?

10. Which drug carries a greater risk of overdose: alcohol or LSD?

Answers

1. Wetting the lips or excessive thirst may be a sign of marijuana use.

2. Periods of sleeplessness followed by long periods of sleep may indicate amphetamine, cocaine, or other stimulant use.

3. True. THC, the active ingredient in marijuana, can affect the brain up to two days after smoking and may show up in the blood many months after the last use.

4. Chemical solvents such as benzene, propane, and those found in glue and paint. More than 20 percent of eighth graders have used such inhalants.[4]

5. Marijuana.

6. Huffing refers to the use of inhalants.

7. Avoiding eye contact may indicate marijuana use.

8. "Jell-O shots" refer to alcohol in "shots" of Jell-O, which facilitates a rapid consumption of multiple drinks.

9. True. Females generally have a larger percentage of body fat, which results in higher blood-alcohol concentrations than males from drinking similar amounts of alcohol.

10. Alcohol. Many deaths each year are caused by alcohol overdose. There is little danger of LSD overdose unless it is combined with other drugs.

You might not *feel* that brave, but ignorance will certainly not give you greater courage. Greater awareness might initially fuel your fear. You may find yourself looking for dealers in the parking lot of the high school or sniffing all your daughter's clothes for that unmistakable scent of marijuana. But as your awareness increases, you will eventually feel a sense of calm knowing. You will stop asking frantically, "What is going on here?" and start calmly sensing, "I know what is going on here." Once you are not afraid to know *what* is going on, you will be ready to look at *why* it's going on.

Remember, even if your daughter does not use alcohol or drugs, she has peers who do. Your growing knowledge will give you a reservoir from which you can offer your daughter a greater understanding of her peers. When you hear stories about her friends who use substances, resist the urge to say, "Oh, how could she do that?" or "That is just disgusting." Your reservoir of knowledge will enable you to say, "I know a lot of girls are tempted by that today" or "Marijuana can make you apathetic about the choices in your life. Do you think that's what is going on with your friend?"

SIGNS OF SUBSTANCE USE

Alcohol
- initial talkativeness and gregariousness
- drowsiness
- slurred speech
- lack of coordination
- odor of alcohol on breath or in sweat

Marijuana
- bloodshot eyes
- smell in hair or on clothing (sweet, pungent odor)
- munchies or sudden appetite
- lip-wetting or excessive thirst
- avoidance of eye contact
- burned or sooty fingers

Cocaine
- jumpy, nervous behavior
- restlessness
- excessive talkativeness; rapid speech
- dilated pupils
- runny or bloody nose
- periods of high energy followed by long period of sleep

Amphetamines
- unusual elation
- jumpiness; shaky hands; restlessness
- fast speech
- poor appetite or weight loss
- insomnia
- periods of sleeplessness followed by long periods of sleep
- poor attention span

Inhalants
- aggressive or hostile behavior
- violent outbursts
- slow movement; lethargy
- slurred speech
- inability to focus
- stupor
- lack of concentration
- seizures
- vomiting
- inability to speak intelligibly

MOMENTS OF MEANING

My friend Carol was in a drug-education crash course. The moments of truth she'd experienced with Blair prompted her to fill her reservoir to the brim with information about drugs. Carol now knew all the names for marijuana:

reefer, herb, weed, grass, bud, pot. She knew what it smelled like. She'd gone on the Internet and looked at pictures of bongs (smoking devices), joints, and roach clips. She knew how much marijuana cost and where the kids bought it. She knew that her daughter could walk to the park behind the high school and for twenty dollars buy enough pot to last a couple days. She anxiously noted the symptoms of drug use in her daughter's behavior—excessive thirst, fatigue, averted eyes. She even learned that her daughter's choices in music were evidence of her drug use.

Carol told me that she had been optimistic when Blair first told her that she liked bluegrass music. "I actually encouraged her to bring her CDs in the car. I liked her new music." Carol went on to explain that she learned that some bluegrass music is part of the culture of pot smoking, that kids listen to the music when they smoke marijuana. "I was, of course, chagrined by my naiveté," she said, "but I was mostly alarmed that Blair was buying into and identifying with the marijuana culture."

The mounting evidence of drug use that Carol had been gathering was finally confirmed when she learned Blair had gone to class high. Now Carol was sure Blair had a drug problem. She knew what the problem looked like and what it smelled like. She knew how much it cost and what music often accompanied it. What she didn't know was *why*. Why did her daughter use drugs? The anguished questions Carol had cried aloud from the deck in her backyard were about to lead her to a deeper understanding not only of alcohol and drug use but of her daughter.

Carol's situation led me to reflect on what I knew about Blair and other teenagers who use drugs. Blair had entered a public high school after attending a small Christian school during her elementary- and middle-school years. Carol had told me that Blair had been overwhelmed not only by the number of students in the school but also with the task of finding her place among the masses. Blair had tried out for cheerleader but had not made it. She had attended an off-campus Bible study but did not really connect with any of the kids. Carol had told me that during the first weeks of school, Blair ate lunch in the cafeteria by herself. (Walk into a high-school cafeteria at lunch sometime and think about how you would feel sitting by yourself in that room brimming with adolescent activity.)

I recalled seeing Blair at a high-school football game. She sat by herself on the periphery of students, and her shame was visible. I knew that Blair's longing to fit in, her failed attempts to find friends, and her growing desperation to be with anyone rather than being alone made her vulnerable to the temptation to use drugs. I also knew that most high schools have a group that is a bit anti-establishment and often welcomes "misfits." Sharing a contempt for the "popular" group, this band of kids bonds over smoking marijuana. It really is a perfect fit when you think about it. The marijuana medicates the hurt over not fitting in, while the group becomes a place to belong.

In their shocking and sometimes frightening behavior,
in the rules of their private world, and in the longing of their hearts,
teenagers are telling us everything we need to know, not just
about themselves, but about ourselves.

—RON TAFFEL, *The Second Family*

My heart ached for Carol and Blair, and I was reminded that growing up can be agonizing for both mother and daughter. When our daughters experiment with or use alcohol and drugs, we have the opportunity to learn more about them—to see our daughters through a new pair of glasses. Arming ourselves with information allows us to see *more* than the symptoms and paraphernalia of drug use; it enables us to see what it all *means*.

MORE THAN STATISTICS

Researchers who study the use of substances among teenage girls have come up with more than overwhelming statistics. As they separate the girls from the boys, they see not only an increase in use of substances among girls but also a clear distinction between the reasons why boys and girls use alcohol and drugs. The National Institutes of Health study I mentioned in a previous chapter reported that *peer pressure* is the most significant reason girls use alcohol or drugs. The study found that girls are most likely to be offered drugs or alcohol by a friend or boyfriend in a private setting. Earlier studies parallel the NIH study, suggesting that few girls drink or use drugs when they are alone.[5]

Although statistics on drug use among teenage girls may have changed slightly in the past few years, the *reason* girls use alcohol and drugs has not. We females were created with relatedness at the very core of our identity. God placed Eve into a relationship with Adam. She was never alone. And her awareness of her need for relationship was more urgent and more compelling than Adam's.

For this reason, whatever the drug or the drug-use rate, females will continue to use alcohol and drugs because they are looking for relationships. They may look in all the wrong places, but nonetheless, they are seeking what God created them to desire.

Another important consideration regarding increased drug and alcohol use among girls is the fact that once girls begin to use substances, they "sink

Just for You

How much do you know about your daughter's relational world? Answer as many of the following questions as you can.

1. Who is your daughter's best friend?
2. What does she value most in a friend?
3. Is there someone your daughter would like to make friends with but hasn't made an effort? What do you think is holding her back?
4. Does your daughter view male friendships differently from female ones? If so, what are the differences?
5. Who are the most "powerful" girls in your daughter's school? What makes them powerful?
6. Who is your daughter's most dramatic friend?
7. What friendship has hurt your daughter the most? Why?
8. Is your daughter usually the one influencing friendships or being influenced?
9. What group of girls in your daughter's school is most likely to use drugs and alcohol? Why?
10. What do your daughter's friends think about drug and alcohol use?

into abuse" much more quickly than boys do.[6] Girls are much more likely to go from infrequent use to habitual use, which means they end up in the clutches of addictive substances earlier and longer than boys.

The research and statistics on drug and alcohol use among teenage girls lay an important foundation for understanding why our daughters use substances and scouting out ways to enter their world. My earlier books in this Hand-in-Hand series—*"Mom, I Feel Fat!"* and *"Mom, I Hate My Life!"*—underscore the importance of relationships to girls and women. It should not surprise us to learn that peer influence fuels the pressure to use drugs and alcohol to numb or fill the longing for relationships or to provide a sense of "okayness" in relationships. As young girls, we start out wanting to be accepted, known, enjoyed, and loved by others. But we learn pretty early on that relationships can hurt or disappoint. Then as we enter the adolescent years, a dangerous message tells us that drinking or drugging can ease the pain of our longing for relationship, gain us acceptance, and guarantee us a place of belonging among our peers.

Although every girl who uses drugs or alcohol is a world unto herself that needs to be explored and uniquely understood, the longing for relationships and the influence of relationships is part of every girl's involvement with substances. By understanding the reason behind your daughter's drug or alcohol use—the longing for relationships—you can take that strand and weave it into a positive identity for both you and your daughter.

Confronting the truth about drugs and alcohol in the adolescent world and cultivating compassion for the meaning behind the substance use is a powerful combination of truth and empathy. I suggested to Carol that she combine what she knew about Blair and her marijuana use and pray for compassionate understanding of the meaning behind it. I shared with Carol my observations about Blair's high-school experience. Carol's voice shook as she responded to my insights. "It's almost as if she didn't have a chance, isn't it?"

Carol started with what mattered most: her heart for her child. She allowed her anger and disgust to give way to sorrow and yearning for her daughter. When she confronted Blair about her behavior, Carol opened her heart to loving her daughter in the midst of the messiness. As Carol let the truth sink in—the truth about her daughter's drug use and what possibly attracted her to marijuana—she was ready to talk to her daughter constructively. It was almost as if the truth had turned on a light, and Carol could see where to go next.

When Carol called to tell me about her conversation with Blair, she explained, "I decided to mostly listen, which really surprised Blair. She had braced herself for me to rant and rave." (One look at the backyard might have tipped Blair off that there was a coming storm!) "I said to her, 'I think it makes sense to me why you were attracted to this group of friends and why you like marijuana, but I want to hear about it from you. Tell me about the first time you smoked pot.'"

Carol told me that Blair looked at her warily. "I assured her that she would not get in trouble for telling me the truth. I told her I really wanted to understand her life." As Blair told her story, Carol's compassion for her daughter grew. "After Blair finished talking, I told her I was sorry for all she'd been through, and that she would not be going to school the next day. We would be spending the day together." I saw the wisdom in Carol's approach. She didn't lecture or immediately impose discipline. She opened her heart, which in turn opened her daughter's heart.

Carol told me about her final words to her daughter at the end of their conversation. She took both of Blair's hands in her own and said, "I know I have a lot to learn. I know I have a lot of work to do. But I'm not going anywhere. You're stuck with me."

JUST FOR THE TWO OF YOU

Set aside some time to discuss with your daughter the questions in the Just for You section that appears on page 69. If your relationship with your daughter is good, you might share with her your answers, confess your ignorance, and use the questions to continue to build your relationship. If your relationship is a bit shaky right now, confess to your daughter that you don't know much about her relationships, tell her that you want to know more, and see if she'll discuss even one question with you. If you and your daughter aren't talking easily right now, be a detective in her life and look for the answers to these questions as you prayerfully commit to being more attentive to her relational life.

After Carol listened to her daughter's story of vulnerability and attraction to the pot-smoking culture in her high school, Carol went outside and sat on her newly cleared deck. She looked up into the cold, Colorado sky and heard a still small voice say, "Don't worry. I'm not going anywhere, either."

"Now what?" Carol asked me. "What do I do tomorrow?"

Carol and I spent the next few minutes talking about where she and Blair might go together and how Carol might continue constructive interaction with her daughter. I suggested that she would need to let her daughter know that she was no longer naive about marijuana or the hold it had on Blair. We talked about "putting feet" to her knowledge of drugs and her daughter, and Carol decided to begin administering drug tests. She also decided that she and Blair would do something special together every week to rebuild their relationship and to give Carol the opportunity to ask Blair about her friends and the temptations she was facing to smoke marijuana.

I heard both anticipation and weariness in Carol's voice. I respected my friend for finding the resolve and resilience to fight this battle, and I knew that behind Carol's weariness was the wise realization that this would be a long battle that would require vigilance.

I will tell you the rest of Carol and Blair's story in the conclusion of this book. But at this point in the story, Carol was in the best place possible for a mother whose daughter is struggling with the temptation to use drugs. She was armed with information, and she was determined to act.

No matter how overwhelmed you might feel by your own daughter's struggle, Carol's starting place provides a good model. Information will arm you for the fight ahead. And determination to do something will keep you from getting stuck in the quicksand of fear regarding your daughter's choices.

MOMENTS THAT MATTER

Over the course of Blair's high-school years, Carol and Blair accumulated many moments that mattered. Blair continued to struggle to fit in. She was vulnerable to the peer group that she knew would always welcome her. Ironically, she eventually had to admit to her mom that she couldn't really fit in with that group unless she smoked pot with them. But Blair also confessed that she liked smoking pot, she liked not caring so much about things, she liked the moments of ease that pot provided. Carol learned all this about her daughter in their weekly talks together. True to her word, my furniture-throwing friend did not freak out at her daughter's disclosures. She asked questions, offered insights, and enforced the consequences that she and Blair had already decided on: random drug tests and a loss of privileges (social privileges, driving, etc.) if Blair tested positive.

Although Blair continued to dabble in the pot culture at her high school, she also stayed connected to her mom. Carol told me about one Saturday night that convinced me she knew more than I did about turning moments of truth and meaning into moments that matter. Blair had walked into the house from an evening out, and she knew immediately that Blair had been smoking pot.

Carol looked straight at her daughter and said, "So, you smoked pot tonight." But her tone was one of compassion. Blair looked at her mom and then looked at the floor before speaking. "Yeah. I'm sorry, Mom. It was so tempting, I gave in. I know I'm grounded. I can't drive until I pass a drug test."

I so respected the climate of openness that Carol had created with her daughter. But once again, Carol was working to turn knowledge into action. She used this moment to let her daughter know that they were not going to sink in the quicksand of marijuana use. "I've been attending Al-Anon meetings," Carol told her daughter. "They are for people whose family members and friends use alcohol or drugs. Since you are so vulnerable to this drug, I wanted to hear from other people about how they've dealt with their loved ones' substance abuse. There are also meetings for people like you who can't stay away from drugs. In fact, there's even a meeting specifically for people who smoke marijuana and use other drugs. I want you to go and hear from other people like you." Carol wisely "caught" her daughter during this vulnerable moment, and Blair agreed. Both Carol and Blair continued attending Al-Anon and Narcotics Anonymous meetings throughout Blair's high-school years.

I know that both Carol and Blair would tell you today that the open relationship between them, their weekly times together, and the Twelve Step meetings combined were a powerful force in pulling Blair out of the grip of drug use and toward a healthier life. If you're like me, you might be tempted to skip to the last chapter and read the conclusion of Carol and Blair's story. Go ahead. I deliberately put the rest of their story at the end of the book. It is typical of families who confront and address drug use in ways that matter. They educated themselves and placed themselves in relationships that could help, but they did not see a happy resolution quickly.

As I said at the beginning of this section, moments that matter accumulate. A mother who wants to be her daughter's ally in confronting and overcoming the temptations to use alcohol and drugs must be willing to hang in there. Sometimes it feels as if you are taking three steps forward and four steps back. As Carol stayed vigilant in watching her daughter, confronting her when necessary, talking to her about the realities of her life, and offering new ideas to challenge the temptations to smoke marijuana, she modeled to her daughter how to live well: one day at a time, with honesty, openness, and a willingness to try better alternatives. Although Blair faltered and stumbled, she got back up and tried again, and in the end all those moments mattered in making a difference.

YOUR DAUGHTER NEEDS YOU

As I sit here at my computer coming to the conclusion of the first section of this book, my mind meanders, and I see a collage of faces of the moms and daughters who have taught me about this subject. I will introduce you to more of them in the pages to come. I know that some of you will identify with the mothers and daughters who are in serious trouble. You know your daughter is drinking and/or using drugs. Maybe she's even been in trouble with the law already, and you fear the consequences she may have to experience in the days ahead.

Some of you will identify with the moms, like Carol, who are in a place of agonized wondering. You're suspicious, watchful, and hoping against hope that you are wrong about what your daughter might be up to.

Some of you bought this book and hid it at the back of your closet. You don't want people to think that your daughter might have a problem, but you're a little afraid that something might be going on with her. Your love and concern for your daughter overrode your fear of what people might think, and you bought this book hoping for some direction.

And some of you who are reading this book know that your child is not using drugs or alcohol, but her friends are. You wonder, and rightly so, how your daughter will survive the adolescent culture with her values intact. I hope this book will offer help and hope to all of you.

No matter what your mothering situation, I am certain of one commonality: *Your daughter needs you.* She may need drug education. She may need random UAs (urinalyses). She may need outpatient or inpatient treatment. She may need stricter rules. She may need you to relax a bit. But one thing is certain: She needs you.

Terri Apter, a social psychologist at Cambridge University, urges parents to realize that the root of drug and alcohol abuse for teenagers is most often "relational anxiety." She explains that teenagers have a deep-seated need for their parents and, simultaneously, a belief that such a need is inappropriate, immature, or for some other reason demeaning.[7] Our job as parents is to

JUST FOR YOU

Write out your commitment to your daughter and keep it handy as a reminder. Be specific. Use examples from your parenting experience. Let your commitment reflect the mother you long to be. Here are a few ideas to get you started:

- I am committed to loving you, even when you tell me you hate me.
- I am committed to keeping you safe, even when you believe that I am ruining your life.
- I am committed to being informed and knowledgeable about your world, even when you think I don't have a clue.
- I am committed to reconnecting with you, even when you slam your door and tell me to leave you alone.
- I am committed to remembering who you are, because you might forget.
- I am committed to helping you take responsibility for your actions, even when it really does hurt me more than it hurts you.
- I am committed to letting go of my agenda for you and looking for your unique interests and abilities.
- I am committed to forgiving the unthinkable and believing in you again, even if no one else does.
- I am committing to praying for you without ceasing.

enter our daughter's world with a sense of mature knowing—knowing her challenges and struggles—and with an unshakable commitment to the relationship. We need to believe (sometimes for both of us) that our relationship with our daughter will sustain us through all of the ups and downs of adolescence—even through the frightening possibilities of drug and alcohol use.

When your daughter is at her worst, scariest, and most challenging, you are in the best position to confirm to her that you're not going anywhere. Your presence will not solve all of her problems or untangle all of the knots. But your presence in and around and through all of the turmoil of adolescence will confirm to her that she is loved. There is no greater gift you can give your daughter. In a strange and sacred way, the most difficult challenges are your greatest opportunities to demonstrate love for your daughter. And loving well is the beginning and the ending of your work with your daughter. When you don't know anything else. When you can't remember anything else. When you're not sure of anything else. Love is what matters most.

Before we dive into more specifics of drug and alcohol use and abuse in the next section, you may need to remind yourself and your daughter that you aren't going anywhere, that you have made a commitment to walk with her through the sometimes confusing and scary days of adolescence—a commitment that even the most powerful earthquake cannot shake. You'll need that commitment because sometimes the ground shakes pretty hard.

Part II

Building a Bridge Between Your Worlds

Tenderness is what follows when someone reveals to you your own inner beauty, when you discover your belovedness, when you experience that you are deeply and sincerely liked by someone. If you communicate to me that you really like me...that you take delight in me, then you open up to me the possibility of liking myself. The look of amiable regard in your eyes banishes my fears, and my defense mechanisms disappear into the nothingness of my non-attention to them. Your warmth withers my self-disdain and allows the possibility of self-esteem. I drop my mask of pretentious piety...start to smile at my own frailty, and dare to become more open, sincere, vulnerable, and affectionate with you than I would ever dream of being if I thought you didn't like me. In short, what happens is I grow tender.

—BRENNAN MANNING, *The Wisdom of Tenderness*

Chapter 5

"Mom, It's No Big Deal!"

We started swindling sips of wine from opened bottles in our parents'
fridges. Our weekend sleepovers became dowsed in alcohol. Our parents
never guessed our little group was cemented with clandestine drinking.
After all, we were the good kids—smart girls with the good grades and
sweet smiles....

With our entrance into high school, we also entered the world of
casual partying, casual drinking, casual drug use. We were typical: We
drank at parties, smoked pot on the weekend.

Sometimes other drugs got mixed up in our lives. When our parents
did find out, we never understood why it had to be such a big deal.

—SARA SHANDLER, *Ophelia Speaks*

I had already been in my cozy, comfy bed for thirty minutes, drifting rest-lessly to sleep, when God nudged me: *Search Graham's car.*

I had suspected that something was going on with my sixteen-year-old son. He hadn't seemed himself. He was unusually fatigued, was irritable at times that made no sense, and was hanging out with a friend I knew was part of the pot-smoking culture at Graham's high school.

I answered back to God's midnight nudging: "But I don't look through my kids things unless they won't talk to me, and Graham's been pretty communicative lately."

Sharon, just look through his car. I really heard God's direction. (You moms know what I'm talking about. God tells us things about our children.)

I dragged myself out of bed and headed downstairs to the garage. I don't know how long I sat in my son's 1990 gray Volvo wagon before I summoned the courage to do a thorough search of his car.

When I found a plastic baggie of marijuana tucked into the pocket of the driver's seat, my heart felt like it had stopped beating. I smelled the sweet, pungent odor. It was a brighter green than I thought it would be. I now know that there was about $40 worth of weed in that baggie. I also found what I now know is a glass pipe, also referred to as a Humboldt pipe. It was blue, purple, and red, in sort of a tie-dyed effect. It was actually pretty. I now know it costs about $60. Finally, I found a bottle that looked like Gatorade. It was called Platinum Magnum Force, cherry flavored. It promised a "300% money-back guarantee." I now know that this is a drink used to purge the system of traces of THC (the chemical component in marijuana that shows up in urine testing). It costs $59.99. By surfing the Internet at 1:00 a.m., I discovered all the ways kids can beat the system, fool their parents, and pass drug tests. When I read that Platinum Magnum Force was formulated specifically for "larger" persons, I started to cry.

You see, my son has always struggled with his weight. And something about the pretty pipe, the illegal feel-good drug, and the Platinum Magnum Force for "larger" persons told my son's story in a way I could never do justice to in writing. His is an unfolding saga of finding himself, developing self-esteem, and learning a way to belong and feel good in a life that has betrayed him with a broken family, that has assaulted him with cruelty from peers and society in general about his size, and that has required an overwhelmingly difficult journey to find his place in the world.

While this is a book about mothers and daughters, my daughter has not used alcohol or drugs. One of the primary reasons she doesn't use substances is because she knows I am an alcoholic, and she is afraid to follow in the family footsteps. (I'll tell more of my story in chapter 7.) But I wanted you to know that I do know what it is like to have a child who is experimenting with, wondering about, and arguing over alcohol and drug use. And although I work with hundreds of adolescent girls who are in counseling largely because of the trouble that drinking and using drugs have brought into their lives and the lives of their families, nothing compares to when it hits home.

When I showed Graham the stash I'd found from my midnight mission to his Volvo, his initial response was predictable and incredulous.

"You searched my car!" And then, "Mom, I don't understand why you are making such a big deal out of this."

I knew the pat answers, and I gave them readily. "I helped buy that car. I help pay for gas and insurance. I pay for the garage that houses that car. I can search your car anytime I want."

I continued my rant. "This *is* a big deal. Marijuana is illegal. You could go to jail. I could go to jail for having this drug in my home. It kills brain cells. It will make you a loser. You'll drop out of school—a private school, which I pay for. You could become addicted. You won't be able to get a job."

Graham's eyes were rolling back into his head. My voice was becoming more and more shrill. I felt like the adults in the Charlie Brown cartoons who speak an incredibly unattractive language that their children can't even understand.

"And why are you buying stuff to fool a drug test?" I kept blabbering. "Platinum Magnum Force—'300% money-back guarantee for larger persons'?"

And then I started to cry again.

I told Graham that we needed to take a break from this conversation and that we would talk about *why this is such a big deal* over dinner that evening.

As I shopped for groceries that afternoon and started preparing Graham's favorite meal (Thanksgiving dinner in the middle of April), I prayed that God would give me more than the Just Say No statistics about the dangers of drinking and using drugs. I prayed fervently that God would enliven my heart and soul to know—really know—why it is such a big deal for our children to use drugs and alcohol. In this chapter I will tell you the answers God has given me over time. But first, the following facts will arm you with information you must know if you are to give strong reasons as to why it's a big deal when your daughter uses these substances.

FACING FACTS

Within five minutes of walking into her public high school (and some private schools as well), your daughter can buy any type of drug or alcohol that you can think of. I could fill this book with statistics about the prevalence and practice of substance abuse among teenagers. Best-selling author Katherine Ketcham has written more than ten books on the use and abuse of drugs and alcohol. She has also developed a curriculum for teenagers with alcohol and/or drug problems. She poignantly states: "I knew a lot about alcohol and other drugs when I started working with kids, but I was not prepared for the magnitude of the drug problem I would encounter. Virtually every adolescent I meet has had some experience with alcohol and/or other drugs. Most of the kids are in trouble with drugs, and an astonishingly high percentage of them are addicted."[1]

In the next three chapters, we will discuss cigarettes, alcohol, and drugs (especially marijuana) much more fully and specifically. For now, consider the following.

CIGARETTES

We've all heard about the risks of smoking—cancer, heart disease, high blood pressure. It's written on the side of the packages in black and white. Nicotine also produces bad breath, yellow teeth, and, eventually, yellow skin and fingernails. According to research:[2]

- Eighteen percent of teenagers between the ages of thirteen and fifteen smoke cigarettes in this country. Only 56 percent of adolescent smokers say they want to stop smoking.
- Increasing numbers of adolescent smokers use unfiltered cigarettes. (They're easier and cheaper to buy at health-food stores and head shops.) According to the Centers for Disease Control and Prevention, these cigarettes have higher levels of carbon monoxide, nicotine, and tar than regular cigarettes.
- Forty percent of teenagers between the ages of fourteen and twenty-two said that popular kids were more likely to smoke than unpopular kids.
- A 2002 report by the Centers for Disease Control and Prevention found that girls who are trying to lose weight are *40 percent* more likely to smoke.
- Currently more than 1.5 million adolescent girls in the United States smoke cigarettes.
- "Sixty-five million Americans use tobacco products, and every year 440,000 of these people die."

Yet in spite of the risks, says Marcel Danesi,

people, especially teens, continue to smoke. The tribal symbolism of the cigarette has not as yet been erased from the memorate. Smoking is a largely unconscious coming-of-age ritual rooted in a body language that keeps the two sexes highly interested in each other. [An adolescent girl's] hair-tossing movements, slightly raising a shoulder…leaning over for a "light."… Smoking allows teens to assume a role in sexual acting.[3]

(If you're surprised or confused by the association of sexual expression with cigarette smoking, just wait until the next chapter!) Nicotine also "stimulates the adrenal glands to release adrenaline, causing an almost immediate surge of energy and euphoria." Recent research has also found that nicotine increases the production of dopamine, the natural feel-good chemical in the brain that enlivens hope.[4]

Smoking is a big deal because it gives your daughter false hope that she can handle social anxiety without putting herself at high risk for a premature death and engaging in a practice that will make her physically unattractive.

ALCOHOL

Drinking, even in small amounts, is hazardous to so many aspects of adolescent health—physical, emotional, and spiritual. Consider these compelling statistics:[5]

- Five percent of all deaths of kids between ages fifteen and twenty-nine are attributable to alcohol.
- Eighty percent of young women in high school reported having at least one drink. Fifty percent reported current alcohol use. By the time these young women are seniors, 33 percent will be heavy drinkers. (Heavy drinking is defined by the *Diagnostic and Statistical Manual of Mental Disorders* as having four or more alcoholic drinks per day).
- Teens who drink are *seven times* more likely to have sex and twice as likely to have sex with four or more partners.
- Almost 50 percent of adolescent victims of crime said they were drinking and/or using a substance at the time they were victimized.
- Within minutes of drinking alcohol, you feel the hopeful effects: "a sense of well-being, relaxation, increased confidence, and reduced anxiety."

- Alcohol destroys cells in the hippocampus, the brain's long-term memory storage area. It's hard to have hope when you have trouble remembering.
- Drinking leads to problems with attention span, focus, organization, and follow-through. Hope erodes when you have fuzzy thinking.
- A recent study suggests that beer drinking can increase the likelihood of dementia later in life.
- Alcohol slows down liver function and can slow down metabolism. (I tell girls that drinking will make them gain weight.) You can't hope for a positive body image if you are a chronic drinker.

Alcohol damages the young brain, interferes with mental and social development, and interrupts academic progress. Alcohol is the fatal attraction for many teens, a major factor in the three leading causes of teen death—accidents, homicide, and suicide.

—JOSEPH CALIFANO,
"Teen Tipplers: America's Underage Drinking Epidemic"

- Alcohol directly damages the heart muscle.
- Alcohol increases anxiety, panic attacks, depression, irritability, paranoia, mental confusion, foggy thinking—all of which are precursors to hopelessness.
- Chronic drinking damages the nervous system. Symptoms can range from mental confusion to loss of motor skills, hallucinations, and brain hemorrhage.

Drinking is a big deal because it gives your daughter false hope that she can handle her problems, deal with her stress, and conquer her challenges without engaging in self-destructive behaviors.

MARIJUANA

Marijuana is the most frequently used illegal drug in the United States. More than 83 million Americans over the age of twelve have tried it at least once. The average age of first use is between thirteen and fourteen. Consider the following effects of marijuana use:

- Adolescents who use marijuana are more likely to engage in deviant behavior, more aggressive, and more rebellious. They also experience relationship problems with parents and associate more with drug-using friends.[6]
- Teenagers who smoke weekly are *six times* more likely to run away from home, *five times* more likely to steal, *six times* more likely to skip school, and *four times* more likely to physically attack others. (This is as true for girls as for boys.)[7]

The use of marijuana can produce adverse physical, mental, emotional, and behavioral changes, and—contrary to popular belief—it can be addictive.

—GLEN HANSON, National Institute on Drug Abuse

- Smoking marijuana first relaxes and then elevates the mood. Some people experience a sense of stimulation with marijuana use, and food, smells, and colors all seem more intense and appealing. Others feel a sense of tranquillity. Users (especially teenagers) may shift between hilarity and introspection.[8] Teens express that they are able to talk more openly and be less intimidated by social settings. Who wouldn't hope for that?
- Long-term research with adolescents who use marijuana finds that these teenagers are less motivated to achieve. Marijuana is called the "antihedonia" drug—it makes you not care about anything. "Pot-heads" are never associated with hope.

Smoking marijuana is a big deal because it distorts the hope that you can feel good about life and yourself without using an illegal drug, which will eventually make you feel that you are worthless and will eradicate your desire to do anything for yourself or others.

FACTS WITH A VISION

Now, when your daughter complains, "Mom, why are you making such a big deal out of one beer or smoking a little pot?" you can give her a few facts and figures. She will roll her eyes. She may debate you: "You drink, Mom, what's the difference?" or "Marijuana is totally natural and legal in most countries around the world" or "It's my body, and if I want to get cancer, that's my choice." *But tell her the facts anyway.* The subconscious is a powerful part of our brains. MTV knows it. Musicians know it. Worship leaders know it. Alcoholics Anonymous knows it. When we hear something over and over again, it traces a pathway in our brains. We just can't control or predict when the information will click in and begin to influence our choices.

Keep in mind that while you have to know the facts, just stating them will make you sound like the adults in the Charlie Brown cartoons who blabber in "parentspeak." You also need a *vision* for who your daughter is and can be. Facts and vision merged together give you power to create an alliance with your daughter against the allure of drugs and alcohol. You fight substance abuse in your daughter's life by *relentlessly* reminding her not only of the facts about drugs, cigarettes, and alcohol but also of your vision for the woman she can become. This combination can help open her eyes, her mind, and her heart to why using substances is such a big deal.

USING DRUGS AND ALCOHOL IS A BIG DEAL
BECAUSE IT KILLS FAITH

"Faith is being sure of what we hope for and certain of what we do not see" (Hebrews 11:1). Faith is being eight years old and believing you can become an astronaut. Faith is being sixteen and knowing—just knowing—that serving dinner to the homeless on Christmas Eve will make a difference in the world. Faith is the fuel that empowers us to make decisions, try different options, and choose pathways that will ultimately shape who we are.

When your daughter drinks three beers and a tequila shooter, she is, on some level, demonstrating a lack of faith in herself—faith that she might be the kind of person who really makes a difference in the world because God has made her unique and wonderful. When your daughter smokes a little weed, she is killing her faith that her mind and effort will get her into a college that will prepare her for a job she actually can't wait to get up and do every day. When she stands out behind the garage and lights up her fourth cigarette of the day, she is killing her faith that she can relieve stress and feel at ease in relationships without the aid of something that is slowly killing her.

When Jaime and her mom first came to me for counseling, Jaime had been making bad choices since the seventh grade. I asked her to tell me about the girl she was when she was twelve years old. She didn't blink an eye when she answered, "I was happy." Her mom's stiffened demeanor softened as she added, "You really were. I remember you were singing all the time and playing practical jokes on your little sister."

"What happened?" I asked.

Now it was Jaime's turn to stiffen. "Nothing" was her one word answer. I knew there was a story here that would explain Jaime's pursuit to kill everything inside of her. Jaime continued, "That girl was stupid. She thought life could be all happy and simple, but it's not."

"So after you smoke pot or get drunk, what do you think about life?" I asked Jaime.

"I think this is as good as it gets. I mean, sometimes I feel a little hungover or sick, but I can't wait until I can drink or smoke again so I don't have to feel."

Jaime's answer broke my heart. "So you use drugs and alcohol to guarantee that you'll never want anything more from life or ever be disappointed again?" I asked.

"I guess you could put it that way," Jaime said. Then she crossed her arms, leaned back on my couch, and added, "It works."

I could see fear and anger cross Jaime's mom's face. What mother wouldn't be shocked and even disgusted by this seventeen-year-old girl's perspective on life. "How do you feel about what Jaime just said?" I asked her mother.

"I think it's awful," she shuddered.

And then I looked at Jaime. "What impact does it have on you to see your mother's fear and contempt?"

"It just makes me want to get away from her." Jaime then hurled these words at her mom: "To tell you the truth, *she* makes me want to drink!"

Sitting in my office were two hurting people who were inflicting even more hurt on each other. Something had happened to make Jaime give up on life, and Jaime's choices made her mother feel like giving up on her. Jaime's use of drugs and alcohol had blurred both of their visions for the future.

Now, maybe, even as a mom who longs for the world for your child, you find your cynicism growing, and you're mumbling, "Well, my daughter probably won't be an astronaut or save the homeless." You see, we moms can lose faith too—no longer being sure of something we hope for (good and glory for our daughters) in the absence of visible evidence. If we are to speak with passion and purpose to our daughters about the reasons not to use drugs and alcohol, we have to shelve our cynicism. If our daughters sense that we, like the culture at large, believe that teenagers are just troubled, materialistic, selfish losers, then we can exhort them all we want to "just say no" to substances, but what they'll hear is, "You're probably not going to get what you want or be what you want, so why fight temptation?"

I knew that part of my privilege in working with Jaime and her mom would be to help them recapture faith. I asked them to pull out pictures of Jaime from birth to the seventh grade and bring them to our next session. They were a little dubious, but agreed to bring the pictures. When they arrived at my office, I asked them to spread the pictures out across the floor. We looked down at baby pictures, grade-school pictures, and pictures of family fun. I asked Jaime and her mom to tell me the stories they remembered from these pictures. It didn't take long before we were transported to another world—a time before Jaime was kidnapped by drugs and alcohol. By the end of the session, we were all down on the floor looking intently at pictures, laughing at stories, and remembering what had been lost in the heartache and bad choices of the past few years. I asked Jaime's mom to stay behind at the end of the session.

"Now you remember who your daughter really is," I said. Then I asked her to do the assignment in the Just for You section that follows. I knew she could do it because a vision of who her daughter really was had just eclipsed her anger and disgust at her daughter's recent choices.

JUST FOR YOU

1. How do you currently see your daughter? Write it out and include her talents, quirks, past accomplishments and experiences, expressed desires, character qualities. What is your vision for your daughter's future?
2. If your vision is somewhat "flat," why do you think it is? For

two weeks pray daily for a vision of faith for your daughter—
hope for what you cannot see. Then try writing your vision for
her again.

3. Keep this vision statement everywhere—in your bathroom, by your
    bedside, in your glove box, in your secret stash of Hot Tamales and
    M&M's (doesn't every mom have one of those?)—and maybe display
    pictures of your daughter (current photos as well as ones from when
    she was younger). If you are going to convince your daughter that it is
    a big deal to use anything that kills her faith in her potential to be all
    her Creator could possibly have in mind, then you have to keep your
    own faith in your daughter alive and vital. Make it a habit to look at
    old pictures of your daughter, cards she has drawn, school papers she
    has written. Recall times when your daughter has revealed the best of
    herself. When your own vision of your daughter is clear and your faith
    in her is strong, then you will be in a much more powerful position to
    tell her over and over again, with personal and passionate conviction,
    why it's a big deal to smoke, drink, and use drugs. Bottom line: These
    substances can take her far away from who she is and who she is
    meant to be. And this is a tragedy that you, as her mother, never want
    her to experience.

HITTING BOTTOM

I worked with Jaime's mom for a few sessions, addressing her fear and anger
and arming her with information and ideas to fuel her vision for her daughter. We asked Jaime to join us after her mom had done some work. Jaime's
mom simply and beautifully shared with her daughter a vision for her future
and her heartache at Jaime's derailed life.

Jaime became visibly agitated during this session. I knew that her
mother's soft and passionate heart was threatening Jaime's hardened and
frightened heart. Jaime had worked hard to hate everyone and not want
much from others. This session disrupted her perspective, and I feared that
Jaime was now at risk of trying even harder to kill anything that might be

growing in her own heart. Using drugs and alcohol is a very effective way to sabotage anything good. Jaime had become a skilled saboteur.

In an effort to preempt a further downward spiral, I said, "Jaime, I know you're going to be tempted to kill anything good that is starting to grow between you and your mom. Please don't."

She didn't answer me. All week I was concerned about Jaime and prayed for her. At Jaime's next counseling session, she confirmed my fears. She told me all about the previous weekend when she had intended to go camping with a few friends. They loaded their gear and headed to the Rocky Mountains, only to discover that if you don't have a reservation, there's no room at the "inn" of the mountain parks. So, Jaime and her "friends" (who turned out to be three older boys) found a room in the Americana Motel in a suburb of

JUST FOR THE TWO OF YOU

Ask your daughter for two hours some evening. Set aside a special, cozy place. Maybe light a few candles, play some of her more mellow favorite music, make tea or hot chocolate, or pour two cold sodas.

1. Together, create a ten-page photo album. On each page place one picture from your daughter's growing-up years. Choose a picture that shows her exuberantly swinging on the swing set, a sweet picture of her nestled in her daddy's arms, a funny picture of her with messy chocolate pudding all over her mouth, an embarrassing picture of her in the sixth grade with big bangs and wearing blue eye shadow.

2. As you look at each picture, mimic a version of that popular TV commercial from *Monster.com,* an employment Web site. You know the one—where children and young people are saying things like "When I grow up, I want to work at a job that pays minimum wage" or "When I grow up, I hope I work for someone who yells at me every day." You might make some of the following statements, which are all true experiences of girls I counsel.

   • "When I grow up, I hope I get so drunk at a party that I take off my shirt and dance on top of the kitchen table."

   • "When I grow up, I want to smoke pot every day at lunch and ask

Denver. One of the boys checked them into this less-than-reputable establishment. One by one they walked past the desk clerk with an air of sophistication that the clerk didn't buy for one minute—or care about, either. He'd rented a room for the weekend. He didn't care what happened there.

Jaime and her friends unpacked their meager belongings and suitcases filled with alcohol. They spent four days—four beautiful, Colorado spring days—in a dirty, seedy motel drinking. They ordered pizzas and worried about the police cars circling the motel during the night. They didn't talk loudly or laugh or turn on the television for fear of drawing attention to themselves. They stayed in their room and drank. Jaime had sex with all three boys.

On the morning of the fourth day, Jaime dragged herself out of bed into the bathroom. She looked in the mirror and saw a person she never dreamed

incredibly stupid questions in my fifth-period English class, such as 'Ms. Lundquist, is a comma a verb or a noun?'"

- "When I grow up, I hope some boys put something in my rum and Coke that makes me dizzy and kind of pass out, so that the next morning I'm not exactly sure what happened with those boys, and everyone starts calling me a slut."

- "When I grow up, I hope I spend five dollars every day on cigarettes, and I hope my car smells so strongly of tobacco that my sister won't even ride in it."

3. After you go through the album, say kindly and fiercely to your daughter, "It is a big deal for you to use drugs and alcohol because it kills your faith in yourself. It can take you so far away from who you were meant to be." Then, don't lecture. Instead, offer your daughter a back rub or a drive to Dairy Queen for an ice-cream cone.

4. Kiss your daughter good night (if she'll let you) and tell her firmly that *you* have not lost faith in who she is and who she will be. Share bits and pieces of your vision for her as you spend more times like this together.

5. Before you yourself turn in for the night, get down on your knees and ask God to keep your own faith alive and burning for your daughter.

of being. Her head hurt, she felt nauseous, her mouth was parched, and she told me that "every inch of my body felt filthy." She added, "Then I remembered what you and my mom told me at our last session: 'You are killing the girl you were meant to be.'"

Jaime slipped out of the Americana Motel at 5:30 a.m., leaving all her stuff in the room. She walked until she found a pay phone and called her parents collect. "Please come get me. I hope it's not too late."

Of course it's not too late for Jaime to recover from the choices and self-harm she inflicted on herself. She has continued counseling and has entered drug and alcohol education and treatment. She may deal with the memories and consequences of her actions for a while, but with good help, she will heal. Her faith in herself will be restored as she does the work of recovering from substance abuse and begins to make good choices.

By faith, Moses's mother hid him for three months after he was born. And then she was willing to do anything—pose as a slave/teacher in the palace, pray for her son, watch him grow from afar, cry herself to sleep at night in fear and in missing him—because she saw that he was no ordinary child, and she was not afraid of all the stories and statistics about drugs and alcohol.

—HEBREWS 11:23 (author's paraphrase, emphasis added)

Of course, Jaime's mom was devastated by Jaime's weekend experience. I don't know of anything harder for moms than watching and waiting while our daughters hit bottom. I thought about the New Testament story of the prodigal, and I suspect that most of us mothers really want our children to be more like the older brother working dutifully in the field rather than the wayward prodigal partying away his future. I remind myself and other mothers that it was the prodigal who returned home to his Father with more faith in his Father and a greater experience of grace than the older brother had in the midst of doing his duty.

Jaime's mom understood something critical about this story after her prodigal daughter called her. She told me, "I could view this horrible weekend with anger and disgust, but I don't. I see it as a means of bringing Jaime home—I mean *really home.*" She is becoming a mom of great faith.

Using Drugs and Alcohol Is a Big Deal
Because It Distorts Hope

We don't have to look far to see evidence that the adolescent world is often cruel and cold. In my first book in this series— *"Mom, I Feel Fat!"*—I encouraged parents to stand in the hallways of their child's middle or high school and listen and observe. If you do, you'll hear unspeakable verbal assaults, you'll see girls get their bra straps pulled, and you'll see boys and girls hug— closely and sexually—while others watch curiously or feel outcast. In the parking lot, music expressing sadistic, sexist lyrics will blare. In classrooms, tired and cynical teachers—who can really blame them?—will overlook the girl in the last row who is "a little out of it" because everyone knows her water bottle is filled with vodka. An overworked and overwhelmed teacher may tell a struggling student to "grow up and stop relying on Mommy to get you out of your schoolwork," embarrassing her in front of the entire class. And then teenagers go home to often empty houses where they will eventually spend eight to eleven minutes talking with their parents that evening.[9]

The lyrics to one of the most popular teen songs of 2001 reflect the haunting loss of hope among adolescents: "I tried so hard and got so far / but in the end it doesn't even matter."[10] This hard-core adolescent angst was expressed to me by one of my fifth-grade clients. Her parents brought her to see me because she seemed depressed. This straight-A student was now making Cs, wasn't sleeping, and wasn't having very much fun anymore. She described her life: "So, I finish the fifth grade, and then I have sixth grade. And then there is middle school and all that homework, and the boy problems start. And then I finish middle school to go to high school. Will I be a cheerleader, a dork, or a volleyball player? Then you work hard in high school and have to get into a college. And in college it's all the same work and grades and trying to figure out where you belong. And then you get a job and have to make money and work all the time. What's the point?"

This eleven-year-old girl was asking about hope. I knew I needed an answer that might keep her from embracing the false hope that was waiting to greet her when she started middle school in just one short year. The answer many adolescents hear from popular culture is that there *is* no hope, except in substance use. We parents know that it's a false hope, a dangerous hope, and a fleeting hope. But we had better admit that, even so, *it is a hope*—a hope that is more available than parents sometimes are; a hope that is more predictable and often more accepting than peers can be; a hope that "works" more quickly than making good choices or, dare I say, even seeking God.

As Jaime continued in counseling, I learned more of her story. When she was in the seventh grade, she had her first boyfriend, who was two years older than she was. "He was really popular, and everyone thought I was really cool because he liked me," Jaime explained. I knew a turn in the story was coming.

"We started going out. We walked home from school together. We would stop in the park by my house and kiss and stuff." Jaime stopped. She didn't talk for several minutes.

"Then what happened?" I asked as gently as I could.

"He asked me to come to his house one day after school. When we got there, no one was home. We started kissing, and then he started doing more stuff. I was scared and told him to stop, but he wouldn't." Jaime was starting to cry. "I tried to push him away at first, and then I just went numb. He went all the way. I was so scared. I pulled my clothes back on and ran home. I never told anyone... But that's not the worst part." Jaime stopped talking again.

I suspected what came next, and my heart was filled with compassion for Jaime and anger at what she had experienced. "What was the worst part?" I asked.

"He...he...," Jaime was crying harder, "he never talked to me again. When I walked past him at school, he would say something to his friends, and they would all laugh at me. I don't know what I did that was so wrong."

When Jaime looked up at me, I could feel the weight of shame she had carried all these years. It was crushing. I wanted to put my arms around her and tell her that she had done nothing wrong. But I knew Jaime needed to understand for herself how this story had pushed her into the arms of alcohol and drugs.

"What have you thought you did wrong?" I asked.

"I thought I was stupid and worthless." Jaime's tone became harder. "I thought no one good or popular would ever want me again. I decided that nothing mattered anymore."

Jaime had just described her loss of faith and hope and her determination to keep either one from growing in her heart ever again.

"Jaime," I said gently, "he raped you."

She looked at me with a mixture of confusion and disbelief. "But he was my boyfriend," she said.

"But you told him no. He kept on anyway, and that is rape. And then he tossed you aside, and that is evil. I am so sorry."

Jaime was quiet for a long time. One tear trickled down her cheek, and then she said, "I never thought of it that way."

"Jaime," I continued, "imagine if this had happened to your younger sister."

Jaime sat upright, immediately agitated. "I would have called the police. I would have told her that it wasn't her fault. I would have kept her from doing what I did."

"Now it's time to use that courage to fight for yourself," I said.

The work Jaime did after this session still amazes me. She told her mom what had happened. When teenagers harbor shameful experiences without an adult perspective to help them sort things out, they often create a false reality and come to harmful conclusions about themselves. Don't assume that you know everything that has happened in your daughter's life. If she seems hellbent on destroying herself, some past event probably made this decision make sense to her. You will probably need an objective person, like a counselor, to help your daughter tell her story and gain a true perspective.

I knew that hope was coming back to life in Jaime when she told me, "Every day I am determined to make choices that don't let what happened to me in seventh grade define me in bad ways. I want to live in a way that proves I am worth something."

Jaime's mom experienced a shift in her hope as well. As she watched Jaime change before her eyes, she told me, "I know that God has been in this whole process, working in and around and through Jaime's bad choices and terrible conclusions about herself as well as my loss of hope and inability to make her change."

JUST FOR YOU

As you reflect on the following questions, be honest about where you place your hope when life is upsetting, disappointing, stressful, unpredictable, and hurtful. Circle the answer that most closely describes you. "Hope is an expectation of receiving, a conviction that there is a way to obtain what we long for. Where we place our hope determine what we surrender to."[11] We were made to surrender to Someone who can be trusted. Sadly, in our confused, chaotic jumble of emotions and experiences, we often surrender to unholy gods. Perhaps the most unholy gods of false hope are drugs and alcohol, but we can also turn to gods of shopping, eating, cleaning, busyness, and unhealthy dependencies on relationships. You will have little power to model authentic, hopeful living for your daughter if your own hope is distorted.

1. What do you do when you feel left out by your husband or friends?

   Eat   Get mad   Organize your cupboards   Talk to him/them about it

2. When you are stressed out, what do you do?

   Sleep   Pray   Exercise   Eat potato chips   Have a glass of wine

3. When you experience a financial stressor or crisis, do you:

   Go shopping   Make a strict budget   Call your parents for a loan

4. When your daughter skips school and gets caught, what do you do?

   Call your friends   Take a nap   Read a novel   Sneak outside for a smoke

5. When you and your husband have a big fight, what do you do?

   Buy a new outfit   Clean the house   Tell all your friends what a jerk
   your husband is

When you are deeply disappointed because you've discovered that your daughter drinks, or you find cigarettes in her purse or marijuana in the seat pocket of her car, you must exercise hope by prayerfully reminding yourself, "Whom have I in heaven but you? And earth has nothing I desire besides you. My flesh and my heart may fail, but God is the strength [the hope] of my heart and my portion forever" (Psalm 73:25-26). When you remember that your hope is in God alone, you are ready to begin to gently, creatively, and effectively dismantle your daughter's distorted hope in drugs and alcohol.

USING DRUGS AND ALCOHOL IS A BIG DEAL
BECAUSE IT LIMITS LOVE

How do you love your daughter after she's come home with alcohol on her breath, or you've found cigarettes in the glove box of her car, or you find out that she didn't spend the night at Brittany's house but went camping with a bunch of guys and girls and probably had a lot more than s'mores for snacks?

Here are some of my favorite ways to "love" my daughter when she blows it:

- I wake her up early with a list of chores and say something in an oh-so-attractive voice, such as, "You'd better start working now because all your free time is mine from this minute until you graduate from college."
- I don't speak to her at all.
- I smile sweetly and say, "I hope you're proud of the embarrassment and trouble you have brought to this family."
- "After all I've done for you, and *this* is how you repay me!" (Inducing guilt is one of my gifts!)

You see, it is our tight, paltry, pinched, vindictive—and scared and confused and hurt—love that makes our daughters ask, "Why are you making such a big deal out of this?" I hope that the facts and ideas in this chapter have given you a better understanding of why it is a big deal when our daughters use drugs and alcohol.

But there is one more question we would be wise to answer. Is it a big deal *to God* when our daughters smoke, drink, or use drugs? And if so, why?

If your daughter lies and says she's at a friend's house and that the parents are home, but then you get a call from the police at 1:00 a.m. saying that the party has been "raided," no parents are there, and that your daughter is at the police station with a "drinking ticket," is that a big deal to God?

Does God care if your daughter craves marijuana and can't wait to get out of class so she can smoke behind the high school?

Is it a big deal to God if your daughter smokes cigarettes? After all, most kids smoke. We hate to admit it. They might not smoke often, but they do smoke. Ninety percent of all smokers begin before the age of eighteen. A 2001 report stated that one in three twelfth-grade women reported smoking cigarettes in the preceding thirty days.[12]

What is the big deal about substance use—to God? What are the *spiritual* consequences of substance abuse? I think answering that question might change how we parent in the midst of the drug and alcohol morass we get pulled into when our daughters enter adolescence.

I sometimes wake in the early morning and listen to the soft breathing of my children. And I think to myself, this is one thing I'll never regret and I carry that quiet with me all day long.

—BRIAN ANDREAS, *Still Mostly True: Collected Stories and Drawings*

Perhaps the best way to begin understanding how substance abuse limits love is to consider how Jesus responds when *we* choose the wrong things time and time again, when we do things that erode who we were meant to be, and when we distort our own hope in God as the Resource of our lives. Does He make a big deal about sin? I was reading *The Ragamuffin Gospel* by Brennan Manning when it finally "clicked" for me (as it will—oh, I promise it will—with our daughters) what God does when we sin: *He pours out His love.*

I have to tell you that I was raised a legalist. I attended a wonderfully academic and astoundingly legalistic college: Bob Jones University. I often wondered, *Isn't there a catch to this unconditional love thing? After all, I've been really bad.*

Perhaps our daughters have been really bad. What if there is no catch? Or as Peter Hiett (my wonderful pastor who relentlessly reminds me of God's love) says, "there is absolutely, truly, and forever no catch. For that means God is not like us—like scared, mad [mothers]. He is absolute love."[13] The really big deal about our daughters' use of drugs and alcohol is that it limits their capacity to give and receive this absolute love. And the Enemy wins twice when we allow our daughters' drug and alcohol use to put us in bondage to guilt and shame so we cannot give and receive love either.

In The Chronicles of Narnia, the wonderful series by C. S. Lewis, Aslan the lion, who represents Christ, is sometimes scary but always loving. He is always singing of his love in between roars and growls (and whatever other noises lions make). Uncle Andrew the magician doesn't like the song, and he tries to convince the children that Aslan's song (God's song) is all about guilt and shame and punishment and roaring and growling. Read what Aslan says to the children about faithless Andrew and others whose hope is so distorted:

> I cannot [speak] to this old sinner, and I cannot comfort him either; he has made himself unable to hear my voice. If I spoke to him, he would hear only growlings and roarings. Oh Adam's sons, how cleverly you defend yourselves against all that might do you good![14]

> You see, they will not let us help them. They have chosen cunning instead of belief. Their prison is only in their own minds, yet they are in that prison, and so afraid of being taken in that they cannot be taken out.[15]

When our daughters use drugs and alcohol, they are in a prison and cannot hear our love—or are afraid to hear it. Likewise, when our daughters use drugs and alcohol, we often cannot speak our love to them—or are afraid to speak it. But there is great hope for change, especially if we let it begin with us.

Do you know why it is a big deal when you sin? Peter Hiett answers that question better than I ever could:

> When we...lust, lie, retaliate, we can't believe in God's love. For God is love. And not believing in God['s love] is not just *a* sin, but *the* sin. So I'm convinced your deepest problem is not the cigarettes you smoke or the alcohol you drink in secret. It's not the slander you speak and the gossip you cherish. It's not the pornography you pleasure yourself with when no one's looking. It's not the baby you aborted; it's not that you

betrayed your brother, cheated on your bride and lied about the whole thing… Your deepest problem is that somewhere deep down inside, you believe Jesus the Messiah rose from the dead just to *kick your [butt]* when, in fact, He rose from the dead so you would believe all is forgiven. It is finished. Justice is accomplished. And the Father is pleading, "Come home, come home, come home!"[16]

Just for You

- Do you believe that God is watching you with a tender eye, checking up on you with a parent's heart of love, weeping over your failures and struggles, and waiting for you to come home so that He can say, "All is forgiven. I love you"? Why or why not?
- Read Luke 15—the story of the prodigal—every day for a month. Ask God to show you how to wait and watch for your prodigal. Consider how God waits and watches for you. Ask God to show you how to welcome your prodigal home. How does God welcome you home when you stray from his love?
- Ask God to infuse your heart with extravagant love for your prodigal as you experience—heart and soul—God's extravagant love for you, a prodigal. Write down the ways God loves you when you are distant from Him, doubt Him, or even disobey Him. How can you translate this unwavering love to your daughter?

Do not allow the Enemy to win twice in this war on drugs and alcohol. Do not let the Enemy of love keep you from giving love to your daughter, no matter how far she has wandered. And as you experience God's love for you, let it lead you in loving your daughter when she makes mistakes, experiments with substances, gets in too deep, or becomes addicted to substances that can deaden her heart, kidnap her soul, and kill her body. Practice loving your daughter fully and freely even when she is acting mean, sullen, withdrawn, rebellious, scary, or out of it. When you know she's lying, using substances, and/or drinking, don't stop loving her. That doesn't mean you don't deal with her behaviors (much more practical advice on this topic is to come); but un-

conditional love is the only foundation strong enough to withstand the bat-
tering of teenage life and culture. If your daughter understands that it is a big
deal for her to use drugs and drink because it keeps her from fully *experiencing* your love and the love of God, then she will be more likely to begin to
change from the heart. This will take time, failures, brokenness, and matur-
ing on her part.

In the meantime, she must not stop feeling confident of your love, or all
may be lost in your relationship with her. Don't be afraid that loving her will
give her permission to act badly. I don't find that anywhere in the Bible. The
apostle Paul explained this radical love that is so "other" from the way we
love. We must plead daily for God to help us experience His love so that we
can lavish it on our daughters and surprise them with it:

> Christ has set us free to live a free life. So take your stand! Never again
> let anyone put a harness of slavery on you.
>
> I am emphatic about this. The moment any one of you submits
> to…rule-keeping system[s], at that same moment Christ's hard-won
> gift of freedom is squandered.…
>
> When you attempt to live [or force your children to live] by your
> own religious plans and projects, you are cut off from Christ, you fall
> out of grace.… What matters is something far more interior: faith
> expressed in love.…
>
> Just make sure that you don't use this freedom as an excuse to do
> whatever you want to do and destroy your freedom. Rather, use your
> freedom to serve one another in love; that's how freedom grows. For
> everything we know about God's Word is summed up in a single sen-
> tence: Love others as you love yourself. That's an act of true freedom!
> (Galatians 5:1-14, MSG)

While something else might "save" your daughter from drugs and alcohol—a bad experience, a time in the corrections system, a testimony from
someone in her youth group—if you lose the opportunity for your love to lead
her to safety, then you have missed something precious. Loving my daughter
to health and life is a privilege that I, for one, don't want to ever lose.

Jaime barely graduated from high school. She had to complete two classes online and do lots of extra credit to make up for all the poor academic choices she had made throughout high school. But she did graduate, and I was honored to be invited to her graduation party. Her friends—some with questionable clothes and demeanors—were in attendance. I smelled cigarettes and alcohol on a few of her peers. Jaime had not yet completely made a break from these friends, although I knew she was abstaining from drugs and alcohol. She regularly passed drug tests and was a star student in her drug and alcohol education class.

Jaime's family was also in attendance. Her grandparents and other relatives were surprised and pleased that Jaime had graduated but were a bit dubious of her friends. Jaime's mother had made an amazing collage of pictures of Jaime that hung on one wall in the living room. I saw many of the pictures we had looked at in my office when Jaime and her mom attempted to recapture faith. Jaime's diploma—a symbol of hope—was proudly displayed on the coffee table in the middle of the living room.

As we all sat in the living room, friends and family began to tell stories about Jaime. I watched Jaime laugh and lap up the attention. she was a very different girl from the one who had first come to see me for counseling. I knew I was seeing the results of her hard work, stops and starts, failure and success. But most of all, I was seeing the evidence of love. Just before I left for the evening, Jaime acknowledged to everyone, "I know that I put my mom through hell. But she kept on loving me. I guess that's why I'm here today."

Our daughters allow us to experience a little bit of hell and a little bit of heaven. I knew that Jaime's mother would walk through hell again if necessary to see the girl before her growing in faith, hope, and love. That may be as close to heaven on earth that we mothers get.

We will be exploring lots more facts, strategies, ideas, and information as we dig into the specifics of teen alcohol and drug use in the following chapters. But if we don't first "get" why it's a big deal—and I mean *really* get it—then we will not be powerful allies in guiding our daughters away from drugs and alcohol and toward being all they are meant to be. So if you need to read this chapter over and over—and over and over—do it. Ask God to help you get it. When you do, you will feel calmer, less angry, and more intentional in your parenting—and maybe even a little energized to start making this the biggest deal of your daughter's life.

Just for the Two of You

1. Ask your daughter what feels like love to her from you. Then practice *showing* her love in those ways during her most unlovely moments. (If nothing else, it will keep her wondering about you!) Here are some of the things my kids have told me feel like love to them from me.

   - cookies fresh from the oven (even Pillsbury "slice and dice" works great)
   - clean sheets on a freshly made bed
   - *my* cleaning up my son's dog's doo-doo
   - popcorn
   - a cold cup of water on the bedside table
   - a full tank of gas
   - mac 'n' cheese
   - a card in the mail from me
   - gum
   - folded laundry

   Make your own list, together with your daughter. Add to it often.

2. Give your daughter opportunities to show love. Even when she is behaving badly, sign her up for a missions trip (you may have to explain a few things to the leader or go along on the trip); go on your own trip to some disadvantaged portion of your city or the country; deliver Meals on Wheels to the homebound; ask your daughter to pick out some clothes/CDs/jewelry that she would be willing to give to someone in a much needier family, box it up, and leave the surprise care package on the doorstep.

Chapter 6

"Mom, I'm Only Smoking Cigarettes!"

As we will see, addiction and attachment; pharmacology and behavior; personality, culture, and genetics all chase each other around like a cat after its own tail when we start to consider the issue of why people smoke.

—DAVID KROGH, *Smoking: The Artificial Passion*

Despite all warnings that smoking-related disease is the number-one killer of women, and that lung cancer has now surpassed breast cancer as the leading cause of cancer death in women, young women continue to light up.

—KIRA VERMOND, "Where There's Smoke, There Are Teenage Girls"

What would you think," I ask the graduate and seminary students in my Substance Abuse Counseling course, "of a mother who brings pictures of her children to her first therapy session?"

I get all kinds of answers from these young counselors-in-training. Most of the answers are not very flattering to the mother.

"She doesn't have a life of her own."

"She's trying to show you her picture-perfect life."

I added a few details for the students. This mother is obviously in emotional pain. She's in the midst of a messy divorce that has shocked her and torn her family apart. The pictures she shows are of her children when they were in elementary school. You know the kind of pictures we've all seen and had taken of us: shiny, scrubbed faces, hair neatly parted and styled, collared shirts in primary colors, and crooked smiles with missing teeth or beginning orthodontia. There are also a few pictures from middle school and high school showing the awkward, inevitable progression from pimply-faced teenager to young man and young woman.

Once again the students look for this mother's pathology.

"She wants to go back to a time in her life when everything was good."

"She's in denial about what has happened to her."

"She's holding on to the only thing she has left."

I surprise the students when I tell them that the mother in the story is me—their teacher, mentor, "expert."

When my marriage fell apart and our family began to feel the strain of being torn apart, my children and I got into family counseling. I have to tell you that being a counselor does not make going to counseling any easier. Consciously, I was not aware at the time of the reason why I grabbed a few school pictures of my children and stuffed them in my purse on my way out the door to see the counselor for the first time. Before I told him any of the details of my divorce—the shock, betrayal, and terror for me—I spread out the pictures of my children on his coffee table as if I were dealing a hand of cards for a fun game of Go Fish.

In that moment I suddenly knew what I was doing—and so did the counselor. I was saying, *It hasn't all been bad. There has been love and laughter and beautiful children along the way to this heartbreaking place in our lives. And there is still something so wonderful: these children whom I love with all my heart and soul and whose mother I will always be.*

Someone wiser and pithier than I once said, "Pictures are our proof that we have been happy." I brought my proof to the counselor before we dived into all the other evidence that wasn't so happy.

And so I tell my counseling students that a woman who takes pictures of her children to therapy probably isn't revealing some deep-seated pathology, but rather her fierce, resilient, shining mother's heart. A heart that holds on through the ups and downs of life, whether they involve a broken marriage or a teenager who is falling apart. A heart that holds on when her daughter brings home As and Bs on her report card and shouts, "Look at me, Mom!" as she does a new trick on the swing set in the backyard. And a heart that holds on when she finds cigarettes in her daughter's car or sees her beautiful girl pull out of the driveway, slip a cigarette into her mouth, and light up with an ease that suggests she's been smoking for a while.

THE FACTS ABOUT GIRLS AND SMOKING

Although overall smoking rates have declined during the past few years, according to a recent study monitoring smoking in the fifteen-through-seventeen age group, more teenage girls smoked in 2000 than teenage boys,[1] and the evidence suggests that this trend is holding steady, if not slightly rising. According to the University of Washington Women's Health National Center for Excellence, *more than one-third* of female high-school seniors are smokers.[2]

Understanding the reasons girls smoke—and are smoking more than boys—is important as we consider strategies to help our daughters stop or stay away from smoking. According to Dr. Elinor Wilson, chief science officer for the Heart and Stroke Foundation of Canada: "Lecturing doesn't help. Punishment doesn't help. It's about closeness and communication—and knowing what your kids are going through and facing."[3] Girls smoke for many of the same reasons they use others drugs and alcohol: to feel okay about themselves, to fit in, and to feel more socially adept. A strong mother-daughter alliance can become a context in which girls develop self-esteem and relational skills. The problem suggests the answer, but this is also a much more complicated issue. Ask any mother with a teenage daughter who smokes.

Recent studies have found a disturbing motivation for teenage girls to smoke: weight control. In a four-year controlled study, researchers asked girls between the ages of twelve and fifteen many questions, including the following:

- How important is it to you to be slim or thin?
- Have you been depressed?
- Have you had trouble sleeping?
- Do you smoke?
- Do you think you will try a cigarette soon?

- If one of your friends were to offer you a cigarette, would you smoke it?

Four years after this study, researchers surveyed the teens again to determine who had become a regular smoker and why. "Teen girls who attached great importance to being thin were *four times* as likely to become established smokers." The study concluded that placing a high value on thinness predicts who will become a teenage smoker.[4]

Helping our daughters develop a positive body image and using the mother-daughter alliance to come up with healthy strategies for weight control can help our daughters stay away from smoking. Once again, the problem suggests a solution. But, again, this issue is more complicated than that. Ask any mother whose teenage daughter smokes.

Just for the Two of You

1. Ask your daughter the questions listed above from the study on smoking and weight control. If your daughter has not considered smoking but worries about her weight, talk about healthy weight-control solutions and begin to build an alliance in this area. My first book in the Hand-in-Hand series—*"Mom, I Feel Fat!"*—is full of ideas to help you help your daughter develop a healthy body image.

2. If your daughter is smoking to control her weight, become educated about the realities of smoking and weight control. *It is a myth that smoking makes anyone lose weight.* This myth developed because many people initially gain weight when they stop smoking, leading us to believe that the opposite is true as well. *Weight loss does not come from breathing smoke into the lungs!* However, smoking *can* work as an appetite suppressant because it releases the chemical dopamine in the brain, which makes us feel good. This is the same feeling we get from eating carbohydrates. Consequently, smoking can become a substitute conduit for the feel-good chemical and can suppress emotional eating.

3. Find as many advertisements for smoking as you can—they're easy to

find. Tobacco companies spend over 6 billion dollars each year on ads that link smoking to fun, friends, and beauty. Point out these links in the ads to your daughter. This exercise is most powerful before she starts smoking. Let her see that every person smoking is tan, slim, and attractive. As you watch television and movies together, notice and point out the context for smoking. Rarely is smoking associated with an unattractive or negative image. (Research indicates that teenagers who watch five hours of television a day are *six times more likely* to start smoking.)[5]

4. Next, show your daughter what women can look like after years of smoking. The Internet is a wonderful *and* terrifying source of information. You can find pictures of just about anything, including some pretty hideous and hilarious pictures of women ravaged by cigarette smoking. (One source for pictures is *www.cnn.com/2004/HEALTH/10/22/eu.smoking.*) Pull some of these pictures off the Net and artfully display them throughout your home. I know one mom who interspersed some of these pictures of women with yellow, leathered skin and yellow teeth, dragging on a cigarette among the pictures of her family displayed on the top of her entertainment cabinet. No lecture needed. Trust God to use the pictures to dismantle your daughter's ill-placed hope in cigarettes. A Canadian study has discovered that when smokers see full-color pictures of how cigarettes affect their mouth, lungs, teeth, skin, and heart, it makes them think more seriously about stopping smoking.

5. If your daughter already smokes, she will be resistant to the exercise above. Ask her if smoking connects her with her friends, if it is a source of fun or relief from boredom, or if it makes her feel more socially adept and attractive. In other words, *ask her to tell her story.* Every girl who smokes has a story of how she started, why she continued, when she wanted to stop, why she didn't, and so on. Again, don't lecture or give alternative suggestions at this point; just try to understand how smoking has become important in her life.

GETTING TO THE HEART OF THE MATTER

The truth is that many parents have given up on being any sort of ally for their smoking teenager. They tell me the same thing their daughters tell me, "Hey, at least it's not drugs. She's just smoking." It's almost as if parents have made an uneasy alliance with their children—"Don't smoke around me, and I'll look the other way as long as you don't do anything scarier." Why would we look the other way when our children are using a drug that is highly addictive and is most certainly lethal in the long term?

I think there are three reasons why we give up on or give in to our daughters' use of cigarettes. First, we decide to pick our battles. Second, we tend to look the other way while our child engages in a very public behavior that is embarrassing or disgusting to us. David Krogh, in his enlightening work on cigarette smoking, writes, "Among addictive practices, cigarette smoking is alone in the degree to which public display of it is allowed."[6] This is true for teenagers as well as adults. Most schools have smoking areas. Even many Christian camps for teenagers include a "smoking area," which gives a nod to the reality that teenagers smoke (three thousand teenagers will try cigarettes today) and that nicotine is extremely addictive. One Toronto study found that more than 20 percent of drug abusers had stronger urges to smoke than to use alcohol or heroin.[7] As Krogh explains: "This very status [acceptable public use], however, probably has made it in some ways a more difficult drug to give up than the more exotic addictive drugs."[8]

The third reason parents often abdicate the battle against nicotine is that they have lost their own battle and are smokers themselves.

In the rest of this chapter, we'll examine these three reasons we parents hold on to as excuses to stay out of the cigarette battlefield. We'll also explore some ideas that can create movement toward positive change. I am not suggesting that we can take on the tobacco companies, advertisers, and our daughters' peers who are smoking. But I am suggesting that we can use this all-too-common experience to connect with our daughters and form a stronger relationship that, regardless of whether it leads them to quit smoking, will certainly create a context in which they can develop a legitimate sense of self-esteem, body image, and social ease without the aid of nicotine.

IS THIS A BATTLE WORTH FIGHTING?

Sometimes we forget that the warning labels on cigarette packs are unique and significant. We don't put warning labels on sugary candy or on cans of soda loaded with sugar and/or chemicals. We put warning labels on cigarettes because they are an undeniably serious health risk. Consider the following statistics:[9]

- Ninety percent of all lung cancers and deaths from lung disorders are linked to cigarette smoking.
- Female smokers ages eighteen to forty-nine are three times more likely than nonsmokers to have brain hemorrhages.
- Smoking causes 30 percent of heart attacks and strokes.
- Women who smoke are more likely to develop osteoporosis.
- Adolescent smokers are twice as likely to be depressed as adolescent nonsmokers.
- Female smokers often take longer to conceive than nonsmokers.
- Adolescent smokers are more than *eleven times* more likely to use illegal drugs and *sixteen times* more likely to drink heavily.
- Once adolescents start smoking, they are twenty-nine times more likely to fail in their efforts to quit than adult smokers.
- *Females are more susceptible to addiction than males.* Research indicates that Caucasian adolescent females "appear to be the most vulnerable of all people to nicotine addiction."

Of course this is a battle worth fighting! It is literally a battle for life over death. One mother came in for counseling with her sixteen-year-old daughter Hillary because she found cigarettes in her daughter's purse. I commended the mom for not pretending that this was a small offense, but at the same time, she needed help letting go of her judgmentalism and nagging. Both were pushing her daughter away. I asked Hillary where she got the cigarettes. Her answer was predictable. "They aren't mine. I was just keeping them for a friend."

After asking her mom to leave Hillary and me alone for a while, I asked Hillary again about the cigarettes. She told me that they were hers, but she couldn't deal with her mom's freaking out. I told her that her mom freaked out because there were good reasons to be afraid and alarmed about cigarette smoking. Then I asked her where she got the cigarettes. Hillary told me, "I either buy them—there are some stores I know that will sell them to me—or I have an older friend get them for me."

"So you lie," I said. "You lie to your mother, to the clerk at the store, and to yourself when you act like smoking is no big deal."

Hillary didn't say anything for a while, and then she spoke, "Yeah, the lying is the worst part. I wish I could just smoke in the open."

I asked her how realistic it would be for her mother to say, "Hillary, can I buy you some cigarettes today?" We both laughed.

I called Hillary's mom back into the office and surprised both of them by suggesting the inconceivable. We all agreed that lying about smoking was a character flaw that could take root and grow in other areas of Hillary's life. I asked if both mom and daughter were willing to address the lying first. They agreed. I asked Hillary to be honest with her mother about when she "needed" cigarettes and to ask her mother to buy them for her. They both looked at me as if I had just suggested that they go rob a bank together.

I wanted Hillary's smoking to be something that connected her to her mother, and I wanted to facilitate the possibility that Hillary and her mother might actually talk about the smoking in ways that could eventually lead Hillary to stop. I told Hillary's mom, "No freaking out. No judgment." Hillary looked relieved. "But, Mom," I continued, "you are allowed to ask questions like 'How long is it between cigarettes?' 'What do the urges to smoke feel like?' 'Is there something going on that you feel especially stressed about?'" And I told Hillary that she had to answer. She had to let her mom in on her internal world.

Then you will experience for yourselves the truth,
and the truth will free you.

—John 8:31, MSG

This strategy might not work with every mom and daughter, but I had a feeling that it would with Hillary and her mom. When Hillary asked her mom to buy her cigarettes, she was telling the truth. The truth is always a precursor to freedom.

Hillary began to tell her mother about the stress she felt when she went out socially as well as the withdrawal symptoms she experienced—moodiness, nervousness, anxiety, insomnia, difficulty concentrating—when she'd gone without a cigarette for a while. Talking openly with her mother helped relieve some of Hillary's stress and helped her admit that she was addicted to nicotine. When Hillary and her mom returned to counseling with an understanding of the underlying issues, they were willing to accept my referral to a physician, who prescribed an antidepressant for Hillary that addressed the physiological roots of her acute social anxiety and also helped with the nicotine withdrawal symptoms. The doctor also monitored Hillary's use of a nicotine gum that she prescribed to help Hillary stop smoking.

ARE YOU EMBARRASSED TO BE IN THIS BATTLE?

I'll never forget my first counseling session with Cathy. She came to see me because her daughter was starting to get in trouble. I asked, "What kind of trouble?"

Cathy told me, "Well, she's not turning in her homework; she's been late for curfew a few times; she shoplifted; and…um…uh…and"—Cathy looked at the floor—"she's started smoking." Cathy's eyes met mine for a second and then darted away.

"What are you feeling?" I asked Cathy that predictable counselor question that is sometimes a really good question.

"I'm just so embarrassed. My daughter has always been one of those girls who sat with the youth group on the front row at church. I never pictured her smoking. She doesn't even want to go to church anymore."

I was not surprised to hear Cathy express her shame over her daughter's smoking, and I wasn't surprised to hear that her daughter didn't want to go to church anymore—a place where she *felt* her mother's shame.

This session began a wonderful season of counseling with Cathy as we talked about her expectation that her daughter be a "front-row kid," especially since her own adolescent years had been marked by failure, promiscuity, and—you guessed it—smoking. As Cathy dealt with her own unfair expectations of her daughter and did some work on herself, her daughter felt released from the shame and guilt that were propelling her further into "acting out."

So how do we get from here to there—from freaking out over cigarettes to setting our daughters free to love and be loved?

Just for You

1. Make a list of your daughter's behaviors that have embarrassed you. Why do these behaviors embarrass you?
2. What impact do you think your embarrassment has on your daughter?
3. When, if ever, did you do something that embarrassed your parents?
4. What effect did their embarrassment have on you?
5. How do you wish they would have responded to you instead?
6. Do you think God ever feels embarrassed by our behavior? If so, what behaviors do you think embarrass him? What does He feel for us when we make foolish choices? (Read Psalm 103:13; Matthew 23:37; and Romans 5:8.)

THE FIVE CS

Becoming our daughter's ally when she is thinking about smoking or is actually smoking requires what I call the five Cs: courage, creativity, curiosity, compassion, and commitment.

COURAGE

When it comes to our daughters and smoking, courage means we don't ignore the smell of smoke on their clothes or in their cars. We ask, "Are you smoking?" "Have you tried smoking?" "Are you thinking about smoking?" Courage means becoming informed about smoking, noticing our daughters' behaviors around smoking, being diligent in highlighting the dangers of this habit, and being ready to talk about it with them. Courage means telling our daughters over and over about the risks associated with smoking—general risks as well as those specific to females. This is not an easy task because our daughters think they pretty much know everything already.

When Crystal was thirteen years old, her parents got a divorce. Her mom was faced with the overwhelming task of being a full-time parent while holding down a full-time job. By the time Crystal and her mom got home from school and work, they barely had enough energy to plop down in front of the television, eat dinner, and go to bed. There was little time or energy for meaningful conversation.

Crystal's mom explained that she started smelling smoke on her daughter's clothes when she did the laundry. "I told myself that some of her friends were probably smoking. I just didn't want to deal with the possible conflict that would come if I asked Crystal if she was smoking." Crystal's mom was in my small-group Bible study, and we all empathized with her fear and fatigue. The week after she told us about her concerns for her daughter, she showed us her heart of courage.

But here's the only thing I can tell you for sure: Whatever is going on, you already have everything you need to meet this moment in your life. You do not require a makeover. You have the heart and you have the brain to be the parent your kid needs right now. Maybe you're not 100% confident.... You don't need 100% confidence. What you need is who you are right now—your full strength and energy.

—ARIEL GORE, *Whatever, Mom*

"God woke me up in the middle of night," she began. (I love these stories because they unite all mothers who have been on the "night watch" worrying and wondering about their children. I used to think that God had a strange sense of timing, but after many seasons of feeling overwhelmed in my own life, I understand His wisdom. The dark and quiet of the middle of the night is sometimes the only time we harried and hurried moms can hear Him clearly.) "He told me to pay attention to Crystal. It was as if He was saying, 'I notice *everything* about you because I love you. Give Crystal the same attentive love.'"

This courageous mom told us that the next morning she awakened her daughter and told her they would be "playing hooky" that day. They went out to breakfast and then to a discount cosmetics store. "I told Crystal that we were going to test all the fragrances and pick out a perfume that fit our unique personalities. We had such fun," she continued. "We tried all the fragrances, and then we each picked one. Next we drove to a park, and I told Crystal that as far as I was concerned, she had always had a distinct aroma. I told her she exuded passion and resilience. I also told her that I knew her dad's and my divorce had brought some stinky smells into her world. And then I told her that I knew she was smoking—I didn't want to give her a chance to lie—and that I knew she was trying to relieve stress and show her independence in the midst of feeling out of control. I asked her to please quit smoking and told her that every week we would plan something to help relieve her stress (like a massage or a hike), and that every month we would add to our perfume collection."

By this point in the story, we were all on the edge of our seats. "My heart was pounding as I presented my case," she concluded. "I think I surprised her. She told me that she was only smoking at lunch and after school and that she would give my plan a try."

Crystal's mom finished her story with further evidence of her courageous heart for her daughter. "Well, I'll be smelling you and your clothes every day," she told Crystal. "If this plan doesn't work, tell me—or you can bet I'll ask—and we'll try something else!"

We ended our small-group time by praying for Crystal, her mom, and one another, asking God to help us follow this example and be "braveheart" mothers.

CREATIVITY

Try creatively working interesting facts into conversations with your daughter while you are taking walks, riding in the car, or stopping for a drink at Starbucks. Okay, maybe that's not as easy as it sounds. Teenagers generally know when we are trying to get a point across. So just be honest. Tell your daughter you know that three thousand teenagers will start smoking today, and you don't want her to be one of them. Give a reason, and then let it go. If your daughter pursues the conversation, great. If she doesn't, at least you have expressed your informed concern. She may not appreciate it or acknowledge it in the moment, but the information will be in her "data bank," and you can trust God to use it.

[We are] servants who waited on you as you gradually learned
to entrust your lives to our mutual Master. We each carried
out our servant assignment. I planted the seed, [another]
watered the plants, but God *made you grow. It's not the one*
who plants or the one who waters who is at the center
of this process but God, who makes things grow.

—1 CORINTHIANS 3:5-7, MSG

According to the American Lung Association, cigarettes contain a number of toxic chemicals. Memorize the following list so that you will be prepared to talk with your daughter about these deadly ingredients. (The fact that you memorized this information will really impress her.)

- acetic acid—used in hair dye
- acetone—a main ingredient in fingernail polish
- ammonia—a poisonous gas
- arsenic—rat killer
- cadmium—a chemical in car batteries
- carbon monoxide—a poisonous gas
- formaldehyde—embalming fluid
- hydrazine—used in jet and rocket fuel
- hydrogen cyanide—a gas used in gas chambers for execution
- nickel—used for electroplating
- pyridine—a chemical in dog-repellant spray
- toluene—a poisonous solvent, once banned from use in nail polish

One mother I know collected all the cigarette butts she could find in her daughter's car and outside the house and put them in a gallon jar. Then she filled the jar halfway with water and continued to put used cigarettes in the jar. She put the jar in the center of the dining-room table as a powerfully visual centerpiece illustrating how filthy the habit is. After six months of quietly adding to the visual aid, this mother came home one day to find the jar gone. At dinner that night her daughter explained, "I threw the jar away. Looking at it day after day finally got to me. I stopped smoking this morning. Do you think we could go to the store and get some gum or lozenges to help me quit for good?" This mother jumped for joy as she got her car keys!

CURIOSITY

Showing curiosity is not simple communication; it's an art. Asking your daughter questions to gather evidence to use against her or to find a platform for lecturing her about smoking will cause her to tune you out—at best—or withdraw completely—at worst. *Listen to your daughter to understand why she's smoking as well as what she's thinking and feeling.* Your daughter is an expert in one thing: being herself. By listening to her story of smoking, you'll discover who she is. There is not a magic set of words you can say to keep your daughter from smoking or to get her to stop smoking. But there is something magical that happens when communication is open between parent and child. And it starts with asking genuine, agenda-free questions and listening with an open heart and mind.

JUST FOR THE TWO OF YOU

The following questions will help you start to learn your daughter's story of smoking:

- Ask your daughter whether she has ever tried to quit smoking and what that experience was like. Ask about jitters, nervousness, and insomnia. If you've had experience quitting or trying to quit smoking, talk about your experience.
- Since smoking is more about being cool and feeling socially okay than drinking or using drugs is, ask your daughter who she smokes with and what it feels like if she doesn't smoke with her friends.
- Ask your daughter if she smokes to lose weight. Ask her what she doesn't like about her body, how much weight she wants to lose, and what her experience with eating and weight loss has been since she started smoking.

After you've heard your daughter's story, tell her about some habitual behavior—overeating, biting your fingernails, drinking, procrastinating—you have tried to change. Tell her what helped you and what didn't. Then ask your daughter what she thinks might help her stop smoking. Talk about ways you can support and help her. Ask her how she wants you to respond if she experiences setbacks.

It's a good idea to write down her suggestions and desires. Tell her you will think about what she wants and pray about how you can support her. As you think of new things you can do that might be helpful, write them down. Share them with her and ask if they would indeed be helpful. Remember that you are listening to understand. As your understanding of your daughter becomes broader and deeper, you will become a rich resource for her.

COMPASSION

Cathy prayed like crazy that she would be able to let go of her embarrassment about her daughter's smoking. As she asked questions to learn her daughter's story, she laid the groundwork for a compassionate connection with her daughter. Cathy learned that her daughter was under the popular misconception that smoking was keeping her weight under control. She already felt fat at times and didn't want to risk feeling fatter if she quit smoking. Cathy's heart of compassion quickly surpassed any lingering embarrassment. Cathy knew firsthand about yo-yo dieting and weight struggles. She shared with her daughter her own desires and disappointments in the body-image battle. She suggested that they embark on a workout program together. She didn't ask her daughter to quit smoking. Cathy wisely found a small gym that emphasized holistic health and would give them personal attention. Cathy prayed that a natural outcome of feeling good from working out, doing yoga, and eating healthfully would be to cut out unnatural, unhealthy habits.

Courage, curiosity, and compassion merged in Cathy's decision. She picked a gym after she talked to the trainer—a woman who had compassion for both Cathy and her daughter. Cathy knew that her increasingly independent, slightly "alternative" daughter needed an environment that would encourage health while not suppressing the "healthy wildness" growing within her daughter. Their new trainer didn't lecture or judge. She just occasionally tossed out tidbits about health and self-care in a manner that didn't remind Cathy's daughter of anything she'd heard at school or church. This caught Cathy's daughter's attention.

Therefore be as shrewd as snakes and as innocent as doves.

—Matthew 10:16

COMMITMENT

Of course, Cathy's experiment in better health leading to better living cost something. It cost time and money. Cathy scrimped, saved, and sacrificed to pay for the gym and the trainer. She made a shrewd bargain with her daughter. She said that if at the end of six months of consistent training, her daughter still wanted to smoke and use the gym, then her daughter would have to pay her own fees. If, however, she quit smoking, Cathy would continue the gym membership with the added reward of a trip to a place of her daughter's choosing.

I often hear from parents that they are tired, that they wish they could just give their teenagers away or back (to whom, I'm not sure). I hear that nothing works and that they've tried everything. After they finish telling me their legitimate woes, worries, and wonderings about the work of parenting, I ask one question: "What's the alternative?"

Moms, just try quitting. Try to stop worrying. Shut out any thinking of ways to connect with your daughter. Stop wanting a relationship with her. You may be able to do it if you do something destructive to yourself and your heart. Otherwise, you won't be able to. God wired you to *want* and *want for* your daughter.

I recently hosted a seminar for parents of teenagers. My cohost was a gifted therapist who works primarily with teenage boys. He challenged parents to estimate about how much time they spent thinking about, planning for, and learning about their teenagers. He asked one dad—a wonderful pastor in our community—who honestly answered, "About thirty minutes a day." He's probably way ahead of most dads. (This statement is not meant to be an indictment against dads. I believe that part of the unique "weight" of being a mother is that we can't compartmentalize our work and ministry from our mothering—they "bleed" into each other. A Chinese proverb says that children bind the mother's feet. No matter where we walk, our children go with us. Dads generally are able to compartmentalize the various facets of their lives. Thank goodness. That allows them to do the work of providing for their families and to offer a needed perspective to moms who sometimes get swallowed up by their children's lives.)

I looked at the mom sitting next to this pastor-dad. I knew that her daughter was giving her trouble and that this mom was at the seminar because she was desperate for help. I asked her how much time she spent thinking, praying, wondering, worrying, and planning. Her eyes filled with tears, and she answered, "It's all I think about."

To escape our demons we seek comfort in our addictions: our alcohol or being right, workaholism or winning, ice cream, television, religion, cocaine, movies, marijuana, money, power, sex, gambling, compulsive reading, or simply having the last word. What is conspicuously missing is an unshaken trust in the merciful love of the crucified redeeming Christ.... Christianity [is] no longer merely a moral code, an ethic, or philosophy of life but a love affair.

—BRENNAN MANNING, *Above All*

That's how moms are naturally wired. So don't fight it. Take the material from this book (as well as the books listed in the resource section) and try everything. And then try again. Never give up on your daughter. Let her know that when you find cigarettes in her purse, when you see her smoking, when you smell cigarettes on her clothes, these things will not faze you or change your love, ideas, concern, and commitment to her.

Oh, by the way, the trip Cathy's independent, alternative daughter decided to take as her reward for stopping smoking was a mission trip to the Ukraine. She'll probably never sit on the front row at church again, but her heart is fully connected to her desire to be alive, wild, and involved in the lives of others. She has, in part, a wise and wild mother to thank for that.

Cathy wrote this letter to her daughter before she went on the mission trip:

I have not always displayed my love for you in ways that could be taken in by you. For most of those times, I am truly regretful. But for some of those times, I can honestly say, "You had it coming." You had to hear my hurt or anger or fear or frustration because to not hear or see it would inhibit you from seeing the seriousness of your actions. You are capable of hurting and helping, of loving and hating, of faking it and being real, of drawing close to God and stiff-arming him, of giving and taking, of thinking only of yourself and thinking of others first—and so am I. Yet somehow, in the midst of it all, God chose to place us in the same family in the same time and space, with a host of others in our lives who are capable of all the same; impacting one another's lives as iron sharpens iron (and often as nails scraping a chalkboard!)

And so, to the extent that you—and I—accept our acceptance by God and each other, we will be free to be who we are meant to be. Not driven and controlled by guilt or rebellion or performance, but free to live as Christ has chosen us to live—fully alive and fully expressing the uniqueness of who we are. There is only one person who can be you, and that is you.

I cannot ever claim to love you as God does—but I love you as totally and wholly as my finite being is capable. I always have, and I always will. Remember how we used to play, "I love you the most...." "No, I love YOU the most...." "NO, I've loved you longer...." "No, I've loved YOU longer...." "No, I loved you first...." "No, I loved YOU first." It never ended, did it? And neither will my love for you.

So there, I win!

Cathy's acceptance of her daughter in the midst of her smoking, along with proactively loving her daughter to health with candor, humor, hard work, negotiation, unconventionality, challenge, and reward "preached" the gospel to her daughter. Her actions made *tangible* the story of the One who loves us in our sin and leads us into light with such surprising grace.

Are You Fighting Your Own Battle?

When Cathy determined to get over her embarrassment that her daughter wasn't a front-row kid anymore, she started asking questions and discovered that her daughter smoked for many of the same reasons Cathy had smoked in her own adolescence. They mostly had to do with fitting in. Telling our daughters about our own smoking, drinking, and drug-abuse history is tricky. We have to carefully analyze whether our daughters can handle our story without using it to justify their own behavior.

When it comes to such a public behavior as smoking cigarettes, chances are that someone in your circle of family and friends knows you smoked. Your relationship with your daughter will be significantly damaged if she discovers that you have talked to her about not smoking while you smoked at one time or are still battling an addiction to cigarettes.

Cathy told her daughter her own smoking story. She told about begging for cigarettes from friends to look cool, because she felt so awkward and out of it socially. When she told her daughter that she also had to wear skirts that covered her knees and wasn't allowed to wear any makeup, her daughter's empathy for her mother deepened. They bonded over how hard it is to find a sense of belonging and how smoking can make you an automatic member of "the club."

You may learn that your daughter smokes alone to ease the pain of loneliness or boredom. A mother of one of my introverted clients learned just that. In response, she suggested that her daughter paint a mural on one entire wall of her bedroom. They went together to buy paint—in lots of colors—and brushes. She suggested that her daughter paint a part of the wall before smoking a cigarette. Her daughter ended up getting caught up in the painting and never went for the smoke. This wise mother used the information she learned from her daughter to suggest alternative remedies for her daughter's legitimate loneliness and boredom.

If you are a smoker, this chapter is not intended to push you further into a box of guilt and shame. It is intended to reveal your responsibility to get out of that box. If your daughter smokes, the best thing you can do is to quit smoking yourself. Avail yourself of all the resources available through your physician and/or a good counselor.

One of my friends recently quit smoking at the age of fifty-three. She never thought she'd quit until she found her grandbaby picking up one of her used cigarettes from an ashtray hidden in the garage. Her mother's heart—still very much alive after all those puffs—moved her to action. (I am told that if there is one thing fiercer than a mother's heart, it's a grandmother's heart.) She told me, "For the last few years, all I could think about was my health and how I was jeopardizing it and probably going to die younger than I wanted to. In a strange way, every cigarette was preparing me to die.

"Now that I've quit," she concluded, "I am preparing to live."

Just for You

1. Write out your own smoking story. Include all of the times and ways you've tried to quit.
2. Make a list of reasons to quit right now.
3. What have you learned about yourself from reading this chapter? Are you compassionate toward yourself? Why or why not?
4. What have you learned that encourages you to try to quit smoking? Are you committed to healthy change on your own behalf?
5. Write a prayer asking God to help you quit smoking. Allow your courageous, creative, curious, compassionate, and committed heart to advocate on your own behalf.
6. Call one or two close friends and share your prayer with them. Ask them to join you in praying for you to overcome your addiction.

Chapter 7

"Mom, It's Just a Beer or Two!"

The media focuses on illegal drugs, but that's the tail.
The dog is alcohol, and the dog is really biting our kids.

—Joseph Califano

Today we know that when a young woman abuses alcohol or other drugs,
the risk to her health is much greater than it is for a man. Yet there is not
enough prevention, intervention, and treatment targeting women. It is
still much harder for women to get help. That needs to change.

—former first lady Betty Ford

Marina never planned to drink six beers at a party, get in a fight with another girl, spray hair spray in her face, get arrested when the police were called by the hair-sprayed girl's parents, and face a lawsuit that would impact her and her family.

Kendra never planned to wander down the beach after sipping rum and hot chocolate with her friends, run into a group of boys on the beach, and be raped by all four of them.

Morgan never planned to get pregnant in the spring before her senior year of high school. She drank and had sex for *the first time* the evening of her junior prom. By the time her classmates were signing their yearbooks at the end of the school year, she knew she was pregnant.

Jessica never planned to get drunk, drive home from a party, and get pulled over by the police. She ended up in detox at the police station, she lost her driver's license, and when the University of Connecticut learned of her legal troubles, she lost her basketball scholarship.

The woman I met this morning in the large urban city I'm visiting never meant to end up a bag lady. I had just sat down on an empty bench in the sun to sip the coffee I'd bought, when someone sat down beside me. I looked up with a start, wondering who it could be, since there were dozens of other empty benches around. When I saw the person who had joined me on *my* bench, I felt a mixture of irritation and repulsion. She was a bag lady, possibly homeless, a street person. Whatever the right term is, she was unkempt, unfocused (she was mumbling something to herself), and an unlikely companion to share *my* bench.

I smelled a mixture of alcohol and days—or weeks?—of unwashed sweat and started to get up to move to another bench. The woman startled me when she spoke: "Miss, do you have some change you could spare? I'm trying to get on the metro to go see my daughter."

I didn't even look at her as I replied, "I'm sorry, but I don't have any money." It was true. I had only my coffee and my hotel room key. The woman began mumbling to herself again, and I got up to leave.

"I didn't plan this, you know," she spoke deliberately and almost passionately.

I looked at her. Behind her leathery face and hazy eyes, I saw the spark of something familiar. I saw a woman, ashamed and desperate, who was caught in circumstances she probably never imagined for herself.

This time I looked at her when I spoke to her. "Didn't plan what?" I asked.

"Didn't plan to become *this,* to live for the booze. To lose my family. To scare my grandchildren. To be crazy half the time and wishing I was crazy the other half. I didn't plan to become nobody."

Her words pierced my heart with empathy as well as gratitude for my own recovery from alcoholism. In an instant I realized that she was not that different from me. I certainly never intended to end up in a detox facility with a potentially lethal blood-alcohol level. My own alcoholism had threatened to drag me to the dregs of humanity, and it left me in circumstances I had never planned for or could ever imagine. My own addiction almost made me lose me.

"Wait here a minute," I said to the woman. "I'm going to run to my room and get some money."

When I returned with ten dollars and my leather-bound copy of *The Message* (Eugene Peterson's wonderful paraphrase of the Bible), she was still waiting on *my* bench. I handed her the money and the Bible and said, "People change all the time."

You may be thinking that she spent the money on booze and never read the Bible, and you may be right. I hope that she bought a subway ticket and went to see her daughter, that she read some words of amazing grace and hope from the Bible, and that something was set in motion to lead her to change. But giving her the money and the Bible was as much about me as it was about her. It was about me remembering that we all suffer from the same condition: We all "fall short of the glory of God" (Romans 3:23). Our falls may look different, but alcohol connected my greatest fall to the bag lady's. I'll tell you more of my story later, but for now I want to assure you that if your daughter comes home with the smell of beer on her breath, if you've found an empty bottle of vodka under her bed, if she's been ticketed for underage drinking or caught at school with alcohol in her water bottle, I have understanding and hope to offer you.

If your daughter talks about the alcohol that is *everywhere* in her culture and wonders why she shouldn't drink, if she feels like she's missing out on all the fun and wonders about having just a few sips of beer, I have understanding and answers for you to offer her.

And if you or your daughter is caught in the quicksand of alcohol dependency—drinking to feel okay, drinking to overcome shyness, drinking to have fun, drinking to get through the day—I have understanding and a path of recovery to share with you. The bag lady actually offered the most important bit of wisdom I could ever give to you and your daughter about alcohol: *Alcohol takes us to places we never planned to go.*

GIRLS AND ALCOHOL

Girls respond to alcohol differently than boys. Girls relate to alcohol differently than boys. During my own drinking days, when I would hear of someone who was struggling in a difficult marriage or with other painful realities, I would think, *Oh, if you only knew about my "friend" [alcohol], you would have some relief from your pain and difficulty.* Due to our biological and relational responses, women get hooked on alcohol more quickly, have a more difficult time disentangling ourselves from the substance, and are ultimately destroyed more quickly than men who struggle with alcohol. Extensive research has confirmed that girls who use substances can sink into abuse and addiction more quickly than boys, even when they consume the same amount or less of a particular substance.[1]

The most recent studies describe alcohol as a "triple threat" to females. Women are more biologically affected by alcohol. "A single drink for a woman has the impact of two drinks for a man"[2] Women get addicted faster than men do, and they are less likely to seek help due to the stigma that is still attached to women who drink too much. "Most experts say the best way to spare women from alcoholism is to get them when they're young. People who drink before they're 15 are *four times* as likely to be alcohol dependent or have alcohol problems when they're adults" (emphasis added).[3]

Here are some other facts you need to know—for your daughter's sake—about the effects and dangers associated with drinking:[4]

- If a boy and girl weigh the same and drink the same amount, a girl will have a higher blood-alcohol level because *females have a missing alcohol-eliminating enzyme* in their stomachs. The result is that alcohol goes directly into a girl's bloodstream. It's as if she is "shooting" alcohol directly into her veins.
- Girls usually have a higher proportion of body fat. Alcohol is easily dissolved in water, but not in fat, which means that people with more body fat will experience a higher blood-alcohol level.
- Alcohol is more damaging to girls' brains than to boys' brains. The hippocampus, the area of the brain that has to do with memory, develops earlier in girls than in boys. So when a girl drinks habitually, she is destroying the part of her brain that remembers who she wants to be, her dreams, her ideals, her hopes, and her desires for the future.
- Blood-alcohol level is affected by a girl's menstrual cycle. Since hormone levels continually vary, girls are less able to predict how alcohol will affect them on any given day.
- Five percent of deaths among adolescent girls between the ages of fifteen and twenty-nine are linked to alcohol.

- Forty-one percent of ninth-grade girls drink.
- One-fifth of ninth-grade girls who drink are binge drinkers (drinking four or more drinks at a time).
- Teenage girls who drink are seven times more likely to have sex they didn't plan on having with boys they might not even know or care about.
- One-fourth of all girls who abuse alcohol have been sexually abused.
- Unplanned sexual activity, date rape, and sexual assault on college-age women who drink has increased *150 percent.*
- Half of all girls who are victims of assaults said they were drinking and/or using drugs when they were assaulted.
- Girls who witness or experience violence (street crime or domestic violence) are two to three times more likely to use substances.
- Girls under the age of eighteen are the fastest growing segment of the juvenile-justice population. More times than not, alcohol was documented as part of their crime.
- Fifty percent of alcoholic adolescent females attempt suicide as compared to 9 percent of nonalcoholic adolescent females.

ALCOHOL *IS* EVERYWHERE AND ALMOST EVERYONE *IS* DOING IT

In *"Mom, I Hate My Life!"*—my second book in the Hand-in-Hand series—I wrote about a night when God "told" me to go find Kristin who was at a "gathering" at the home of a girl named Dorrie. I had asked Kristin if Dorrie's parents were going to be home, and she said what almost every teenager says in response to that question: "Yes, I think so."

Since then, I encourage parents *not* to ask that question. Either ask for the telephone number to call the parents of the home in question or assume that the parents will not be home. Today's teenagers generally want to congregate only in homes where parents are not there or, as I am discovering with increasing distress, in homes where the parents themselves are heavy users of alcohol and/or drugs.

When I made my surprise visit to Dorrie's house, a boy with a beer in his hand greeted me with an expletive: "@*#%, it's somebody's mother!" As I pushed my way into the foyer and asked the boy to go get Kristin Hersh, I saw a group of about five kids in the kitchen with cans duct-taped to their hands. Too many images, fears, and words were flooding my brain to register what was going on with these kids at the time. I got my daughter (who, after her initial shock and embarrassment that I had tracked her down, admitted she was relieved that I had come to get her), and we left. The next day during our "debriefing" session, I asked about the cans duct-taped to hands.

The Office of National Drug Control Policy (ONDCP) tells us that the estimated eleven million children whose parents abuse alcohol or illicit drugs face heightened risks of drug abuse themselves.

—Meredith Maran, *Dirty*

"Oh, it's a drinking game," Kristin explained. *(A drinking game!* my mind silently screamed. *Whatever happened to Nintendo or even spin the bottle?)*

"Everyone duct-tapes a beer to each hand," my daughter continued. "You can't take the duct tape off until you finish the beer."

Without a moment's hesitation, I told Kristin exactly what I was thinking. "What kind of a world is this where teenagers duct-tape beer cans to their hands and call it a game? Where *were* Dorrie's parents? How did you guys get the beer? Why didn't you call me immediately to come get you? Do you know where this type of behavior leads? This is how girls get raped! Do you want to become an alcoholic? Do you know what it's like to be a female alcoholic? Well, I do. And it's not fun. You could end up jobless, homeless, crazy."

Kristin was wisely quiet until I calmed down. (It took awhile!) Eventually I had to admit to myself and explain to my daughter that *she* was going to have some tough decisions to make regarding what kind of relationship she was going to have with alcohol.

"What do you mean by *relationship* with alcohol?" Kristin asked.

I knew the time was coming for me to tell my daughter more of my own story.

ESTABLISHING CLEAR CONSEQUENCES FOR DRINKING

It is important that, as a family, you establish clear consequences for drinking. Write them out. Have everyone sign them. Following are three ideas to get you started. The consequences you use with your daughter may need to change in response to the realities of her social life.

First offense. When you smell alcohol on your daughter's breath or she fails a Breathalyzer test, she loses her social privileges for a week. I believe it is important to keep consequences for teenagers brief. A week is a long time. When a teenager (particularly a strong-willed, rebellious one) is faced with consequences of weeks or months, she begins to think, *What difference does it make? My life is ruined. I might as well do whatever I want.* Privileges are restored and maintained every time she passes the Breathalyzer.

Second offense. Your daughter loses social privileges and the use of the car for a week. Privileges are restored and maintained each time she passes the Breathalyzer. She is also required to attend an Alcoholics Anonymous meeting. You can find a meeting in your area by calling the number for AA listed in the white pages. Ask for an "open" meeting and, if possible, a meeting of young people. Tell your daughter that you don't think she's an alcoholic, but you want her to see how alcohol takes wonderful, amazing people to places they never planned on going.

JUST FOR THE TWO OF YOU

If your daughter is thirteen or older, watch the movie *Riding in Cars with Boys* together. (You may want to preview the movie first, and if you are uncomfortable with your daughter seeing any part of it, you can mark that section and fast-forward through it.) This is an excellent, realistic movie about a girl with goals and plans, who, after a few drinks at a dance, compromised herself and ended up pregnant. The decision to drink changed the course of her life. This movie does not romanticize the harsh realities of being a teen mom. After you watch the movie with your daughter, do not lecture. Ask her a few questions. Here are some to get you started:

1.   What changed the life direction of the character in the movie?

2. What do you think she would do differently if she could rewind her life and do it all over again?
3. What other people were affected by her choices? Were they affected negatively or positively?
4. If there had been no alcohol in this movie, how would the story be different?
5. What are some goals you hope will come true in your life?
6. What if you made the same choices as the character in the movie? What impact do you think these choices would have on your life goals?

Third offense. Your daughter loses social privileges and the use of the car for a week. She must also enroll in a drug and alcohol education program. Your daughter will think this is extreme, but if you review with her (and yourself) the statistics about alcohol use and girls, you will find support for acting quickly early on. See the resource section at the back of this book for information on finding a program. We will also examine treatment options in greater depth in chapter 11.

DRINKING: A LOVE STORY

When Kristin first asked me about what I meant by a "relationship with alcohol," I immediately thought of the poignant and powerful book *Drinking: A Love Story,* in which Caroline Knapp describes her relationship with alcohol:

> I loved the way drink made me feel, and I loved its special power of deflection, its ability to shift my focus away from my own awareness of self and onto something else, something less painful than my own feelings.... By the end [alcohol] was the single most important relationship in my life.[5]

I explained to my daughter that, believe it or not, that smelly, sticky, sometimes sour, sometimes bitter, sometimes sweet substance courts you, makes you promises, gets you to depend on it, and makes you think you need it. Then before you know it, it begins to erode your self-confidence and damage you physically, emotionally, and spiritually. And once that happens, it won't let you go.

For me, the first glass of wine was all it took. I was a young adult, newly married and living two thousand miles away from friends and family while my husband attended law school. I was filled with emotions I did not understand and could not control. I was afraid, anxious, and lonely.

One night about six months into our marriage, Dave and I went to a thriller movie, and I became more and more uptight as the film went on. By the time I rose from my seat, I was feeling dizzy, tingly, and sick. I told my husband I needed to get to the emergency room right away. After a race to the hospital and a shot of valium to calm me, I described my almost constantly anxious emotional state to a young intern. He gave his recommendation: "If you were my wife, I'd tell you to go home and have a glass of wine."

I had never drunk alcohol before. I was raised in a very conservative church that frowned on all alcohol consumption. But my desperation to get rid of the anxiety eclipsed my conscientious objections. In the aftermath of what I now know was a panic attack and a developing anxiety disorder, I was ready to try the well-meaning physician's "prescription."

After I'd downed my first glass of wine, I realized I'd found something I had been looking for all my life. For the first time, my busy, busy brain stilled. My worries didn't feel so all-consuming. My high expectations didn't seem like such a big deal. My loneliness was replaced by a warmth that seemed to spread from my heart to my toes. I wondered why everyone didn't have a glass of wine.

It made sense to me to have a glass of wine every night. And it also made sense to exchange the tall glass of wine for a short glass of hard alcohol. I told myself that the vodka contained fewer calories (not true), but the truth was that I liked the more intense rush and faster relief that hard liquor gave me.

I drank every night for the next three years. Slowly—and it was slowly at first—I drank a few more sips every night. After we moved back closer to my extended family, I continued to drink. Although I told myself that I needed this and there was nothing wrong with it, I hid my bottles and drank in isolation.

Once every few months I would drink a little too much and awaken with a pounding headache and upset stomach. Then I would cut back. And when I got pregnant, I quit drinking altogether. No problem. After I had a beautiful baby girl, the stress and anxiety of adding this new life to ours made drinking seem all the more necessary again. Once again, I began to drink every night. And then I decided to have a "few sips" when Kristin took her nap.

Alcohol became my best friend. My reward. My solace. My comfort. I wondered how other people managed their lives without drinking.

During this time I was active in church, taking care of my family, and involved with friends, but I kept my alcohol abuse a secret.

I started feeling very shaky in the mornings. I knew this probably had something to do with my drinking, although I was completely ignorant about the phenomenon of alcoholism. The guilt and the shakes worried me. I remember so many Sunday nights when I would take a few more sips and then throw my almost-finished bottle in the trash, set the trash can at the curb for the garbage collectors, and determine to be done with this unholy god of false hope forever. I also remember, as if it were yesterday, waking at 4:30 on Monday mornings, desperate to drink, desperate to stop, craving alcohol like crazy. I would slip out the front door of my suburban home, fish around in the trash for a bottle that wasn't quite empty, crouch down by the garbage can, and swill the alcohol—right there on the curb in my nightie!

One morning after I had taken Kristin to preschool, I came home to discover that I had forgotten to give her a show-and-tell object for class. I poured myself a short one and thought, *She can show it tomorrow.* Guilt (and the Holy Spirit) overwhelmed me. I wondered with horror, *What kind of a mother pours herself a glass of vodka instead of taking her daughter's show-and-tell treasure to school?*

"Not the kind of mother I want to be!" I said aloud. My love and longing for my daughter welled up within me. I poured out the vodka and quit drinking. *No problem,* I thought. I had no idea, yet, that this first conscious experience of my fierce mother's heart was no match for my addiction to alcohol.

I did quit for a while, and then I got pregnant with Graham. With more responsibility came more anxiety, and I was reminded of my "friend." I forgot how alcohol had become my enemy. After Graham was born, daily drinking became my routine again almost immediately. I was so grateful that my children went to bed so early, so I could drink.

During this time I learned the story of my mother's adoption and found out that her birth mother died from alcoholism at the age of fifty-two. I didn't know anything about alcoholism, but I thought I might have it. I worried about my children. I didn't even really enjoy drinking anymore. I was more anxious than I had ever been. But the only thing that gave me moments of relief from the anxiety and the guilt was drinking. I didn't see how I could stop.

Near the end of my drinking, the days began to blur together. It seemed I was only drinking and surviving the drinking. After one horrible weekend of drinking steadily, I knew I needed help. I asked my parents to take me to the hospital, where I was admitted into a detox ward. The amount of alcohol in my blood was at a level that normally is lethal. It is a miracle I did not die.

While in detox I was introduced to the Twelve Steps of Alcoholics Anonymous and learned more about what the founder of AA called the "cunning, baffling, and powerful" disease of alcoholism. Finally I admitted I was an alcoholic. I had been seduced by a drug that promised to make my life easier but ultimately almost took my life. I have been in recovery from alcoholism ever since. I'm not doing life perfectly, but I'm staying sober and progressing spiritually one day at a time.

After Kristin had heard some of my story, she said, "But Mom, my friends aren't like you. They just have a few drinks. Sometimes they get trashed. But they can stop."

Kristin's response indicates why telling our story to our teenagers is not effective in and of itself. Teenagers believe that they are different, invincible, and won't make the same mistakes their old parents did. To get through to them, we must find ways to connect our stories to theirs. I asked Kristin to think of drinking as a relationship and to spend some time consciously looking for the different stages of relationship that she and her friends had with this slippery, seductive substance. Although Kristin didn't drink, I knew her friends did. I hoped my own story would connect with Kristin's as she came to understand that I really did "get" what was going on with her friends and that her decision not to drink was actually a life-and-death decision for Kristin, because of her genetic vulnerability to alcoholism.

The Courtship Phase

Most girls drink because someone else suggests it or invites them to drink. The National Center on Addiction and Substance Abuse at Columbia University suggests that girls differ significantly from boys when it comes to how they obtain access to alcohol, tobacco, and drugs. Girls are more likely to be offered alcohol by girlfriends or boyfriends.[6] Girls initially drink to be "a part of" the group, to make their boyfriends happy, to experience a sense of belonging. One of my clients described her first drinking experience like this:

> When I got to the party, everyone had these red plastic cups. I mean *everyone* had one. I looked to see if there was a "drink table" and couldn't find it. Everyone seemed so friendly and happy. I felt awkward and like I didn't know what to say. I didn't know a lot of people who were there. Like a little puppy dog, I kept following my friend who brought me to the party. She left me for a few minutes, and I thought I was going to freak out. I didn't know what to say to anyone.
>
> When she came back, she had two red plastic cups. She handed me one and said, "Loosen up and stop following me around." I took a sip and almost choked. I knew that I was drinking alcohol. It burned clear down to my stomach. But then I felt kind of warm all over. I took a few more sips, and I started to relax. After a few more cupfuls, I felt like I could talk to anyone. It was great. How can anything that makes you feel so good and makes you relax and able to talk and be with people be wrong?

My client had been courted by a substance that promises what we females long for more than anything else: relationships. In my first book, *Bravehearts,* I write about the unique longing of the female heart for relationships. Deep within all of us is a voice that whispers, "Ask me, notice me, listen to me, enjoy me, pick me, pursue me, love me, stay with me, and receive all of this from me as well." For many of us, alcohol promises to be a connection to what we want most: relationships. When you merge the promise of connection, the relaxation of inhibitions, and the peer-pressure invitation of girlfriends and boyfriends, you have a potent concoction that lures many girls into the beginning of a relationship with a potentially life-altering, even deadly, substance.

For girls who choose not to drink, life can be very lonely. I know that some of you who are reading this book have daughters who are not drinking or smoking. You are reading this book to help support them and keep them from these temptations. You need to know that your daughter's choice not to drink makes her vulnerable to loneliness. She will decide either to avoid much of the social scene altogether or to abstain from substance use in social settings. But both of these decisions result in loneliness. Don't be deceived if your daughter is involved in cheerleading, parachurch organizations, or school activities. Although these settings are monitored as closely as possible, they are not immune from the influence of alcohol. My daughter was a cheerleader during her high-school days and told me of countless games, bus rides, and activities in which many of the participants where under the influence right under the noses of adult supervisors. Kristin told me about the drinking among her peers not to "narc" on them but to confide in me her loneliness in the midst of all the "revelry."

Just for You

Now is the time for you to evaluate your own relationship with substances. You will be authentically powerful in your daughter's life only to the degree that you have looked at and worked on your own life.

1. Have you ever used alcohol or any other substance to ease social anxiety?
2. Do you avoid social gatherings because of anxiety?
3. Do you use alcohol, drugs, and/or food to medicate, numb, and soothe your emotions?
4. If you answered yes to any of the above questions, what do you need to do to change your life so that you can offer hope to your daughter? (For helpful information, see the resource section at the end of this book.)
5. If you answered no to any of the above questions, what do you do to overcome your social anxiety, gain a sense of belonging in groups, or feel okay about yourself?

Whether your daughter is drawn to alcohol because of its promise of connection or she is abstaining and suffering the consequent loneliness, your task if clear. Once again, the problem offers the solution. As mothers, we have to develop relationships with our daughters that offer *more* than a relationship with alcohol can. We'll talk much more about this later in the chapter.

The Dating Phase

The problem with alcohol is this: Nothing else works quite like it. When a girl learns that alcohol makes her a part of "the club," that she can talk to anyone more easily, that she feels at ease in all sorts of situations, it's difficult to convince her that prayer or meditation or positive self-talk is a better solution. Alcohol offers a girl, who has been created for relationships, two very important payoffs: relief from the pain and hardships of life, and a sense of control in a world that is out of control. Once she has experienced these payoffs and learns that she can rely on alcohol to come through for her, it becomes very difficult to disentangle herself from it.

Alcohol makes everything better, until it makes everything worse. When a girl drinks, within minutes she feels a sense of well-being, relaxation, increased confidence, and reduced anxiety. Every teenage girl who walks into my office tells me the same thing when we start to talk about why she is drinking: *"I just want to have fun."* I have come to understand that this is "code" for many other longings:

- "I want to forget about all my problems"—boyfriends (or no boyfriends), parents fighting, bad grades, or a friend's betrayal.
- "I want to be a part of something fun."
- "I want a little relief from the pressure to be good, get good grades, and look okay to my peers."
- "I want to feel good about the way I look, about who I am among my friends, about what I have to say."

As human beings we all *crave* relief from the challenges of life. The Greeks believed that the gods gave them wine to help them forget the misery of existence. We are the generation that was indoctrinated by the McDonald's jingle: "You deserve a break today," and we have raised a generation that demands immediate gratification. This is what lures so many girls into a relationship with alcohol, which initially provides immediate relief. In fact, the female hormone estrogen increases sensitivity to drugs and alcohol and, in turn, intensifies cravings. When a girl drinks habitually while her estrogen levels are elevated, her sensitivity to alcohol remains even when her estrogen level is lower.[7]

Ironically, the deepest "relief" alcohol ultimately provides is that it destroys the passion our Creator instilled in us to desire much more than escape and temporary "fun." As alcohol use escalates, the deeper passions of the heart for loving self, others, and God in glorious ways are dulled. The bottom line: Alcohol effectively keeps girls from wanting *more*. Eugene Peterson expresses it most poignantly in his paraphrase of Romans 1: "They traded the glory of God who holds the whole world in his hands for cheap figurines you can buy at any roadside stand" (verse 23, MSG). Some of my saddest clients are girls in their twenties who tell me, "I started out wanting to stay a virgin until I got married and to abstain from drugs and alcohol, but once I started drinking, it all slowly got away from me. Now I just want a job so that I can get a car and be independent from my parents."

---

*One of the most powerful lessons we can give to our children
about alcohol, or any other topic, is by our own example.... May
I suggest that change is not just a youth thing, but a life thing. We
are "becoming" throughout our lives, even as parents and grandparents. As soon as we stop, we stagnate and begin to die.
Growing and improving along with our children brings
legitimacy, closeness, and trust to our relationship.*

—STEPHEN G. BIDDULPH, *Alcohol: What's a Parent to Believe?*

When my daughter's last high-school prom was approaching, it was a dramatic, traumatic time. (Nothing new there!) But what made this prom so dramatic and traumatic was an invitation from a boy named Andy, who had been prom king two years in a row. He was outgoing, funny, popular, and the boy Kristin was sure she wanted to go to her senior prom with. So when he asked her to go with him, she accepted with joy!

Gradually, Andy made the prom plans known to Kristin. A group of about twenty would go to a restaurant before prom, attend the dance, and then head to a cabin in the mountains for the night. The group was going to skip the school-sponsored Afterprom and head straight for a night of drinking and partying.

Kristin came home in tears after she learned of the plan. "This isn't what I wanted. It's not what I'm going to do," she declared with fierceness. "I am not going to miss my Afterprom and sit around and watch a bunch of people get drunk." She collapsed on her bed in tears. "Oh, Mom, why can't I just go along with everyone? It would be so much easier. This is going to turn into a drama, and it's not how I wanted to end my senior year."

I replied quietly, "Because you want *more*."

Kristin told me later that this short sentence revived her, restored her sense of self, and guided her in the events that followed. She told her date that he deserved the prom he wanted and that she did too, and that it sounded as if they wanted two different proms. She told him that he was free to ask another girl. He called her two days later and told her that he respected her and still wanted to go to prom with her. Five other girls followed Kristin's lead and told their dates the same thing. Unfortunately, not every boy responded like Andy did. Kristin and Andy had a blast at prom, and afterward Andy told her that it was the only high-school dance he had ever attended sober and that it was the best high-school dance he had ever attended!

If your daughter is trying to withstand the temptations of drinking, I hope Kristin's story encourages you and reminds you of the powerful role you can play in creating a relationship with your daughter that continues to offer her *more* than the temptation to drink, which will always be lurking right around the corner. If your daughter is already caught in alcohol's seductive embrace, it is not too late to interrupt her relationship with this substance and offer her *more*.

One of my clients told me about sneaking down to her garage to grab three beers before she went out to a movie with friends. She said matter-of-factly, "I needed to drink to have fun." When she left for the evening and her mother called out, "Jenna, have fun!" this seventeen-year-old girl whose heart had been hijacked by her relationship with alcohol told me that she suddenly felt overwhelming hatred for her mother. Why? Her mother hadn't done any-thing. But alcohol had, and she could not receive love from her mom.

When Jenna's mom later learned of her daughter's premovie drinking, she was surprised and chagrined. She didn't know that her daughter was drinking at home *before* she went out, and she didn't know that her daughter was feel-ing a powerful contempt toward her because of her ignorance and lack of intervention. When our teenagers are acting out and engaging in outrageous activities, it is easy to forget that they are actually crying out for someone to be stronger than they are. The adolescent world is a scary place to be left alone.

Jenna's mom is one of the most creative mothers I have worked with. As soon as she learned of her daughter's behavior and decoded its meaning, she got busy. She ordered a Breathalyzer test kit off the Internet and told her daughter that she would routinely test her *before* she left the house. If Jenna failed the test, she would not be allowed to go out and would experience additional consequences, including the loss of more social privileges. If she passed the test, she would get to pick from her mom's grab bag of confidence boosters. Jenna's mom explained to me that she had been a Mary Kay cos-metic consultant in her "previous life" (before teenagers) and that she had a vast assortment of makeup, skin-care products, and other items. These items went into the grab bag along with breath mints, upbeat CDs, coupons for a free facial or pedicure, and pithy, encouraging sayings, such as "Hooray for your fierce spirit!" and "Shoot for the moon. Even if you miss, you'll land among the stars!"

Jenna's mom met her daughter's behavior head-on. By purchasing and administering the Breathalyzer, she told her daughter clearly, "*I* am stronger than you." By offering her daughter the grab bag of confidence builders, she assured Jenna that there is so much *more* to building confidence than chug-ging down a few beers.

Another great example of a mom who offered *more* to her daughter is my friend Jill. Jill knew what it was like to feel awkward in social settings, and she especially felt uncomfortable "in her body." She felt big and clumsy, even though she was a normal-size woman. Knowing that her fourteen-year-old daughter felt equally self-conscious and was being tempted to find relief in using alcohol with her friends, Jill decided to sign *herself* up for a dance class.

After the six-week session, she felt so much more confident that she not only danced around the house (slightly embarrassing her children), but she joined a book club at her local library. She shared with her daughter how much more confident she felt in every way and convinced her daughter to sign up with her for a hip-hop dance class. Jill used her own experience to help her daughter develop self-confidence in a healthy way and to strengthen their relationship *before* her daughter found herself in the arms of the sinister, seductive companion, alcohol.

The second reason girls give for drinking besides "I just want to have fun" is *"I just want to be in charge of my own life."* When a girl drinks, she quickly learns that she can turn uneasiness into ease, sadness into hilarity, shyness into talkativeness, and a feeling of being left out to a feeling of belonging. She can be in control of a world that, more times than not, feels out of control.

When a girl uses alcohol to gain a sense of control over her life, she is telling everyone around her, "I don't like the world I've been left in. I will find a way to make it better." Parents need to listen to what she *isn't* saying in specific words and investigate to learn if she has experienced any type of violence, abuse, or other emotional devastation.

When Joan and Jessie came to see me for counseling, we were able to quickly get to the heart of Jessie's experimentation with alcohol. Her parents had just gone through a divorce, and she was doing the "custody shuttle," spending one week at Mom's and the next at Dad's.

"I bet you hate that—" I began.

Jessie interrupted me with a barrage of complaints, "Yeah, I really hate it. I'm always losing my stuff or forgetting where it is. And it embarrasses me when my friends ask, 'So, are you at your mom's or dad's this week?' My parents are the ones who wanted the divorce, but I'm the one who has to pay for it."

I knew that Jessie's understanding of her parents' divorce was simplistic, but I also knew that her experience of their divorce left her feeling totally out of control. I asked Jessie, "So when you pick up a beer at a party, is that your way of saying, 'This is one way I can be in charge of my life!'?"

"Exactly," Jessie answered.

I asked Jessie if we could meet with both of her parents and talk about a new custody arrangement. Jessie's eyes got wide as she asked, "You would do that for me?"

When your daughter feels powerless, one of the greatest gifts you can give her is to show her how she can empower herself in a positive way. I asked Jessie to come up with a proposal that would satisfy her and be fair to both of her parents. When she came in for the family session, she brought a very official-looking proposal. She suggested that she spend one month at a time at each parent's home but spend at least two weekends during that month at the other parent's home. Everyone agreed to the proposal, and I could tell immediately that Jessie felt more empowered in her life.

After a month of passing Breathalyzer tests and abstaining from alcohol at parties, Jessie told me about the continuing growth of her own personal power. "It feels kinda powerful to not drink at parties," she explained. "I am in control of *myself*. I can help my friends who drink. I don't have to hide from or lie to my mom. It feels good." I was thrilled that Jessie was responding with a positive identity and role for herself to a life that sometimes feels out of control.

"I'm thinking about becoming a lawyer," she concluded. "I think I would be good at helping people negotiate their problems."

I don't know whether Jessie will go on to law school, but I agree with her that she'd be a great negotiator. And more important, Jessie is developing a vision for herself that will outlast all the Friday-night parties during high school.

The cycle of alcohol use and abuse during the "dating" phase of the relationship works like this: I deserve relief, so I choose the fastest and most effective route available (drinking) and end up saying and doing things I regret, which makes me hate myself and feel shame, which makes me mad at the world, which makes me need relief even more.

It's worth repeating: Alcohol makes everything better until it makes everything worse. The very promises that lure your daughter into this relationship will become curses if she becomes a habitual drinker. The promise of relief and escape will be replaced by increased anxiety and problems. Alcohol is both a stimulant and a depressant. Simply put, it confuses the brain. The girl who drinks habitually (every day or every weekend) becomes dependent on alcohol for relief from stress and worry. Frequent use is predictable among teenagers since some surveys report that adolescent drinking accounts for *80 percent* of excessive use of alcohol in the United States.[8]

When your daughter is in the dating stage of her relationship with alcohol, she *craves* relief, escape, a sense of okayness. You cannot make everything okay for her, relieve all her stress, or take away all her struggles and challenges. But you can offer her a powerful antidote to this developing, dangerous alliance with alcohol: relationship. You can *crave* her, and you can *chase* her.

Forming an Alliance Against Addiction

Addiction happens when the *craving* and *chasing* parts of the brain get hijacked by a substance. Ask any addict. Life becomes reduced to craving the addicted substance and chasing it. Our brains are wired to crave and chase, but God intended for us to crave those things that bring us life (relationship with Him and others) and chase them as we seek meaning, generosity, wisdom, compassion, and creativity. William Barclay's translation of Acts 17:24-28 describes our divine design: "It is He who gives to all men life and breath and all things.... He created them to seek God, with the hope that they might grope after Him in the shadows of their ignorance, and find Him." This is redemption in all its glory.

Redeemed Craving

Remember when your daughter was little and she craved *you?* She would follow you into the kitchen, the bedroom, even the bathroom. It seemed as if she couldn't get enough of you. Her brain was activated to crave what she knew she could rely on to provide sustenance, comfort, and security. The problem is that most parents do not learn to reciprocate. We are relieved when our children no longer pull on our "skirt tails" and call after us incessantly, "Mommy! Mommy!" We do not know that showing we crave *them* can immunize them from craving substances that will ultimately entangle them in destructive relationships.

Perhaps *craving* your daughter sounds strange or sick. I remember when I committed myself to give in to the instinct of my mother's heart and crave my daughter. Kristin was in the third grade, and I was in Idaho speaking at a women's retreat. During an afternoon break I went to see the movie *The Horse Whisperer* at a local theater. In one scene the preteen daughter asks her overbusy mother, "What happened to you, Mom? Why do you act like everything is more important than me?"

My heart burst. I knew in a flash that I was like the mom in the story. And I knew what had happened. First, I had watched my own mother parent my brother during his days of rebellion, failure in school, and drug addiction. I watched her be hurt and become cynical. She'd often see a sweet little child and comment, "Just wait until he [or she] becomes a teenager." I had distanced myself from my daughter to keep her from breaking my heart as my brother had broken my mom's. Second, I had suffered the worst of my own alcohol addiction when Kristin was a toddler. Guilt shadowed me constantly. I felt unworthy of being a mom—much less a *great* mom—to this wonderful girl.

In that movie theater I bowed my head and confessed my sin. My own heart—so guarded and guilt-ridden—was holding me back from a wholehearted commitment to mothering. From that moment on I have thrown myself into mothering, although not perfectly. I never resist an impulse to let my children know I *crave* them.

Eric Poole, a criminal justice professor who had studied kids from the toughest neighborhoods, found some interesting conclusions. In those neighborhoods, whether a child joined a gang had almost nothing to do with the size of his family, the number of parents at home, their education or income. Rather, it had to do with whether the child had anyone in his life who would be disappointed if he joined a gang.

—STEVEN W. VANNOY, *The 10 Greatest Gifts I Give My Children*

What about you? Do you also feel guilty because of past failures or sins against your children? Of years of plopping your children in front of the television instead of offering them your presence? Does your own experience of being mothered keep you from mothering your own children with all your heart? Have your daughter's harsh words and unthinkable behaviors compelled you to steel your heart against further hurt?

In the next section you'll find some ideas to help you demonstrate your heart for your daughter. You will know that your desire is healthy if the energy of your heart is not to fix her, protect her from the inevitable hurts of life, indulge her, smother her, or keep her from the outside world. Confess your holding back. Let go. Let your mother's heart lead you to love your daughter.

By the way, it is especially important to demonstrate your craving for your daughter when she is unlovely. When she snarls, comes home drunk, snaps at you with contempt, or withdraws completely, don't hold back. If you're worried that your love will give her permission to keep sinning, read the New Testament book of Galatians. Read it again and again. Perhaps you'll finally "get it." God's love for us is not based on or limited by our performance. Likewise, your love for your daughter, if it is to set her on a course toward true self-esteem, cannot be based on or limited by her performance. She will experience logical consequences if she continues to make bad choices. She already knows you don't approve of her drinking. But does she know that you love her anyway?

REDEEMED CHASING

Remember that when your daughter was little, she didn't just crave you. She *chased* you. She chased you while you were trying to read, while you were cooking, while you were putting on your makeup, even while you were going to the bathroom. Just as her brain was wired to crave you—a safe source of sustenance and security—her brain was wired to chase you, to find in you what she needed to be fed and feel safe and loved.

Now it's your turn to chase your daughter to rescue her from forming a relationship with alcohol. I'm not talking about becoming like a yippy little dog that follows her wherever she goes. Once again, you can evaluate your pursuit of your daughter when you examine the energy of your heart. If your energy is focused on fixing your daughter or controlling her or keeping her from the logical consequences of her choices, then your pursuit is not healthy. The chasing I'm referring to is intentional, thoughtful, purposeful, and creative.

When your daughter is using alcohol, you will be tempted to give up, hand her over to someone else, or distance yourself in disgust (much like I felt with the bag lady). You may need to find a counselor or a treatment facility (we'll talk more about this in chapter 11), but your daughter will not stop needing *you*. Whether your daughter is in the grips of a destructive relationship with alcohol, is flirting with a relationship, or is wondering what the big deal is, the most important thing you can offer her is yourself. Offering yourself to your daughter might seem like the least likely solution to your daughter's temptation to drink. Teenage girls have a way of letting us know that they are embarrassed by our clothes and our music, and even by the way we chew our food! While your daughter may reject you, hurt you, and hurl words that deeply wound you, do not be deceived: *You are what she needs.*

When Kristin began telling me about the partying behavior of her friends, I worried that her own values and fear of drinking would not outlast the persistent temptation. One Saturday morning during Kristin's freshman year of high school, I awakened her before sunrise. She was a bit disoriented and irritated with me. I urged her, "Put on some sweats and get in the car. I have a surprise for you."

"It'd better be a good one," she snarled. "This is my only morning to sleep in."

I drove her (in sullen silence) to a state park in our city called Red Rocks. In the middle of the park is a large amphitheater surrounded by majestic red boulders. The view from the theater stretches out toward the city of Denver and beyond. I led Kristin to the top row of the amphitheater and poured us both a steaming cup of hot chocolate.

Kristin's irritation had not abated. "What is this all about?" she asked.

JUST FOR YOU

1. What is keeping you at a distance from your daughter right now? Her behaviors, her hurtful words, her withdrawal?

2. Pray every day that God will give you a sense of your mission to love your daughter as well as the courage and creativity to act on that mission even on difficult days.

3. Do you believe that your daughter needs *you?* If not, why? Have your own failures or experiences in mothering or being mothered caused you to feel this way? If so, how are you offering yourself to your daughter? How are you withholding yourself?

"Just wait," I whispered as I prayed like crazy that God would do His part.

We watched in silence as the horizon lightened and the sun tinted the clouds with pink. It took about thirty minutes for the sunrise to unfurl in all its glory. Teenage girls are captured by beauty. That's why, in part, they love fashion magazines and corny posters with sentimental slogans. I was prepared to allow God's backdrop to frame the offering of my presence to my daughter.

"Kristin," I said, "I know that the temptation to drink is everywhere. I wanted to bring you to see this sunrise to remind you that God is faithful to show up every morning. He will be with you in the midst of all the temptations. And I will be available to come pick you up if you get into an uncomfortable or dangerous situation, to make our home inviting to you and your friends, and to answer your questions about drinking from my own experience. I know I don't understand all the complexities of your world, and I don't always say and do the right things, but I will always be with you in spirit, praying for you, and I will show up whenever you want me to."

He didn't, and doesn't, wait for us to get ready. He presented himself for this sacrificial death when we were far too weak and rebellious to do anything to get ourselves ready.... We can understand someone dying for a person worth dying for, and we can understand how someone good and noble could inspire us to selfless sacrifice. But God put his love on the line for us by offering his Son in sacrificial death while we were of no use whatever to him.

—ROMANS 5:6-8, MSG

This past summer, after Kristin graduated from high school, we had a wonderful weekend away together. I asked her what had been most helpful to her during the ups and downs of high-school life. She listed her friends, her extracurricular activities, and her car, and then she told me, "Remember that conversation we had at sunrise at Red Rocks? There were a lot of times when I wondered what it would hurt to have a few sips of alcohol—like everyone else was. But I always told myself, 'The sun *will* come up tomorrow, and I know God and my mom are watching me.'" She continued, "Sometimes it annoyed me that I couldn't get your voice out of my head, but most of the time I was glad."

Don't ever doubt that your daughter needs your annoying, corny, pesky presence! Commit to showing your daughter at least once a day that you *crave* her, and then purposefully, wisely, and creatively *chase* her. If you think she doesn't deserve this kindness, let me assure you that *kindness is never wasted.* She may not change her behavior immediately. But as you persistently demonstrate your craving for her and chase her unconditionally, you have the potential to literally change her brain chemistry and pull her out of the arms of a relationship with alcohol. Psychiatrist and neuroscientist Daniel Amen asserts that "spending actual physical daily time with your child will have a powerfully positive effect on your relationship.… It has been shown that enhancing emotional bonds between people will help heal the limbic system."[9] (The limbic system in our brain processes our emotional memories and sense of bonding.)

In the Just for the Two of You section that follows are a few ideas to get you started with craving and chasing your daughter in active and fun ways. If you get stuck, think about how you would like your husband or a friend to demonstrate that he or she wants you and is willing to go to any length to prove it. Remember: This is not about what your daughter deserves, but about how much you love her—no matter what!

JUST FOR THE TWO OF YOU
Craving Your Daughter
- Wrap up one of your daughter's favorite treats and tell her, "I know you sometimes crave M&M's. Enjoy! I want you to know I crave time with you, and I long for you to be happy and have a great life."
- If you have a picture of yourself when you were pregnant with your daughter or an image of her ultrasound, give her a copy. Tell her how you longed for her and anticipated her arrival.
- Write a message on her mirror with lipstick. Tell her that she is beautiful and that you will be praying for her all day long.

- Buy a blank puzzle and write a message to your daughter on it. You could tell her about a special time you'd like to have together or write a coupon for something she would enjoy. Have fun giving her a piece to the puzzle each day in surprising or creative ways. Let her see your joy in surprising her and your anticipation of her joy.
- Every day for a month, write your thoughts and prayers for your daughter in a journal. Present it to her at the end of the month. Tell her you wanted her to know that every day you are thinking about her and praying for her without ceasing.

Chasing Your Daughter
- Drop by your daughter's car in the high-school parking lot and leave a note, a flower, or a balloon bouquet.
- If your daughter has a cell phone, text-message her every day. Tell her she's gorgeous, loved, prayed for, etc.
- Mail your daughter a care package—at home. We all love to get special treats in the mail. Lavish her.
- Celebrate your daughter for no special reason. Plan her favorite meal. Set a table for two using your best dishes, or pack a picnic just for you two. While you're eating tell her everything you enjoy about her.
- Set up a special retreat for your daughter in her room. If she's going through a rough time, place a cozy comforter on her bed, light a fragrant candle, and buy her a new journal. Leave her a note telling her that you know she's having a hard time and that you hope this little "retreat" in her room will help.
- Bring her breakfast in bed.
- Detail her car for her—vacuum it, clean out the trash, place a new air freshener on the dashboard.

Don't Give Up Before the Miracle

As you're approaching the end this chapter, you may be feeling like many of the moms I talk to every week—tired, overwhelmed, and a little cynical. I sometimes feel that way too. My kids hurt me, make scary choices, and ignore all my accumulated experience and wisdom. I want to give up. But I have evidence I can't ignore that compels me to get up in the morning and try again. (You do too, though you might not know it yet!)

While doing research for this book, I came across this statement: "After fourteen to twenty drinks in an hour, even people who drink heavily and chronically and who have a high tolerance for alcohol (that is, alcoholics) may lose consciousness or lapse into a coma. *For three out of four people, .50 is a lethal dose*" (emphasis added).[10] When I read this statistic, time stopped for me, and tears streamed down my face. When my husband dropped me off at detox, my blood-alcohol level was .675. Odds are I should have died. But God wanted me to live, I believe, to love my children.

Your story may not be so awful or dramatic, but God has obviously placed you with your children at this time and place to love them, no matter how hard or scary or lonely it gets.

When we listen as if we were in a temple and give attention to one another as if each person were our teacher, honoring his or her words as valuable and sacred, all kinds of great possibilities awaken. Even miracles can happen.

—JACK KORNFIELD, *A Path with Heart*

During the initial days of my recovery from alcoholism, I was easily discouraged. I was tempted to drink, I was compelled to feel emotions I had numbed for years, and some days it felt as if I was going through the motions and not getting anything in return. A well-known Alcoholics Anonymous slogan kept me hanging in there: "One day at a time." We also say "Don't give up before the miracle" to remind us that even when it's hard to see the light at the end of the tunnel, we need to keep walking—putting one foot in front of the other—because eventually miracles do happen. For the recovering alcoholic, the miracle is waking up one day and realizing that you actually feel good physically, you can think clearly, you're making honorable choices in relationships, and you trust God more than ever. You have *become* a person you never thought you could be when you were slowly killing yourself with alcohol.

Parenting a teenager can be a lot like the work of recovery. We moms are confronted every day with new challenges in parenting, our hearts are often filled with angst for our dear daughters, and it does sometimes feel as if we are going through the motions and not getting anywhere. *Don't give up before the miracle!* As you walk hand in hand with your daughter, inviting her to live with faith, hope, and love, you will become a woman of greater faith, hope, and love.

"Mom, Everyone Tries Drugs!"

I hate that I have no one to talk to, I hate that I have no one to call, I hate that I have no one to hold my hand, hug me, tell me everything is going to be all right. I hate that I have no one to share my dreams with, I hate that I no longer have any hopes or dreams, I hate that I have no one to tell me to hold on, that I can find them again. I hate that what I have turned to in my loneliness lives in a pipe or a bottle. I hate that what I have turned to in my loneliness is killing me, has already killed me, or will kill me soon.... More than anything, all I have ever wanted is to be close to someone.

—JAMES FREY, *A Million Little Pieces*

A mother bringing her daughter to counseling is not unusual. In fact, I often ask mother and daughter to come together for counseling sessions. What was unusual when Stacie's mother brought her daughter to my office was that Stacie was twenty-one.

Stacie didn't have a driver's license. It was revoked when she was arrested for driving under the influence with a blood-alcohol concentration of .325. Stacie didn't have a car because she sold it to a drug dealer for $300 to pay a debt for cocaine—and it was a 2000 Honda Accord! Stacie worked at Blockbuster for $6.25 per hour. She'd lost her "good" job because she had been caught drinking and was frequently late for work. Stacie didn't have a house because her duplex, along with all her possessions, burned to the ground during a cocaine binge that Stacie went on with her boyfriend. Stacie's mother didn't have much hope for Stacie. I'm sure that if she could have left her at my office for weeks or even months, she would have gladly done so.

Stacie and I spent many sessions talking about the consequences of her drug and alcohol abuse. Stacie's primary complaint was that she could no longer smoke pot. She had been sentenced to drug and alcohol education classes that required random drug tests. If Stacie failed a drug test, she would be spending time in jail. Stacie loved marijuana and was counting the days until her classes were over.

The first significant session that Stacie and I had began with her telling me about her visit to a psychiatrist. She told me she had requested sleeping medication because she was having terrible dreams. The psychiatrist wanted me to call him and give approval for the medication. I told Stacie that I was dubious about the medication because it was another drug that could stimulate the craving in her brain for other mind-altering, mind-numbing drugs. Then I asked about her dreams. It turned out that they weren't really dreams. As Stacie was trying to fall asleep, she would start to remember all of the things she did while she'd been under the influence of drugs and alcohol.

"I can't stand thinking about it all!" She spoke with more passion than I had seen in any of our previous sessions. "I just want to forget."

"There is an alternative," I suggested gently.

"What?" She looked at me as if she really wanted to know.

"You could talk about it?" I said.

"With who?" she genuinely wanted to know.

"With me," I said and then looked at her. A ruin right before my eyes. A girl intended for glory and goals, for romance and relationships, for adventure and aspirations, now broken down because of drugs and alcohol.

"Ah, you don't wanta hear about it all," Stacie said, her voice hoarse from smoking cigarettes. And then she left. Stacie often left our sessions early. I suspected that she left when she thought we might be close to connecting.

Two Stories of Adolescent Drug Abuse

Stacie's story of addiction and recovery is a good one for you to know because it highlights many facets of teenage drug use. It's a hard story to tell because drugs and alcohol took Stacie to places most of us have never imagined and don't want to think about. Her story is also an encouraging one because Stacie has hung in there. She recently celebrated one year of continuous sobriety.

She now has a car and a driver's license. She has a job with potential. She just completed two college classes. But that's all the stuff that's happened on the outside. I can't wait to tell you about what is happening on the inside. Stacie has become a glorious ruin.

In this chapter I also want to continue telling some of my son's unfolding story as we have faced his experimentation with marijuana. Graham's story is a good one for you to know as well because it highlights how teenagers and their mothers get introduced to the world of illegal drugs. His story is a hard one for me to tell because he is my son. But his story is also an encouraging one, because in the hardship and the horribleness we have faced together, I am more sure than ever of what I believe about alcohol and drug use and abuse: *The answers are found in relationships that heal from the inside out.*

According to the 2002 Monitoring the Future Survey,
nearly 25% of 8th graders have used illegal drugs.
For 12th graders, the statistics are more frightening—53% of
high school seniors admit to having used illegal drugs.

—FROM WWW.MONITORINGTHEFUTURE.ORG

I deliberately chose these stories, one about a hardcore drug (cocaine) and one about marijuana, a drug that's often characterized as benevolent. This book will not go into details about all the drugs available to teenagers today (see the resource section for materials that can educate you further. But I hope the issues we consider in this chapter will give you a foundation for understanding teens and drug abuse. I spend a little more time on marijuana, partly because we live in a culture that believes marijuana use is no big deal. In fact, to many people it's kind of a joke. I have never met with a teenager using harder drugs who did not begin by smoking marijuana. Teenagers are often more willing to try marijuana because it is perceived to be less harmful. In addition to the statistics on marijuana use listed in chapter 5, a study published in the Journal of the American Medical Association in 2003 found that early marijuana smokers were twice as likely to use opiates like heroin and five times as likely to use hallucinogens like LSD.[1]

I believe the dramatic increase in illegal drug use between middle school and high school can be linked to the use of marijuana. Once an adolescent becomes part of the culture of drugs, no drug is off-limits. Many of my clients tell me that it is among their pot-smoking friends that the pressure to use other drugs begins.

Should you be concerned if your teenager gets caught "trying" drugs? What if she claims (and she will), "I just tried it once. Everyone tries it"? When our teenagers try drugs, they are uniquely at risk because of their age. Here are a few facts to fuel your concern, vigilance, and interventionary action right from the start:[2]

- Drugs change the chemistry of the brain. Because the adolescent brain is still developing, even infrequent drug use can change the brain, hard-wiring it during the developmental stage and changing its chemistry for life.
- The female hormone estrogen increases sensitivity to drugs, which increases the craving for drugs.
- Girls who use drugs (even one time) are at greater risk for dangerous sexual activity.
- Girls are more likely than boys to become addicted to prescription drugs.
- Girls and young women are more susceptible than boys to adverse health consequences as a result of drug use.

Among teens, the average first use of marijuana is at age thirteen.
One in ten adolescents has used an inhalant (glue, gasoline, paint thinner).
Seven percent of twelfth graders have used methamphetamines.
Five percent of tenth graders have tried LSD.
Twelve percent of adolescents have experimented with ecstasy.
The percentage of teens who have tried cocaine has increased to 9.4 percent.
Approximately 4 percent of teens have tried heroin.
Twenty percent of teens have tried illegally obtained prescription drugs.

—COMPILED FROM KATHERINE KETCHAM AND NICOLAS A. PACE,
Teens Under the Influence

Stacie's story is typical of teens who use drugs. She began smoking pot in the ninth grade. Her parents were naive about drugs and alcohol and did not suspect that her falling grades and apathetic attitude were due to a growing habit of illegal drug use. By the time Stacie was a junior in high school, everyone at her school knew she was a "pothead." Her parents thought she was rebellious, listened to the wrong music, and hung out with the wrong friends. They did not know she had bonded with these friends and attached her identity to this group of kids who disdained the "popular" kids, liked mellow music by groups like Phish and The Grateful Dead, and organized their interactions around smoking pot. These peers had become Stacie's "second family."

As it is with many girls, Stacie's introduction to harder drugs came through a boyfriend. Her resistance to drug use had been eroded by her habitual use of marijuana. When her boyfriend suggested she try cocaine, her vulnerability to drugs and her desire for a boyfriend were too powerful a combination to defeat any lingering inhibitions about drug use.

SUBSTANCE ABUSE AND REVERSE SPIRITUALITY

Teenagers who use drugs are seeking something spiritual, which is both good and bad news. How do I know that your teenager—your rebellious daughter with drug paraphernalia hidden under her bed—is seeking something spiritual? Because to be human is to seek the spiritual. The apostle Paul says it this way:

> But the basic reality of God is plain enough. Open your eyes and there
> it is! By taking a long and thoughtful look at what God has created,
> people have always been able to see what their eyes as such can't see:
> eternal power, for instance, and the mystery of his divine being.
> (Romans 1:19-20, MSG)

The hurting, risk-taking, rebellious, curious teenager is allured by drugs because of the promise of something spiritual, powerful, mysterious, even divine. The very nature of drugs and alcohol ("spirits") awakens something in the inner person. The danger is that it is a reverse spirituality that leads to even greater spiritual bankruptcy.

God's intention is that our spirit connect with His Spirit first: "God's Spirit touches our spirits and confirms who we really are" (Romans 8:16, MSG). Our spirit life is enlivened to impact our soul, our relationship with ourselves and others. A healthy spirit life is marked by giving and receiving love. The spirit life and soul life then empower the body to be a living temple: "Take your everyday, ordinary life—your sleeping, eating, going-to-work, and walking-around life—and place it before God as an offering" (Romans 12:1, MSG).

Drugs and alcohol reverse spirituality. These substances enter the body first and then numb or deaden the soul life. Pain is initially lessened, but relationships are false, and the desire for anything more is effectively numbed, even killed. But drugs and alcohol don't just deaden the soul; they infiltrate the spirit, opening up the user to a spirituality that is from the god of this world. It is no coincidence that the word *witchcraft* used in the New Testament (Galatians 5:20) is the Greek word *pharmakeia,* the same word from which we get our word *pharmacy.*

Now before you freak out and panic that your daughter is into devil worship or witchcraft because she is doing drugs, hear me out. She *is* under the influence of the Enemy who wants her to be in a terrible conflict. The conflict is described in Galatians 5:17-23:

> For the sinful nature desires what is contrary to the Spirit, and the Spirit what is contrary to the sinful nature. They are in conflict with each other, so that you do not do what you want....
>
> The acts of the sinful nature are obvious: sexual immorality, impurity and debauchery; idolatry and witchcraft; hatred, discord, jealousy, fits of rage, selfish ambition, dissensions, factions and envy, drunkenness, orgies, and the like....
>
> But the fruit of the Spirit is love, joy, peace, patience, kindness, goodness, faithfulness, gentleness and self-control.

When Stacie told me I wouldn't believe some of the things she'd done, I told her that I already knew. I opened my copy of *The Message* to Galatians 5:19-20 and asked, "Are your waking nightmares about 'repetitive, loveless, cheap sex; a stinking accumulation of mental and emotional garbage; frenzied and joyless grabs for happiness; trinket gods; magic-show religion; paranoid loneliness; cutthroat competition; all-consuming-yet-never-satisfied wants; a brutal temper; an impotence to love or be loved; divided homes and divided lives; small-minded and lopsided pursuits; the vicious habit of depersonalizing everyone into a rival; uncontrolled and uncontrollable addictions; ugly parodies of community'?"

Tears trickled down Stacie's face, and she asked: "How did you know?"

THE ANSWER IS IN THE PROBLEM

When a teenager is using drugs or alcohol, true healing comes via the path of true spirituality—from the inside out. Sometimes external behaviors have to stop and be stopped for a while before we can get to our daughters' inner worlds. While teenagers may not know it or be able to put words to it, they are seeking a spiritual experience. They are vulnerable to drugs when their spiritual life is either superficial and therefore not very satisfying or when they have been wounded spiritually and are trying to put salve on their wounds.

Before we can talk to our daughters about drugs or encourage them to "just say no," there are two essential prerequisites. First, we must let go of the harsh judgments and crippling stigmas often attached to those who use drugs. Second, we must be primarily concerned with our daughters' spiritual lives. Once again, the answer is clearly in the problem. Drug abuse is a spiritual problem that demands a spiritual solution.

LETTING GO OF JUDGMENTS AND STIGMAS

Stacie knows that she is judged by the way she looks on the outside. Her hair is sometimes pink, sometimes red. She has a pierced eyebrow and a tattoo of an angel on each arm. She is also judged by her criminal record: stealing, DUI arrests, reckless endangerment, drug possession and use. Stacie also judges herself. She often repeats to me all she has lost—her driver's license, college credits, job, cool house, friends, car—because of her drug abuse.

She is also marked by the stigma of drug abuse. The Oxford dictionary defines *stigma* as "a mark or sign of disgrace." The word comes from the practice of slave owners hundreds of years ago branding their slaves with a "stigma" of cuts that made scars that would identify the slaves if they tried to run away. Slaves carried their stigmas throughout their lives.

Stacie described her stigma to me:

- She overheard her mother talking about her: "She's not all bad. You just have to look closely to see anything good."
- After Stacie's first arrest, the youth leader at her church asked Stacie's parents to keep her away from the youth group because she was a bad influence on the other kids.
- After Stacie's house burned down during her cocaine binge, she got a tattoo on her arm showing the date of the fire. I asked her why she wanted to memorialize that date. "I never want to forget how stupid I am and how much I hate myself," she answered.
- Stacie's friends have abandoned her because she acted too crazy when she was using.

The stigma of drug abuse from her family, her friends, her church, and herself was keeping Stacie from healing and developing self-esteem and true spirituality.

When I first learned of my son's experimentation with marijuana, my inner voice shouted, *You can't do this to me right now. I am writing a book on teenagers and drug use. You are going to undermine my credibility.* Bless Graham's heart! Having a writer, speaker, and teen counselor for a mother is not an easy cross to bear. We stereotype and stigmatize our children when we make their drug and alcohol use about us.

I had to let go of my judgmentalism, and let go fast. As long as I made Graham's choices about me, my reputation, and my credibility, I would never get to the heart of what was going on with him. Graham recently wrote a poem about *my* difficulty in handling his difficulty with marijuana. One line summarizes it well: "I find it hard to take action / when everything I do defines you."[3]

Never forget that our children can tell how we *feel* about them, and *that* is what they respond to. They can tell if they are being coped with, manipulated, hidden away, lied to. They can always detect hypocrisy. Consequently, what your daughter responds to indicates how you are *regarding* her.

Carefully consider the questions and exercises in the following Just for You section. If your feelings and regard for your child are negative, you will not be able to help her.

JUST FOR YOU

1. Close your eyes. Picture what you think a drug addict or alcoholic looks like. Now find a picture of your teenager. What stigma are you branding her with?

2. How has your judgment and stereotyping about the kind of people who use drugs impacted your conversations with your daughter, your tone of voice, and your vision for her future?

3. Do you regard your teenager as a person just like you, who has hopes and needs? Or is she a threat, a nuisance, a problem?

4. Are you willing to let go of your stereotypes and judgments of your daughter? What are you most afraid of if you do let go? Do your fears have to do with what others think of you? Are you making your daughter's problem about you?

5. Write a letter to your daughter confessing your harsh judgments and asking for her forgiveness. Note that small-mindedness, depersonalization (the same as stereotyping), and false community are in the same category as drunkenness and uncontrollable addictions listed in Galatians 5.

6. How healthy is your spiritual life? What "god" are you relying on to deliver your daughter from the temptations of drug use? A counselor, drug tests, a church youth group, your own prowess as a detective?

7. Do you really believe you are powerless to "save" your daughter? If not, what influence do you have? How is it working? Where does that leave you?

8. May I suggest that you say the following prayer for your kids every day? It is my version of the third-step prayer used in the Twelve Step program of Alcoholics Anonymous. I, personally, have to say this prayer at least ten times a day: *God, I offer Graham/Kristin to Thee to build and do with as Thou wilt. Keep me from making it about me so that I can see their hearts and better do Thy will. Remove their difficulties so that victory over them may bear witness to others they might help of Thy power, Thy love, and Thy way of life.*

LETTING GOD BE IN CHARGE

On Stacie's second counseling visit, her mother brought me a stack of papers to read. After skimming the papers, which were all about schizophrenia, I asked why she had brought them to me. "We think Stacie might be mentally ill. We want your opinion."

Granted, people on drugs can act crazy. And many drug addicts and alcoholics are mentally ill. But Stacie had been given a clean bill of health by two psychiatrists, and yet her parents still held on to their suspicions, preferring to have a mentally ill daughter rather than a drug addict.

When I gently asked her mother why they could not accept that Stacie was a drug addict, her mother replied, "Because then we don't know what to do. If she's schizophrenic, we can get her on medication or send her somewhere. If it's just the drugs, we really are powerless."

In this chapter I am going to give you a number of tools to use in helping your child fight drug abuse. There are things you can do. There are things you can say. But ultimately, your teenager is in God's hands. Your daughter's drug use is an opportunity to build your own faith, to trust in a Power greater than you are, and to wait for God's deliverance.

"O our God…we have no power to face this vast army that is attack-
ing us. We do not know what to do, but our eyes are upon you…."
"Take up your positions; stand firm and see the deliverance the
LORD will give you.… Do not be afraid or discouraged.…
For the battle is not yours, but God's."

—2 CHRONICLES 20:12,17,15

Within twenty-four hours of learning of Graham's use of marijuana, I had grounded him, ordered drug-testing supplies, contacted two counselors, and drawn up a contract regarding Graham's social activities and his use of his car. I was exhausted. I was acting as if it all depended on me. I will share with you some of the strategies Graham and I agreed upon because they are good ideas. But Graham put a stop to my frenzied activity when he wisely said, "You know, Mom, I'm going to have to find a reason for myself not to smoke pot. Your reasons won't cut it for me. You're not in charge of everything." Thank goodness Graham knew what he was talking about.

Admitting our powerlessness is how we accept that we do have a problem and begin to discover what the problem is. In some cases we are going to find out that there is a better action to take, that we have been doing it the wrong way. In some cases we may discover there is nothing we can do—we are powerless over the situation. In either case—whether we take a better action or admit that there is nothing we can do—we are on the road to recovery.

—Joe McQ, *The Steps We Took*

Establishing Clear Consequences for Drug Use

Even though there are aspects of your child's life over which you are powerless, it is still important that you create logical consequences that will be enforced when your child uses drugs. As we discussed in the previous chapter, it is wise to put a "contract" on paper and have everyone in the family sign it. Here are a few ideas to help you establish consequences for your daughter if she uses drugs:

- *First offense.* Immediately order reliable drug tests off the Internet. (See the resource section for more information.) Let your daughter know that she will be tested anytime, especially when she returns home from school and social activities. Explain to her that one humbling consequence of getting caught using an illegal drug is that you will have to be present when she urinates to make sure you are getting a legitimate sample. Also, explain to her that you will routinely send the sample to a lab to determine whether any substances were used to "fool" the test. Restrict social activities for a week. Privileges are earned by passing drug tests.
- *Second offense.* Enforce the loss of social privileges and the use of the car for a specified period of time. Privileges are earned by passing tests. Attend a Narcotics Anonymous meeting together. You can find an

"open" meeting by calling the Narcotics Anonymous listing in the white pages and asking for the location of a meeting near you.

- *Third offense.* Continue drug testing and enforcing the loss of privileges that must be earned back. Enroll your daughter in a drug and alcohol education program. Explain to her that you are going to take her continued drug use very seriously and that the next offense will result in a treatment program (more about this in chapter 11).

As a result of getting caught with marijuana and drug paraphernalia in his car, my son had to experience the consequences we agreed upon in advance. Besides being grounded socially for two weeks (unless his friends came to our home while I was there), Graham had to have random urinalysis tests that either I or his new counselor could administer at any time. These tests would be sent to a lab to determine whether substances were taken to try to beat the test.

HELPING YOUR CHILD HEAL FROM THE INSIDE OUT

While it is imperative to establish and enforce consequences for drug use, I am convinced that your daughter will not listen—really listen—to what you have to say about drugs unless you address what's going on *inside* her as well. If your daughter is using cocaine or smoking pot, I promise you that she was wounded in her spirit long before she ever became a drug user. I know that this is a strong statement to make and one that I cannot prove scientifically. But after talking to hundreds of girls and listening to hundreds of alcoholics and addicts, and based on my own personal experience, I know it's true.

Stacie grew up in a very religious family. In fact, she was home-schooled until the ninth grade. She attended church three times a week and memorized many Scripture verses. Stacie became a Christian when she was eight years old, but she felt that no one at church ever talked about *real* life issues such as loneliness, anger, or sex. While visiting relatives when she was six years old, Stacie was exposed to pornography. She started masturbating shortly thereafter and continued to do so on a fairly regular basis throughout her teen years. Who could she talk to about her questions about her own body and about the pictures she saw in that magazine? Her mother was a busy, strict, critical parent who sometimes disciplined Stacie by spanking her with a hairbrush.

When Stacie was in the seventh grade, she told one of her friends in her youth group about the pornographic magazines. That friend told her mother, and her mother began to "share" with other mothers in the church her concern that Stacie was a lesbian. When Stacie and her family learned of the rumors, Stacie's mom chastised Stacie for telling her friend about the magazines, and she scoffed at the gossip. The fissures in Stacie's spirit were becoming jagged and painful, influencing what Stacie believed about herself, the church, and God.

When Stacie began attending public high school in the ninth grade, she quickly found acceptance with a group of kids who smoked pot every day during their lunch hour. When Stacie smoked, she felt happier, calmer, relaxed, and at peace. She felt embraced by a community in which the only requirement was smoking a drug that made her feel wonderful. No rumors, no judgments, no off-limit topics.

Stacie started smoking every day too. In order to get marijuana, she started selling it. It was when she was arrested for possession with intent to sell that she was kicked out of her church youth group. At that point, the fissure became a canyon that separated her from any desire to know God or be known by Him.

After Stacie told me the beginning of her drug-abuse story, I said, "Your parents should have left that church."

She looked at me, eyes wide open, and said, "They would never do that for me."

To what lengths are you willing to go to become your daughter's ally against drug use? My son was right. Our children need to find their *own* reasons to stay away from drugs. But they are more likely to find those reasons if we create a context that clearly reveals that nothing is more important to us than they are—not our jobs, our church work, our reputations, our money, or our hobbies. Consider carefully what you are willing to lose and to what lengths you are willing to go in order to make your daughter your top priority and to provide a context in which she could choose to be safe from drugs and alcohol. Be honest with yourself. What is more important?

I have been privileged to learn from people like Brittany's parents, who were active in a parachurch youth organization. They were in the upper echelons of leadership. But when they learned that Brittany had been ridiculed and rejected by the group, they resigned from leadership. Brittany's mom made the night the youth group had met each week a special night for her and Brittany to do something together.

Krista's mom worked hard to become the chief financial officer of a large insurance company. She worked long hours. But when she discovered that Krista and her friends were smoking pot at their home several days a week after school, she resigned from her position and took a job that allowed her to be home when Krista was home.

When Cami's mom discovered that Cami was smoking pot on a regular basis and was in a peer group reputed to also use cocaine, she picked Cami up from school one day and drove eight hundred miles away to another state. She and Cami spent the rest of the semester living with relatives, getting their relationship on track, and making decisions about the future, including changing schools.

When I learned of my son's marijuana use, I reflected on some of the fissures in Graham's spirit that made him vulnerable to alcohol and drug use. Graham's dad, Dave, and I had been divorced a year by this time. Dave and I had taught seminars on marriage. We promised our children often that "we will never get a divorce." It is not important for me to go into the details of the tragedy in our family, but it is important for me to say that broken promises to our children crush their spirits and leave them vulnerable to the promises of drugs and alcohol. They begin to see the world in a jaded way that makes them feel justified in their self-destruction.

Graham told me that when he smoked, he felt at peace. I replied, "Things haven't been very peaceful in our family for a long time, have they?"

He just looked at me as if to say, "No kidding."

I asked him what I could do at this point to make home more peaceful. He told me, "Stop complaining about Dad and the divorce. Don't be bitter or resentful." He was clearly telling me that my sick, wounded spirit was contaminating his. I knew I needed to continue working on myself if I was to be of help to him.

Graham also told me that "all" of his friends at school smoked pot. He told me that it would be hard for him to remain friends with them if he didn't smoke. I knew Graham was vulnerable to marijuana not just because of the wounds from our divorce but because of the welcome from his peer group and their pressure on him to be a part of the group by smoking pot. I knew Graham was using drugs to impress his friends and to join them in not being part of the "preppie" popular group. I also knew I would be completely ineffective in talking with Graham about his friends and their destructive influence until I did something about my own inner world and its toxic contents

JUST FOR THE TWO OF YOU

The following exercises are not for the faint of heart!

1. Ask your daughter if you have broken any promises to her, which left her feeling hurt or disillusioned. If she says yes, confess your failure and ask her forgiveness.

2. Ask your daughter, "If it were possible to make a tangible representation of your spirit, what would it look like?" Gather materials—paints, clay, paper, chalk—and work together on creating a representation of an unharmed, free spirit. Also make a representation of a wounded spirit and talk about the wounds. Make a representation of a spirit battered and influenced by drugs.

3. Ask your daughter if there are situations in which she feels rejected or judged? Ask if there's anything she would like you to do in response to these realities.

4. Ask your daughter what would make her room feel safe, peaceful, and restful. Work together to create that kind of environment.

5. Ask your daughter to write out a description of her ideal friend. Suggest that she chronicle her current friendships and see how they match up to her ideal friend. Ask her to share with you some of the character qualities of her ideal friend. Then make it your task to pick a quality each week and live it out with your daughter with passion, intention, and creativity.

that were seeping out onto my son and propelling him further into the arms of his "second family."

One mother I know did exercise 5 in the Just for the Two of You section on the previous page. One week she picked the quality of loyalty, and every chance she got, she stuck up for her daughter with other family members and with a teacher who gave a lower grade than expected. She also made a sign for her daughter's room that took up an entire wall. The sign pledged her loyalty to her daughter. Yes, her daughter rolled her eyes and thought her mother was acting "silly." Yes, her daughter filed away her mother's actions in her brain, and that file will be there when her "friends" let her down. Because there is one thing that is certain: Friendships forged through drug use will fail.

Though the exercises mentioned in the Just for the Two of You section will not magically solve your daughter's drug problems, they can open the door for her to hear what you have to say.

When I first tried to talk to Graham about his marijuana use, he had all the same arguments that teenagers who use pot typically give:

- *"Marijuana is natural."* (It actually has 421 different chemicals in it. Drug users round the number down to 420, and that is why April 20—4/20—has become National Pot Smokers Day.)
- *"Marijuana is legal in other countries."* (Actually, other countries, like Australia, are discovering that marijuana users are twice as likely to use heroin and five times as likely to use LSD.[4])
- *"It doesn't hurt anyone."* (Actually, marijuana changes your brain chemistry, often causing you to crave other drugs. Smoking five joints a week causes you to take in as many cancer-causing chemicals as someone who smokes a full pack of cigarettes every week. Smoking marijuana causes lung problems and chronic sinus problems. Marijuana dramatically increases the heart rate. Marijuana results in decreased testosterone levels. And pot is firmly linked to "amotivational syndrome," which leads to depression, anxiety, and hopelessness.)
- *"It isn't addictive."* (The truth is, every year the number of kids entering treatment facilities for drug use with a primary diagnosis of marijuana dependency is increasing. Research also shows that marijuana

use is *three times* more likely to lead to dependence in adolescents than in adults. Among those who have used the drug at least five times, the rate of dependency is estimated at 20 to 30 percent! No wonder the Office of National Drug Control Policy concludes that marijuana *is* an addictive drug.[5])

When I shared these facts with Graham, he didn't hesitate to pull out the most effective weapons in his arsenal. "What about *you*, Mom? Have you ever smoked pot? You drank. You're an alcoholic. And you seem okay now."

As I've said earlier, answering our kids' questions about our own drug and alcohol use is tricky business. I believe that if we have an addiction, we are obligated to tell them our story so they're aware of their genetic vulnerability. But we must also keep in mind that they see themselves as different from us and more immune from the potential ravages of drug and alcohol use.

I told Graham that I had smoked marijuana a few times and that, in fact, I had smoked once when I was babysitting for neighbors. The neighbors called my parents, and within a week I was whisked off to a two-week camp in the mountains for teenagers. Graham rolled his eyes and said, "You'll never do that to me, will you, Mom?"

"Addiction is serious, Graham. That is what I *know* from my own drug and alcohol use. It almost killed me. It kept me from being a good mother, a good friend, and a good person. I know enough to take it seriously. And if I ever believe that you are not communicating honestly with me about this and are hellbent on using drugs, I will take drastic measures."

Once again my son rolled his eyes. But he was silent. "I already have something up my sleeve," I added. My smile gave me away. He knew that I was not shipping him off but that I was definitely up to something.

A few weeks later I was scheduled to speak at a church in the suburbs of Chicago. I decided to take my son along, and I asked my brother Jim to join us for the weekend. I paid for his plane ticket and for a room in the city for him and my son while I was working in the suburbs. I told my brother, who is a recovering drug addict, about Graham's experimentation with marijuana and asked for Jim's help. I didn't tell him what to do (a very difficult task for me), and I left his time with Graham in God's hands.

Uncle and nephew had a blast. They rode the train all over the city, they went to a concert of a local band in a neighborhood I would not have ventured into, and they stayed up late and talked a lot. Jim took Graham to meet a guy who was the lead singer of some '90s band. They admired all of his memorabilia, but Graham could not help but note that he was "not all there." When he asked Jim about it after they left, his uncle explained that the musician's mind was half gone from drug use. Then Jim took Graham to meet a guy who is still in the music business. (My brother had an alternative industrial band during his drug-using days and knows a lot of people in the business.) This guy showed Graham his studio and then looked at my brother and said, "Man, you're a lot different from the last time I saw you. You were so strung out that your eyes were actually looking in opposite directions."

My brother answered, "Well, that's mainly because I'm in recovery from drug addiction, and I got serious about Christianity. I realized that what I was looking for in using drugs was something spiritual, and for me that could only be legitimately found in Christ."

I'm certain my brother didn't lecture Graham about his mistakes. I'm also sure he didn't tell him everything I would have wanted him to. But they connected. Graham came home excited about participating in an inner-city youth group my brother is beginning, and he is ready to set a goal with me for an "extreme dream" end-of-summer reward if he stays away from drugs and alcohol. He doesn't want a new car or money or a fancy stereo. He wants another getaway with his uncle.

Connection is the antidote to negative peer pressure. Graham is beginning to heal from the inside out.

If you suspect that your daughter is abusing drugs, it will be hard for you to wait for the truth to be revealed. While your daughter is using, she will withdraw from you and be suspicious of your love and support. Guilt confines her to a box that distorts her view of herself and others. Your daughter may see you as the enemy, as boring, judgmental, or unenlightened. It is essential that you do not put yourself in that box—that *you* know you are her ally, open to a growing, creative relationship filled with compassion and discernment, particularly when it comes to her drug use.

As Stacie began to open up about her experiences as a drug user, it did not take long for the truth to come out about her "friends." Most of Stacie's friends abandoned her when she lost her home, job, and car. As Stacie remembered what had really happened during her using days, she also re-called times when her friends had stolen from her or left her when she was experiencing bad side effects from the drugs or alcohol. And some of Stacie's most painful memories were of her sexual experiences with men when she was under the influence. She knew she had put herself at risk of being vio-lated and used in unspeakable ways. At the end of one session, Stacie told me that she really didn't have any friends anymore, that she craved marijuana because it was really all she had left.

"Not all," I said gently. "You still have your family. I know they've hurt you and made a lot of mistakes, but they wouldn't have brought you to coun-seling and paid for it over the months if they didn't care about you. Maybe it's time to tell them your story."

It took a few weeks, but Stacie finally agreed to tell her story to her mom in my office. It was an amazing two hours of intense emotion. All three of us cried. Stacie's mom said, "We would have done things so differently if we had known all we know now. I'm sorry we hurt you and didn't know how to help you."

Here is an irony that shows the power of God. We have taken the problem—whatever it was we were powerless over, whatever was destroying our self-worth, destroying our lives, giving us guilt and fear and shame, and making us feel like a zero—and finally become will-ing to let go of it. We have come to believe, have made a decision, and have taken the actions. Then after we have gotten God's direction in our lives…we find out the thing that seemed the worst, that we hated the most, is really the jewel of our life. In the end it is the only thing we have enough understanding of to offer to the rest of the world.

—Joe McQ, *The Steps We Took*

Stacie confessed, "I hurt you, too. I'm sorry."

Stacie and her mom agreed to get together once a week for a movie or a meal to try to build a new relationship.

I watched Stacie slowly begin to heal as she continued to recover from her drug and alcohol addiction. Transformation began when I made a simple request of her: "Stacie, I have a fifteen-year-old client who really likes smoking marijuana. She's putting up all the usual arguments about why it's okay. Will you talk to her?"

"You want *me* to talk to her?" Stacie was incredulous.

"Yes. Tell her your story."

Stacie met with my client in my office. After the first ten minutes, I left them alone. I could tell that Stacie was going to be great. She was honest, funny, and real. The next week when we met together, Stacie smiled and said, "I think maybe I want to go to school to do this for a living. I could talk to kids about drugs. I maybe could help a few people." Stacie was healing from the inside out.

Just for You

Your daughter has used or is using drugs. Her friends are using drugs. You know that much. Is she addicted? Is the problem serious enough for intervention or a treatment facility? We will answer these questions together in part 3 of this book. For now you need to concentrate on laying the foundation for effective communication with your daughter about this serious and potentially life-threatening subject. You will not have peace or clarity about making the difficult and important decisions about your daughter's treatment if you have not first answered the following questions for yourself.

- What wounds have made your daughter vulnerable to drugs?
- What wounds have drugs inflicted on your daughter's spirit and soul?
- If possible, identify the conflict your daughter is caught in as she uses drugs, doing things she doesn't want to do and not doing things she wants to do.
- Have you let go of your harsh judgments and stereotypes about drug users? If you haven't, what's keeping you from letting go?
- Have you told your own story of drug or alcohol abuse in a way that lets your daughter know that you understand the seriousness of addiction and will go to any lengths to keep her safe? If you don't

have experience with drugs or alcohol, have you let her know that you are committed to learning all you can so that you can help keep her safe?

- How have you demonstrated in tangible ways that you are willing to go to any lengths to keep your daughter safe?

- What logical and appropriate consequences have you set that everyone agrees upon? What incentives or rewards have you included if your daughter refrains from using drugs or alcohol?

- What resources have you found to help your daughter? Have you found people with stories of recovery from drug and alcohol abuse who are willing to be involved in your daughter's life?

- Do you continually surrender your daughter to God to do His part in the areas of your daughter's life and heart over which you are powerless?

- What is the state of your own spiritual health? Are you living from the inside out? If not, what are you willing to do to revitalize your spiritual life *now?* When our children are in crisis, we often let ourselves go. This is a big mistake. We cannot help them if we are not spiritually fit. Talk to your husband or ask a friend about supporting each other in a rigorous program of spiritual fitness—even in the midst of your daughter's crisis. Meditate on Scripture. Pray. Be in community where you can share your fears, foibles, and needs.

Part III

Conquering Roadblocks to Relationship

More than ever teens and parents are ending up on different sides of the battlefield. The growing gap creates a kind of teen code that parents find difficult to crack. This code does not consist of numbers and symbols and Navajo words; it's actually a lot more complex—it defines how we think and act, why we get tattoos and piercings, why we experiment with dangerous stuff, and how and why we are who we are, teens of today.

I was not looking for—and didn't find—any kind of magic words for you to say to make everything perfect between you and your teenagers. I just wanted parents to understand that it really is possible to have good communication with us, as impenetrable as we seem. And it starts with listening.

—Rhett Godfrey, *The Teen Code*

Chapter 9

Bad Company

*Like soft-shelled lobsters in their molting season, teenagers are tender. They
don't know how to be in the world. They cast around for guidelines. If they
don't find them at home, they can be easily pushed and seduced by peers.*

—ROBERT SHAW, *The Epidemic*

Stacy came to counseling because she was in big trouble. Two weeks prior
to our first appointment, this fourteen-year-old had left the movies with
a friend and two seventeen-year-old boys. She had gone to one of the boy's
homes, smoked pot, and made out with the boys.

Stacy's mom knew something was amiss when Stacy was not at her usual
pickup spot after the movies. This mom waited for her daughter for thirty
minutes before Stacy came walking down the sidewalk to her car. Stacy
reeked of marijuana and guilt and would not look at her mom when she
asked, "Where have you been?" As Stacy's "story" of what she'd been up to
quickly unraveled, Stacy became more defiant, and her mom became more
panicky.

Both emotions were evident when Stacy and her mom came to my office
for their first counseling appointment. Stacy sat on my couch with her arms
crossed and her face closed off from any emotional expression. Her mom's
voice became more and more shrill as she shared her perspective. "Stacy has
just gotten in with the wrong group of friends. She is grounded from using
the telephone, the Internet, and the television. She can't go to movies anymore, and she can't ever hang out with Tiffany [her partner in crime] again.
That girl is bad news."

At this, a tear trickled down Stacy's cheek.

"What are you feeling sad about?" I asked Stacy.

"My mom has taken my life away. I don't care about the Internet or TV, but I want to talk to Tiffany. My mom has gotten everything she wants. I just sit in my room and stare at the wall, and she's happy about that. But I don't have anything I want. I hate her. I can't wait until I'm eighteen and can move out."

I had that feeling in the pit of my stomach that I always feel when I know that both mother and daughter are on dangerous ground. I knew that Stacy's mom was in danger of losing her daughter to a world of defiance and destructive behaviors and that Stacy was in danger of losing herself as well.

Sometimes parenting our daughters when they are in the peer-pressure cooker is not just hard, it is overwhelming. It's one thing to make your daughter feel significant, to create a sense of belonging at home, and to help her develop self-esteem when she's somewhat open, but what if she's downright defiant? What if her friends encourage her to hate you and are pulling her into scary and dangerous situations?

The goal of the interactions suggested in this book so far has been *to connect* with your daughter so that forming an alliance is possible. But sometimes teenagers get so deep into a world of disobedience and self-destruction that they can't get out of it by themselves. It will be impossible to connect with your daughter until she is disentangled from toxic influences. In this chapter we will examine the evidence of unholy alliances, consider appropriate responses you can give in the face of these alliances, and determine ways for you to begin to build a holy alliance with your daughter.

Unholy Alliances

When Stacy and her mom first met with me, Stacy actually gave me all the evidence I needed to know that she was involved in an unholy alliance with her friend Tiffany. Sometimes our daughters' most hurtful words reveal powerful truths that uncover necessary solutions. I think the most disorienting words parents can hear from their daughters are, "I hate you." Whenever I hear those words in the counseling office, I first examine what I know about the family. I look for evidence of an abusive or neglectful home. I had already met with Stacy's mom and stepfather and felt confident that this was a "good enough" family. (I use the term *good enough* to describe families in which parents are doing their best to deal with the tumult and responsibilities of raising teenagers.) Stacy's mom was involved in Stacy's life and had been close to her before her last year of middle school. Her stepfather had been in Stacy's life since she was four years old and had also had a good rapport with Stacy until recently.

"I Hate You!"/"I Hate Myself!"

I suspected that when Stacy hurled the words "I hate you" at her mom, she was really saying, "I hate who you have seen me to be." Stacy had a solid moral grounding and an involved, supportive parental presence in her life. As she made the series of choices that led to that fateful night when she was supposed to be at the movies, she knew that she was drifting away from her moral grounding and was betraying her parents. The contempt that arose within Stacy was more about her own choices and behaviors—about who she was becoming—than about who her parents had been.

Parents make a big mistake when they fight on their rebellious, unstable daughter's turf. When your daughter claims that she hates you, your compassion and conviction will be aroused if you recognize that what she really hates are choices she is making. There is something woven into the fabric of our souls that will not allow us to rest in the midst of sin. We can become experts at distracting ourselves from this unrest with an infinite number of defenses. For teenagers, a powerful defense against their own guilt and shame is "I hate you."

God's law is not something alien, imposed on us from without, but woven into the very fabric of our creation.

—Romans 2:15, MSG

After my first meeting with Stacy and her mom, I asked her mom to make her best effort to look beyond Stacy's hurtful words and decode her daughter's expression of contempt. I asked her to write down everything she thought Stacy might hate about her own behavior and to connect these thoughts to stories and character traits from Stacy's childhood. Here is part of her list:

- Stacy would hate lying. I remember when Stacy was seven years old and lied about breaking a dish in the dining room. After she confessed and I forgave her, she said, "Mommy, I feel sick inside when I lie to you."
- She would hate getting into a car with boys she didn't know well. Stacy's cousin was killed in a car accident when she was seventeen, and since then, Stacy has been hypervigilant about car safety.
- She would hate smoking pot. We have had so many conversations about drugs, and Stacy has expressed her disgust with drug use on many occasions.
- She would hate losing our trust. Stacy told me at the beginning of the school year that she was so happy that we had a good, trusting relationship.

JUST FOR YOU

If your daughter has expressed hatred for you, take a few moments to do the exercise I suggested to Stacy's mom. Then ask yourself the following questions:

1. What have you felt toward your daughter when she has demonstrated the behaviors you listed? Have you felt contempt? disgust? hatred? fear?
2. As you decode her behaviors and how she might feel about herself, how do your feelings for your daughter change?
3. How will you be empowered to better help your daughter by not taking her expressions of contempt personally?

"I CAN'T WAIT TO MOVE OUT!"/"I NEED TO GET OUT!"

When a teenager claims in the midst of turmoil, "I can't wait until I'm eighteen and can move out!" she is often speaking a language many parents don't understand. Of course, this extreme expression may reflect some rebellious desire for independence from rules and family responsibility, but often it is about wanting to get out of the situation *she* is in. As our daughters get deeper and deeper into destructive and dangerous behaviors, a growing dread rises in them that they have chosen a lifestyle they can't get out of. To get out means disowning friends, which is anathema to teenagers. To get out means acknowledging that getting in was wrong or foolish. To get out means having to start all over again finding a group and an identity within the complex adolescent culture.

Once again, when parents try to fight on their daughter's turf with statements like "I can't wait until you're eighteen either!" or "Go ahead and move out. See what life is really like," they fuel disconnection and miss an important opportunity to see that their daughters are often saying one thing with their words while they're expressing something else entirely different beneath the surface. I know it's crazy making.

When I looked at Stacy and learned about her family, I knew she did not really want a dark life of meaningless sex and dangerous drug abuse but felt she was already immersed in a world from which she could not extricate herself without destroying her friendships and her reputation among her peers. This felt like too high a price to pay. In Stacy's mind her choices were lose-lose. She was trapped.

In the fall of 2004, tragedies related to alcohol abuse occurred on both campuses of Colorado State University. During fraternity and sorority "partying," two freshman students died from alcohol poisoning. Investigations of

Just for the Two of You

1. Ask your daughter if she feels she can be honest with you about what goes on with her and her friends. If she doesn't, ask her why.
2. Ask your daughter what would happen to her if she told on her friends, if she cut herself off from her friends, or if she lost her friends.
3. Use your daughter's answers to the previous questions to evaluate her personal resolve to say no and her felt ability to separate herself from bad friends or dangerous behaviors.
4. If her resolve is weak and her felt ability is small, how could you help her distance herself from her current situation? Could you provide alternative activities? be the "bad guy" by imposing stricter rules? change her school or youth group?

both deaths uncovered an underworld of heavy drinking and risk-taking behaviors, but peers of the dead students denied the heavy drinking. A writer
for the *Denver Post* described the overwhelming peer pressure to drink and
keep quiet about any misdeeds:

> The school has a hotline for students [to report pressure to drink in fra-
> ternities and sororities], but that may not be worth the social conse-
> quences. If you turn the group in, then the pledges will turn on you,
> and I know some students end up dropping out [of school altogether].[1]

My heart breaks for the families of the students who have died, and then
I think of my adolescent clients who are far less mature and equipped to confront temptations than college students are. If college students confess that
they cannot expose or extricate themselves from peer pressure, how can we
expect young adolescents to do better?

I asked Stacy's mom about the lengths she was willing to go to rescue her
daughter from her escalating situation. She told me she had already looked
into a different school for her daughter, and we talked about the pros and
cons of changing schools. One mistake parents make is blaming their child's
behavior entirely on bad friends. Stacy's mom knew that Stacy was making
bad choices because she desperately wanted to belong and perhaps was a little
uncertain of her own values. But I agreed with her that Stacy's influencers
played a major role in the direction her life had taken and that maybe the
only way to disentangle from this peer group was to transfer to a new school.

"I Can't Live Without My Friends"/
"I Need Something to Live For"

When a girl begins high school, she is desperate to find a peer group and a
few close friends. Once those attachments begin to form, she breathes a sigh
of relief that she will be okay in her new world. When those attachments are
unhealthy and lead to dangerous and destructive behaviors, she continues to
associate her sense of okay-ness with her friends and their behaviors. When
her behaviors are found out and her friendships threatened, she is terrified
that she won't be okay.

I knew that Stacy's tears and desperation over her friend Tiffany were about more than wanting to see her friend. They were about needing to belong and feel okay in her world. Stacy meant it when she claimed that her mother was taking away her life. She felt that losing her friends meant losing her life.

We found that the single most important factor [on drinking and drug use] is the behavior of their five closest friends.

—CHRISTOPHER NEWTON, "Feeling the Pressure"

I began my second session with Stacy by asking her what she liked to do when she was angry or happy, lonely or bored. She told me she loved to draw. I expressed interest in her drawing and asked if she would be willing to take an excursion from the counseling office to our local Hobby Lobby. She agreed, and we picked out a sketchbook and some colored pencils. Along the way we talked about Stacy's friends—Tiffany, in particular. I told her I was sure Tiffany had some good qualities, but it seemed that when the two of them got together, they got in trouble. She was not happy when I told her I supported her parents' moratorium on the friendship.

JUST FOR YOU

1. Brainstorm how you can facilitate new friendships for your daughter. Consider her school, her youth group, her hobbies, and her extended family.
2. Practice your responses to your daughter's emotional pain. Offer validating statements, such as "I'm sorry you are feeling that way. It must really hurt." "I'm glad you're telling me what you're feeling." "This is a really rough time for you. My heart aches for you."
3. Consider your daughter's hobbies and interests. What healthy outlets—art, music, physical exercise—can you help provide for her emotional expression?

I asked her to use the times when she felt angry or lonely because she couldn't be with Tiffany to draw. I said, "Anything goes. Draw what you are feeling." I knew Stacy would feel anger, loneliness, despair, even rage, and that she needed to express these emotions. I also knew that the expression of these feelings would eventually lead to their healing.

The next week Stacy came in with a sketchbook full of drawings. The sketches were dark and foreboding. I asked Stacy how she felt about starting over with new friends, and she wept and raged. "I hate it! I am all alone. My life is over!"

I asked Stacy to keep drawing to express her emotional state. Over the next weeks, as Stacy transitioned into a new school, her drawings continued to express anger and despair. We talked about her emotions, and I encouraged her to keep drawing. Slowly, as Stacy inevitably made new friends and the wounds of her separation from her old friends and their behaviors began to heal, her drawings became more hopeful.

One of the most important responses in mothering during emotional turmoil is, "I know you feel bad right now. You will not always feel this way." It is easy for both mothers and daughters to become enveloped in the mood of the moment. As we remember that emotions come and go, we have faith in the possibilities of the future.

—SHARON HERSH, *"Mom, I Hate My Life!"*

I realize that I saw Stacy only one hour a week and did not hear or see her emotional distress as her parents did. I urged them to let Stacy feel what she was feeling and to keep encouraging her to do her drawing assignments. Her mom made sure that Stacy was well stocked with sketchbooks and pencils. The foundation for Stacy's successful transition from her old friend group to a new one was threefold:

1. Her parents needed to provide a new context in which Stacy could make new friends. They chose to transfer Stacy to a new school.
2. Stacy needed to be able to feel and express her grief over losing her old friends and her fear about making new friends.
3. She needed a healthy outlet for her expression.

EVIDENCE OF BAD COMPANY

Sometimes a bad experience, like Stacy's night away from the movies, will tip parents off that their daughter is keeping bad company. But you can watch for other clues that your daughter is being influenced by peers who might lead her in dangerous or destructive directions. Here are a few signs to look for:

- Review your daughter's grades. If she has been an A and B student and her grades are now mostly Cs and Ds, she may be keeping company with friends who are changing her attitude and approach to school.

- Observe your daughter's style. If your neat daughter becomes messy or changes her style of dress, ask about her friends and their style. A messy or more casual style does not necessarily signal a problem, but it does indicate that your daughter is being influenced by new peers. You will want to watch to see if their influence extends to behaviors, language, or attitudes that trouble you or are contrary to your family's values.

- Look for evidence of smoking (the smell of smoke on your daughter's clothes, in her car, or on her breath; cigarette butts; lighters), profanity (written on notebooks or in notes), and inappropriate music in your daughter's car or among her belongings. These things can indicate a change in peer groups.

- Listen to your daughter's stories. Teenagers almost always reveal what is going on in their peer group as they talk about what is happening to their friends. Just because your daughter's friends are getting in trouble does not mean that your daughter is, but if she defends their behaviors or expresses anger and outrage at authorities who have intervened, then you can suspect that she is dabbling in those behaviors as well. If your daughter refuses to talk about her friends, her secretiveness is cause for concern about their behaviors and their influence on her life.

- Most important, take note of how your daughter interacts with you. If her attitude toward you becomes hateful, secretive, or disrespectful, you would be wise to consider her friends and their influence on her.

WHAT'S A PARENT TO DO?

When you suspect or know that your daughter is keeping bad company, you must be proactive in her life. If you aren't, you may miss a critical opportunity to form an alliance with her. Early intervention can keep disastrous events from unfolding, but even if you have waited until your daughter is repeatedly getting in trouble with her friends, it is not too late to address this issue. As you take action, your daughter may get angry with you, you will probably have conflicts, and you will have difficult decisions to make. Keep in mind that you are doing the hard work of forming a holy alliance with your daughter and that this work is not for the faint of heart. You will have to dig deep in your mother's heart for the fierceness and determination to effectively love your daughter when she is acting her most unlovable.

DON'T LOOK THE OTHER WAY

When your daughter's grades start to slip, her language changes, or her behaviors become deviant, consider her peers. Has she made new friends? How are they influencing one another? Let your daughter know that you are noticing the changes in her choices and behaviors as well as observing her friends and their influence on one another. Will your daughter think you are being controlling and invasive? Yes. Stress to her that you understand the importance of friends and that just as you would not look the other way if she became attached to destructive substances such as drugs or alcohol, you will not ignore her friends if they influence her to make bad choices.

JUST FOR THE TWO OF YOU

When your daughter is not in trouble or under suspicion because of her friends, find a good time to tell her about *your* experience with friends. Tell her about friends who have had an unhealthy influence on you.

1. Why were you vulnerable to their influence?
2. What allowed you to see their negative influence?
3. How did you extricate yourself from the relationship?

Tell your daughter about friends who have had a positive influence on you.
1. What qualities made these friends a good influence?
2. What positive things happened when you were with these friends?
Ask your daughter about her friends.
1. Does she think any of her friends are a negative influence? In what ways?
2. Is she able to stand up to them and resist their negative influence? Why or why not?
3. What friends in your daughter's life does she think are good influences? Why?

DON'T MAKE YOUR DAUGHTER'S FRIEND THE ENEMY

Even if you are certain that your daughter's friend is a bad influence, do not attack that friend. Your daughter may feel compelled to choose her friend and stand against you. Instead, focus on the *behaviors* your daughter and her friend or friends engage in together.

Denise and her fifteen-year-old daughter, Debbie, came to see me about a conflict over a friend. At a recent sleepover at Abby's house, the girls had climbed out Abby's bedroom window to meet a boy whom Abby liked. Debbie drank some beer while she was with her friends and came home with alcohol on her breath. Her mom was waiting for her in the living room after having been called by Abby's mom who was looking for her daughter.

During our counseling session Debbie was distraught because her mother had branded Abby a "bad girl" and had forbidden Debbie from ever being with her again. We all agreed that Abby had made some foolish choices and that Debbie had blindly gone along with them. Then I asked Denise if she would be willing to give Abby and her daughter a second chance and allow Abby to come over for the evening. Denise agreed, and we talked about possible activities that would allow Debbie and Abby to have fun while Denise closely supervised them. After three of these get-togethers, Debbie and Denise came to see me again. Denise was beginning to trust Abby and support her friendship with Debbie as long as the girls followed her rules. Denise told me, "I think both girls just need a strong parental presence."

I have found that when girls are willing to let their parents be involved and set boundaries with their friends, they usually have pretty good friends. Conversely, when girls don't want their parents around their friends or involved in any way, parents should smell trouble.

DO SET APPROPRIATE CONSEQUENCES

When your daughter gets into trouble with a particular friend or group of friends, it is appropriate to suspend or regulate activities with that friend or group. You can let your daughter know that she can reestablish the relationship as she works to build trust with you by making good choices, acknowledging her foolish choices, and interacting with you in a respectful manner. Your daughter may not want to admit that her choices with that friend or group of friends have not been good, but she needs to know that you see the relationship as potentially toxic and will not stand by while it takes over. She may be angry with you for setting boundaries, but she will be grateful that you are more powerful than her friends.

Consequences must touch a child and must be enforceable.
This creates connection—a pause in the action that brings
adults into the foreground and diminishes the extraordinary
gripping power of the second family [peers].

—DR. RON TAFFEL, *The Second Family*

Mothers, especially hover mothers or mothers who parent from beneath, sometimes worry that if they set good boundaries and appropriate consequences with regard to their daughters' friends, their daughters will be mad at them or not like them. That may be true. In this case, however, your daughter does not need you to win a popularity contest with her or her friends. She needs you to be a powerful presence in her life.

DO PREPARE TO TAKE EXTRAORDINARY MEASURES

When your daughter's friends wield a bad influence despite your attempts to encourage good friends, to invite her friends into your home, and to set boundaries and appropriate consequences, you may have to take extraordinary measures. As the quotation from teen specialist Ron Taffel suggests, peers can have an extraordinarily powerful grip on an adolescent, and parents must sometimes take extreme measures to loosen that grip.

One of my heroes in mothering is Phyllis. When her daughter Ceyerah was in seventh grade, Phyllis noticed that she was increasingly influenced by her peers to make choices contrary to their family's values. Ceyerah never got into big trouble, but she showed signs of choosing her peers over her own values, even in the face of consequences. This wise mother decided to intervene before the choice became too scary or threatening. While her relationship with her daughter was still on solid ground, Phyllis proposed that they home-school for a year and highlighted all the positives that would await them apart from the regular school routine. Her early intervention solidified her relationship with her daughter and helped Ceyerah to internalize her own values before she headed to the hallways of high school.

Most of us don't seek such radical solutions until the situation is a bit more perilous. Extraordinary measures may include choosing a new school or home-schooling, removing your daughter from an environment by sending her to live with other family members, or enrolling her in new extracurricular activities.

Where there is no vision, the people perish.

—PROVERBS 29:18, KJV

While you are in the midst of making these difficult decisions, keep a clear vision in mind for your daughter. This is about her, not you. Remember that you are not out to control or punish her; you want to *preserve her options*. While she is involved with bad company, you have to be in crisis-management mode, which means surviving the crisis of the moment without having a lot of time or energy to think about the future. When you use *your influence* to keep your daughter from destructive peer influences, you are remembering her future and honoring her potential to be all that her Creator would have her be.

Addiction

Sharing the story of what happens in addiction, what brings a person to change, and
what life in recovery is like is a ritual that enables the holy presence to come forth.

—Linda Schierse Leonard, *Witness to the Fire*

I know a sixteen-year-old girl who shoots heroin between her toes twice a day because that is the only place left on her body that will receive the drug.

I know a cheerleader at her suburban high school who "does" cocaine every weekend. She will often go straight from the basketball game to the party to "do a line."

I have a friend whose son asks to borrow the car every night so he can "clear" his head. He just admitted that what he really needs is to smoke a cigarette before he can go to sleep.

I have a twenty-two-year-old client who has taken some form of diet pill every day for the last ten years. She is terrified to stop because she's afraid she'll get fat.

My daughter has a friend who drinks every night during the summer. She's had sex with boys she didn't know, been ticketed by the police for drinking, and run into a fence while driving, but she doesn't think she has a problem because she drinks "only during the summer."

I just got a phone call from a panicked youth leader who learned that one of the girls in her youth group smokes marijuana *ten* times a day. She wonders what she should do.

I also know a thirty-two-year-old woman who ingests a handful of laxatives every night and spends hours of her day in the unspeakable ritual of binging and purging to satiate her hunger and maintain her weight.

I read about a thirty-four-year-old superstar gymnast who could not go a single day without four hours of exercise or she would have an anxiety attack.

I had a friend in a church we once attended who told me she *had* to read her Bible for thirty minutes every day because she was afraid of what God would do to her children if she didn't.

I have an adult client who gets home from work, shuts her door on the world, and watches television for six hours until she falls asleep.

The evidence of addiction is everywhere in our culture. The American Medical Association reported in 2002 that not a family in America is untouched by addiction. But I suspect that you are not reading this chapter to gather statistics or to hear stories of other addicts. You are interested in one story, your daughter's. Is your daughter addicted to substances?

Welcome to America, where on any given day, one million people are in treatment for drug or alcohol abuse. The number one health problem in the nation, substance abuse causes more death and illness than any other preventable condition.

—MEREDITH MARAN, *Dirty*

In this chapter we will look at the external evidence for addiction to smoking, alcohol, and drugs. I will also talk about the internal realities that are going on in your child if she is addicted. Understanding the external evidence arms you with information to make choices about appropriate treatment options. (We will discuss this in the next chapter.) Understanding the internal realities will empower you to become your daughter's ally in a frightening and dangerous time in her life—and yours.

ADDICTION AND YOU

Before you can be authentically powerful in helping your daughter identify her addiction and guiding her toward recovery, you must evaluate your own heart and its attachments. In my first book, *Bravehearts,* I wrote about all the things we can give our hearts to in response to loneliness, pain, disappointment, or longing:

We seldom leap into affairs of the heart. Most often such affairs are subtle, gradual relationships that develop as a result of the choices we make about where we will spend our passion. We can have affairs of the heart with food, shopping, sexual fantasy, being liked, helping others, work, gambling, alcohol, drugs—the list is endless....

An affair of the heart is any relationship, behavior, or experience that supplants healthy relationships and replaces God as central in our lives.[1]

Lori's mom brought her to see me for counseling because Lori was getting into trouble—going to parties and coming home visibly under the influence of alcohol or marijuana. After spending a few sessions with Lori, I asked her mother, Karen, to come in for a visit. Understand that Lori had told me nothing about drug and alcohol use in her family. I'm sure I asked, but Lori never indicated there was a problem. I suggested to Karen that since Lori had had repeated incidents with substance use, she take Lori to an Alcoholics Anonymous meeting. I told Lori that if she was uncomfortable going, I would go with them, since I am a recovering alcoholic and attend meetings regularly.

As soon as I disclosed my history with alcohol, Karen visibly relaxed. Her shoulders slumped, tears welled up in her eyes, and she admitted, "I'm a binge drinker. I get really drunk a couple of weekends every month. I think I need help too."

I suggested that Karen get some individual counseling, begin attending AA meetings, and get a sponsor to guide her through the Twelve Steps of recovery from alcoholism. Making an immediate start on her own recovery was the only way she would be ready to help her daughter. Karen's shoulders visibly stiffened at this, and her resistance came out in her next statement. "Well, I can probably just cut back or stop on my own, and then I can help Lori."

You need to know that I am pretty passionate about getting mothers healthy so they can be all God created them to be for their daughters. I decided not to confront Karen directly, but to go in through the back door of her daughter's story. I said, "You know, Karen, if Lori doesn't get help pretty quickly, this is what could lie ahead for her and you: She will start drinking more flagrantly—maybe during the day or even at school. With the zero-tolerance policy in schools these days, she'll probably get expelled. Because alcohol is a depressant, she'll start feeling joyless, stop enjoying people and things she once really liked. She may get in trouble with the law—tickets for drinking and/or driving under the influence. If that happens, there will be court costs and legal consequences. Her grades will likely drop if she continues to use alcohol, and some of her friends will fall away. Her new friends may introduce her to other mind-altering substances. She'll be moody, irritable, and tormented by self-hatred because she will not like the direction her life is taking. She may even consider suicide."

JUST FOR YOU

1. Do you need to acknowledge a destructive relationship with alcohol, cigarettes, food, spending money, work, relationships, or something else that has you in bondage?
2. Has a friend or family member ever suggested that you might be "a little addicted" to something?
3. Have you ever found yourself caught up in something you thought you would never do? How did you get trapped by that activity?
4. Do you have behaviors that you feel you must hide from others?

The greatest gift you can give your daughter is to acknowledge your own unhealthy dependence on a substance, behavior, person, or experience and begin recovery. You do not have to be fully *recovered* to help your daughter. But you do have to be in the process of being honest with yourself, being open to the help and guidance of others, and being committed to doing whatever it takes to get yourself healthy.

(*Note:* This chapter will not include any Just for the Two of You sections because its primary purpose is to help *you* come to a place of peace and authenticity in your own life with regard to any unhealthy dependencies you may have. Once you do this, you will be in a much better position to gather evidence about what is really going on with your daughter and to arm yourself for the choices you will be making about the help that is most appropriate for her.)

While I was describing this all-too-predictable path for an addicted teenager, tears started flowing down Karen's cheeks. "I've experienced all of those things you are talking about. I probably had a drinking problem as a teenager, but no one really noticed because my parents drank a lot. I don't want my daughter to repeat this cycle." Karen agreed to first get help for herself immediately. As Karen began her own recovery, she would be better able to be authentically powerful in her daughter's process of recovery.

EXTERNAL EVIDENCE OF ADDICTION

Some of the external evidence I will cite in this section will be familiar to you. You've probably seen or even taken those self-tests that indicate whether you might have a problem. It's important to preface the external evidence with the reminder that teenage addiction is different from adult addiction. *Addiction progresses faster in teenagers.* The progression for adults can take years. Because a teenager's brain and organs are still developing, they are acutely vulnerable to the toxins of drugs and alcohol. *The female teenage user is at the greatest risk.* As we've discussed in previous chapters, females are impacted more intensely and become addicted more quickly than males.

Read this chapter carefully. Don't shrink back from taking an honest inventory of what you see in your daughter's life. It may be a matter of life and death. (The resources section of this book also lists Web sites or publications that describe the specific indicators for addiction to every substance imaginable and provide tests and checklists that will help you evaluate your daughter and, if applicable, yourself.)

Watch carefully for the early signs of addiction. Is your daughter shaky, agitated, nervous, having trouble sleeping, experiencing gastrointestinal distress and psychological anguish (guilt, shame, self-hatred, contempt for others, a sense of hopelessness and despair)?

If your daughter drinks often (at least once a week), you will begin to see growing evidence of a life increasingly out of control: legal problems, phone calls from teachers about "out of it" behavior, declining grades, lack of self-care. If you are paying close attention to your daughter, you will likely notice some or all of the following signs of addictive behavior:

1. Restlessness and discontentment—All addictive drugs leave you craving more and feeling anxious when the effect of the drug begins to wear off. Your daughter may seem more irritable, react in ways that seem out of proportion to the event at hand, or be uncharacteristically nervous. She may have all kinds of excuses to "go out" as she tries to get her hands on her drug of choice.

2. *Bloodshot eyes*—All drug and alcohol use causes bloodshot eyes either from the actual use or from lack of sleep if the drug of choice is a stimulant. Take note if your child is wearing sunglasses all the time or you find bottles of Visine or other eye drops.

3. *Anti-establishment attitude*—One mother told me that her daughter was "all of a sudden" against the police, the pastor, the government, and even the television for the "stupid" commercials on marijuana. Your daughter may say she hates her teachers, her coaches, and even some of her friends. One of my clients who was using cocaine every weekend made this statement about a girlfriend who confronted her about her drug use: "Oh, she's such a hypocritical, judgmental person."

4. *Weight loss or gain*—When my daughter graduated from high school, she discovered that many of her friends felt the freedom to party all summer long. She made this observation about many of her girlfriends who were drinking beer every night: "They are gaining a lot of weight." Conversely, the use of stimulant drugs (cocaine and methamphetamines) will make teenagers lose weight quickly. Associating marijuana with the "munchies" is accurate, and marijuana use often leads to weight gain.

5. *Low motivation*—One of my clients described her typical summer day/night. She would stay out until curfew smoking pot and sometimes drinking. She'd return home and eat and watch television until 2:00 or 3:00 in the morning and then sleep until 2:00 or 3:00 in the afternoon. When I asked what she liked about that schedule, she said, "I don't have to worry or care about anything." Chronic alcohol and drug use make a teenager's life about one thing: drugs or alcohol and the experiences attached to it. Motivation to work, carry on conversations, exercise, do anything creative, or pursue an authentic spiritual life evaporates.

6. *Angry or violent outbursts*—When your daughter cannot get access to drugs or alcohol, she may throw a temper tantrum that makes no sense to you. It isn't about immediate events; it's about the withdrawal she's experiencing and her craving for the drugs or alcohol. Girls generally turn inward when

they are emotionally unstable, and they may self-injure. (I discuss self-injury and "cutting" in my second book in this series, *"Mom, I Hate My Life!"*) Girls who cut themselves do so to get relief from pain, anxiety, restlessness, and boredom, and they feel a high from the whole experience of cutting themselves. In their book on self-injury, Karen Conterio and Wendy Lader report, "There is a strong correlation between self-injury and other types of addictive behavior: a good percentage of our patients abuse drugs and alcohol."[2]

7. *Self-hatred*—As your daughter's grades slip, she will get into trouble at school, at home, and even with the law, and as she does things under the influence that she would never do otherwise, she will be eaten up with guilt and shame. Guilt and shame often come out in adolescents as expressions of self-hatred. Your daughter might say such things as "I am totally disgusting. I hate myself." When questioned about the impetus for her comments, she will probably withdraw and shift her self-contempt in your direction: "You don't get me at all, Mom. No one does." Repeated interactions like this are compelling evidence that something is going on that is tormenting your daughter with guilt and shame.

8. *Fads and fashions*—The drug culture, in particular, has its own fads and fashions. For example, as mentioned in chapter 4, bluegrass music is strongly associated with the marijuana culture. One of my clients also told me that fellow users greet one another in the hallways at school by making the motion of "toking" on a marijuana joint (pretending to take a drag), which communicates to one another that they will be getting high soon.

9. *Increased tolerance*—As your daughter continues to use substances, her body will require more and stronger alcohol and drugs to get the same effect. Symptoms may include drinking more than one drink at a time, shifting from beer to vodka, or combining alcohol with other drugs. You will find this evidence by smelling your daughter's breath, looking at the reading on a Breathalyzer, and searching for "empties" in her car or room. If consequences are enforced, a girl may try anything to get her "buzz." One of the most common drugs used among teens is over-the-counter cold medication: Nyquil, Robitussin, or Coricidin D. Teenagers call Coricidin "Triple C" because it contains a decongestant, antihistamine, and cough suppressant. Teens will take up to forty of these pills to get the effect of being "drunk."

10. *Stealing and money problems*—Drugs are expensive. Cigarettes cost

about five dollars a pack. If a teenager needs a pack every other day, that's more than thirty dollars a week. If adolescents aren't stealing their alcohol from their parents, alcohol is expensive as well. Most teenagers don't drink just one beer, so the cost for a night of partying will be in excess of twenty dollars. Marijuana is expensive. In the Denver area, a bag of weed costs forty dollars. All other illegal and over-the-counter drugs cost money. If your daughter is going through cash, stealing from you or other family members, or selling things to get money, this is strong evidence that she is using regularly.

11. Withdrawal—An adolescent who is in trouble with drugs or alcohol will not want to eat with the family, attend church, or participate in family life. She may hole up in her room, and listen to music. She will be extremely secretive about phone calls and e-mail. Your daughter may also withdraw from you to keep you from seeing her symptoms of addiction.

There can be no acting or doing of any kind, till it be recognized that there is a thing to be done; the thing once recognized, doing in a thousand shapes becomes possible.

—THOMAS CARLYLE

---

12. Physical complaints—Your daughter may complain about not sleeping. An addict might use drugs or alcohol right before bed, thinking it will help her sleep, but substances actually "wake up" the liver in the middle of the night as the organ attempts to metabolize the toxins. Your daughter may complain of an upset stomach, nausea, or diarrhea. It stands to reason that the organs that eliminate waste will be affected by toxic substances ingested into the body. If your daughter begins to shake her feet a lot or has jittery hands, she may be in the withdrawal and craving stage of an addiction. Alcohol and marijuana leave the user with the worst dry mouth imaginable. Your daughter may be licking her lips a lot, carrying around a sucker, or drinking more water than usual after a night of using.

13. Denial—You can have all the evidence in the world, and your addicted teenager will deny she has a problem, insisting that her substance use is not a big deal. Denial is part of addiction—perhaps one of the most difficult aspects to address. Remember that denial of the problem *even when consequences are administered* is evidence of a growing destructive relationship with alcohol or drugs.

I encourage you to pray for a sense of *knowing* about your daughter's status regarding substance abuse and addiction. God will bring facts and stories and examples to mind. Be courageous. *Knowing* is the beginning of recovery because it can lead to appropriate intervention, which is always necessary when a teenager is addicted. We will discuss intervention and breaking through denial in the next chapter.

14. Lying and broken promises—However you want to label it, an addict—even a teenage addict—makes a lot of promises to quit, cut back, never use again, get better grades, talk to a counselor, and so on, but doesn't follow through. Your daughter may make promises and sound sincere (she really does feel sincere), but she is unable to keep her promises. It's important

JUST FOR YOU

1. Spend time thinking about each of the signs of addictive behavior. Write down any facts, stories, and experiences that supply "evidence" for each category. Ask friends and family for their perspectives. Pray that God will bring to your mind whatever is necessary for you to clearly see your daughter and her relationship with drugs and alcohol. You *need* this information if you want to help her.

2. Are you afraid? That's kind of a rhetorical question, isn't it? If you are afraid, act like you are courageous, and you will discover that you are indeed a mother of great courage.

3. Read the Psalms. Start with Psalms 40–50. Here is my own "mother's translation" of Psalm 43: "Vindicate me, O God, and plead my cause against ungodly addiction; rescue me and my child from deceitful and wicked peers or adults who might tempt my child with drugs and alcohol. You are God my stronghold. I feel like I'm hanging on by my fingernails. I get downcast and disturbed. But I will put my hope in God and praise you. Please don't let go of me, my Savior and my God."
   You may want to write down your own paraphrases of scriptures that are meaningful to you and reflect where you are in life right now.

to realize that addiction is powerful—more powerful than any promise your daughter can make. That is why intervention and treatment are necessary. Whether or not she acknowledges it, she feels horrible about herself every time she breaks a promise.

As you watch for evidence of your daughter's increasingly dependent and abusive relationship with alcohol, don't let the evidence paralyze you. Don't let the good times fool you either. One hallmark of the family disease of alcoholism is denial of the "elephant in the living room." We are so grateful for the happy, calm times that we don't want to address the ugly, chaotic times that have just occurred.

INTERNAL EVIDENCE OF ADDICTION

What's happening on the inside of your daughter's life is more difficult to detect. Take it from me, as an addict and as one privileged to hear the stories of so many addicts—both recovering and not—that there are four internal realities always present in the heart and soul of the addict. Knowing how addicts *see themselves* will help you when you decide to intervene in your daughter's life and seek treatment for her. Once again, this is a time for you to honestly evaluate your own story so you can be in the most powerful position possible to help your daughter face and fight this formidable foe.

1. *"I am crazy."* The stories of addiction are, at times, unbelievable. I have told you some of them in this book. One of my clients became so drunk and disoriented at a party that she drove home—only not to her own home, but to someone else's. She walked in (unbelievably the door was unlocked), walked upstairs, and got into a bed. When she was awakened in the morning by an alarmed family and a police officer, she had no idea how she had gotten into that home.

While your teenagers may laugh about the predicaments their substance use gets them into, believe me that in the middle of the night, when no one is around, they wonder if they are crazy. One of my clients expressed the saddest, most poignant words about this state of heart after telling me about one of her exploits when she shoplifted thousands of items from Target while she was high on cocaine and ended up in juvenile detention: "I just want to be like everyone else. Is there a pill I can take that will make me normal?"

2. "I am unforgivable." Addiction takes us into a dark labyrinth. One of my clients said to me, "I am nothing but a screwup. I have stolen money from my grandmother to buy booze. I've had sex with boys I don't even know. I am a complete failure."

I replied, "You're right. You are a failure. But you are so much more than that."

She sat upright on my couch and asked indignantly, "What do you mean, I'm a failure?"

It's the denial and the shame that keep us locked into thinking that no one can ever forgive us. First, we are terrified to admit—especially to another

JUST FOR YOU

1. What's the worst thing you've ever done? Does anyone know? Have you forgiven yourself? Do you believe that God and others have forgiven you? In his essay "A Reflection on Guilt," Dominic Maruca explains, "The memory of things past is indeed a worm that does not die. Whether it continues to grow by gnawing away at our hearts or is metamorphosed into a brightly colored winged creature depends on whether we can find a forgiveness we cannot bestow on ourselves."[3]

2. You will be able to speak to your daughter about God's forgiveness and to forgive her yourself (an important part of healing your relationship) only to the degree that you know you are forgiven! I urge you to read the chapter titled "The Redeemed Heart" in my book *Bravehearts,* not because it is an extraordinary chapter, but because I was an extraordinary sinner. I sinned in my addiction against myself, my children, my friends, my family, and God, and I found the forgiveness Maruca wrote about. Or, better said, it found me. And it will find you, too, as you confess your failings and open your heart to the One who said, "I can't tell you how much I long for you to enter this wide-open, spacious life.... The smallness you feel comes from within you. Your lives aren't small, but you're living them in a small way. I'm speaking as plainly as I can and with great affection. Open up your lives. Life openly and expansively!" (2 Corinthians 6:11-13, MSG).

person—that we are sinners. And, second, we can't believe that anyone can *really* know all about us and forgive us, much less love us.

3. "I am alone." Even if your daughter tells you that her drug and drinking "buddies" are there for her, she knows that if she stops using or gets into trouble, they will be gone in an instant. And she feels alienated from you because she's not being honest about her life. One mother told me she thought her daughter hated her because all the daughter did was push her away with words like "I can't stand you. I wish I wasn't in this family. *Leave me alone!"*

The addict so completely believes she is alone that if you try to hang in there with her, she will work even harder to push you away to *prove* that she is alone. Obviously, this is a devastating dynamic for both you and your daughter. That's why it is critical that you get plenty of support for *yourself* while you are the target of her self-hatred, self-rejection, rage, and hopelessness.

JUST FOR YOU

My parents suffered alone for years, not telling anyone about their children's struggles with drugs and alcohol. My brother had stolen from them, committed other crimes, and brought drugs into their home, but they told no one. They were afraid of being judged and didn't know that hundreds of other families were suffering alone as well.

1. Whom have you told about your concerns about your daughter? What has been helpful to you? Unhelpful? What can you do to pursue relationships that support you during this time of crisis?

2. Now is a good time to begin attending Al-Anon meetings. These support and recovery meetings are for family members and friends of alcoholics and other addicted people. Call Al-Anon (listed in the white pages), and they will direct you to a meeting near you. I know it will be hard at first for you to be among "strangers" while you are at your most vulnerable. You may not agree with everything that is said, but disclosure itself is powerful. Often it is in the process of telling the truth about our lives that we discover the truth more fully. As you prepare to help your daughter with her drug or alcohol problem, you

must be in relationships that support *you*. Even if your spouse or other family members will not go with you, go anyway!

3. One of my favorite books is *Telling Secrets* by Frederick Buechner. This would be a wonderful book for you to read as you begin to disclose to others your needs and to seek support. Buechner writes of his participation in Al-Anon: "Just by getting yourself there…, you have told an extremely important secret, which is that you cannot go it alone. You need help. You need them."[4]

By the way, my parents now talk often about their children, their children's struggles, and their growth, recovery, and transformation. Sometimes I wish they wouldn't talk about me so freely!

4. "I am hopeless." Because of the components of addiction we talked about earlier—of trying again and again to stop drinking or using and promising again and again to stop and not succeeding—an addict believes she is hopeless. The apostle Paul described the hopelessness this way: "For sin, seizing the opportunity afforded by the commandment [promising to do better, obey, etc], deceived me, and through the commandment [fear of punishment and rejection] put me to death" (Romans 7:11). You need to know that your daughter's repeated failures to change may actually intensify her addictive behavior, threatening to lock her in a box of perpetual hopelessness.

HOW THE LIGHT GETS IN

This has not been a warm and fuzzy chapter. I imagine that as you take inventory of your daughter's life as well as your own, you find it to be messy, humbling, scary, and confusing. But I promise you that this is how the light of hope gets in. Seeing your daughter's external signs of addiction and getting a glimpse into her internal horror house is the beginning of taking her hand and gently or even fiercely leading her to help, change, and recovery.

The novel *How the Light Gets In* by M. J. Hyland is about a sixteen-year-old girl from a dysfunctional family who ends up in the grip of alcoholism. In one scene she tries to explain her first AA meeting to a friend.

The friend asks, "What did you *really* do?"

"We said the Serenity Prayer and then drank cups of tea and talked a bit more."

"What is the Serenity Prayer?"

"Do you really want to know?"

"Sure I do."

"It goes: God, grant me the serenity to accept the things I cannot change, the courage the change the things I can, and the wisdom to know the difference."[5]

Taking inventory, telling secrets, admitting the truth, stumbling, and getting back up again are not tasks for the faint of heart. But they are tasks for mothers, particularly mothers of daughters with alcohol and drug problems. And they are the tasks that let in the light, tasks with great reward: a healthy, whole daughter who wants to really *live*.

There is no doubt that addiction—and all of the components discussed in this chapter—is stronger than you are. *But it is not stronger than God.* As you prepare to become your daughter's life-saving ally, remember that you also have an Ally. "For God, who said, 'Let light shine out of darkness,' made his light shine in our hearts to give us the light of the knowledge of the glory of God in the face of Christ.... Therefore we do not lose heart. Though outwardly we are wasting away, yet inwardly we are being renewed day by day" (2 Corinthians 4:6,16).

If you're not feeling renewed day by day, I encourage you to start praying every day—maybe many times a day—the prayer the teenager in Hyland's novel learned at her first AA meeting: *God, grant me the serenity to accept the things I cannot change, the courage to change the things I can, and the wisdom to know the difference.* Serenity, courage, and wisdom are essential ingredients of an effective hand-in-hand alliance with your daughter. If she is addicted to alcohol or drugs, she needs you to develop these spiritual qualities in your life more than ever before. Her life may depend on it.

Chapter 11

Treatment

From there Jesus took a trip to Tyre and Sidon. They had hardly arrived
when a Canaanite woman came down from the hills and pleaded, "Mercy,
Master, Son of David! My daughter is cruelly afflicted...." Then the woman
came back to Jesus, went to her knees, and begged, "Master, help me."

—MATTHEW 15:21-22, 25, *The Message*

✦

My emergency pager went off at 9:15 p.m. I recognized the telephone
number. It was the home phone number of a fifteen-year-old client
who had been in crisis off and on for more than a year. I called the number,
and Lindsey's father answered the phone. He told me that "Lindsey was
arrested tonight for a 'minor in possession' of marijuana. She's home now, but
she wants to talk to you. She wants to know that everything is going to be
all right."

I asked to speak to Lindsey, "Would you like to come to my office? We
can talk this thing through."

"Yes," she answered shakily.

Lindsey's dad got back on the phone and said, "I'll bring her right over.
Thank you."

What Lindsey didn't know was that her father and I were speaking in
code—a code of sorrow and anticipation. Lindsey's family had made arrangements for Lindsey to be escorted to a treatment facility in less than forty-eight
hours. We were talking to each other in a language Lindsey couldn't understand that said, "Let's just get her through the next two days."

Two days later at 5:30 a.m., two professionals from the treatment facility
came to Lindsey's house. Her parents awakened her, told her to get dressed,

and explained that she was going somewhere to get help and would need to leave everything else behind.

I feel honored and humbled to know parents like Lindsey's. During the past year they had tried counseling, offering grace, showing "tough love," enforcing consequences, doing random drug testing, and revoking privileges, but Lindsey still seemed hellbent on self-destruction. One well-meaning counselor heard about Lindsey's struggles and asked her mom, "Lois, are you *in* this—willing to do what it takes?" Lois humbly and kindly answered, with tears streaming down her face, "Yes." She told me later that she wanted to say, "Ask your wife when she's been in labor for twelve hours and is still six centimeters dilated if she's *in* this."

Lois was in the excruciatingly painful labor of delivering and finding deliverance for a hurting and troubled child. Like the mother in the scripture at the beginning of this chapter, Lois was willing to risk everything, be humiliated, beg, plead, and go to any lengths to get help for her daughter. I watched Lois over the course of a year consider every option for her daughter—counseling, medication, out-patient treatment, spiritual deliverance, homeschooling—and then, after repeated nights of worrying about her missing daughter who came home with alcohol on her breath or with behavior altered by some substance, Lois *knew*. She knew she had to do the unthinkable: send her daughter away to get help.

Carol Kent, in her book *When I Lay My Isaac Down,* writes eloquently and poignantly of the desperation that leads a mother to get help for her child, whatever the cost:

> There are times in life when all of us are called upon to make heart sacrifices. Some of those sacrifices are things we choose because of a cause we believe in or a desired end that makes our decision worthwhile. However, most of us will face an "Isaac experience," when a crisis is thrust into our lives without warning and without survival instructions. Our "Isaacs" are the heart sacrifices we make when we choose to relinquish control and honor God with our heart even when all seems lost. We have to decide if we will let go of our control over a person, situation, or event, or if we will hang on for dear life and refuse to relinquish something we cherish.[1]

In this chapter we will look at the indicators that treatment—inpatient or outpatient—is needed, how to find treatment, how to intervene and get your daughter into treatment, and how to live in the midst of this relational and emotional upheaval.

INDICATORS THAT TREATMENT IS NEEDED

In the previous chapter I referred to checklists and self-tests that are available to help you determine whether or not your daughter might be addicted to specific drugs or alcohol. In addition to these tools provided by experts in alcoholism and drug addiction, I offer my own list of indicators I use to help parents make difficult decisions about whether they need to intervene in their daughter's downward spiral.

In the foreword to the handbook of Alcoholics Anonymous, the authors suggest that the only requirement for membership and recovery is "an honest desire to stop drinking." We alcoholics learn in recovery that we *ourselves* have to become desperate enough to go to any lengths to get help, follow directions, and start to get better. *We* must choose our path. There is, of course, a difference when the alcoholic or addict is a teenager. Parents have the responsibility to love their children and keep them safe. When a teenager is using drugs and alcohol, she is not safe. When parents allow the behavior to continue, they are not loving. The following Just for You section includes my checklist of indicators that your child needs intervention and treatment.

JUST FOR YOU

1. Have there been more than five episodes when your daughter has been drunk or high? The research cited earlier in this book suggests that if an adolescent uses a substance more than five times, she is at risk for dependency.
2. Have you set reasonable consequences (drug tests, loss of privileges, etc) to no avail?
3. Have you lied, paid fines or legal fees, or "covered" for your daughter because of her drinking or drug use?

4. Is your daughter failing in school due to drug or alcohol use?

5. Is your daughter draining the life from your family because of her behavior? You may need to ask your other children this question. Sometimes parents become so enmeshed with the "problem child" that they do not see the mounting problems of anger, resentment, and hurt in their other children.

6. Does your daughter acknowledge that she has a problem? Has she agreed that she needs and wants help?

7. Has your daughter made any effort to address her addiction? Has she fully participated in counseling (this means going without complaint and taking suggestions from the counselor), attended Twelve Step meetings, and asked for prayer and support from family and friends?

8. Has your daughter acknowledged which friends do drugs or alcohol and been willing to disentangle herself from them?

   If you answered yes to the first five questions and no to the final three, this tells me that you are desperate and afraid and that you are in the process of *knowing* that your daughter needs intervention and treatment.

TYPES OF INTERVENTION

There are three types of intervention you will have to consider for your daughter:

1. Preemptive (or brief) intervention
2. Radical intervention
3. God's intervention

You will find entire books written about the first two types. The third type is often not included or given "equal weight" in the vast body of literature about addiction. Understanding your options and coming to your own conclusions about the type of intervention you will need to use with your child (she may need all three) is essential if you are to parent intentionally and effectively.

Adolescents are experts at inducing panic in parents. When I was training for a triathlon and learning to swim, my instructor told me over and over, as I flailed in the water and cried that I could not do it, "Your panic is soaking up all of your energy. You can't move effectively when you are in panic mode."

If there's one thing I learned from being a teenager, from mothering teenagers, and from writing books about teenagers, it's how necessary it is—and how far we have to go—to give every child not just what's easy for us to give, but what he or she truly and uniquely needs.

—MEREDITH MARAN, *Dirty*

If you are reading this chapter right now and hanging on to every word, you may be in panic mode. I hope the information that follows will help you come to some sense of knowing, planning, and direction that will ease your anxiety and mobilize you to move forward effectively on behalf of your daughter.

PREEMPTIVE INTERVENTION

Preemptive intervention (or "brief" intervention, as it is referred to in therapeutic circles) is effective only in the early stages of drug and alcohol abuse. Preemptive intervention lets your daughter know that you notice what she's doing, that you have a plan to help her, and that you hope she's listening. Preemptive intervention takes place the morning after your daughter has come home with beer on her breath, has been at a party where teenagers were disbursed and ticketed for being under the influence or in possession, or behaves in a way that leaves you suspecting she has been using drugs or alcohol. Do not try to intervene while your daughter is under the influence. Both she and you will say things you don't mean.

Brief intervention might sound like one of the following:

- "Last night when you came home, I smelled beer on your breath. Drinking is illegal and dangerous, and I don't want you to drink. I have ordered a Breathalyzer test kit and will be using it when you come home from a night out. If you continue to drink, there will continue to be consequences (loss of driving, social privileges, etc.). Do you want to talk to a counselor about peer pressure and your choices?"

- "Last night you got a ticket for being in possession of marijuana. You will have to go through the legal process. We'll be right there with you, but you will have to pay the financial costs and participate in whatever the court requires. I am very concerned about you and your judgment. Do you want to go to a drug and alcohol education class?"

During brief intervention, you must say what you see, be honest about what you are feeling, clearly state consequences, and offer an opportunity for further help. If you try to push or manipulate, your daughter may push back or become more secretive. If you shame her, she won't believe you are a source of real help. If you look the other way, you will both be lost. The authors of an excellent book, *Changing for Good*, explain why good parents might look the other way: "Enabling continues when the helper fears that any challenge to the behavior will risk a break in the relationship. If the problem is ever to be resolved, however, it will be because the helper dares to intervene."[2]

JUST FOR THE TWO OF YOU

Have you laid the groundwork for a clear understanding between you and your daughter about how you intend to deal with any alcohol or drug use? Following are some questions to discuss together. Ask your daughter these questions when things are more open and emotionally stable between the two of you. Tell her that the purpose of this discussion is for you both to be honest with each other and to make sure that she clearly understands the direction her choices will take her.

1. What do you understand our house rules to be with regard to your use of drugs and alcohol?
2. Do you think these rules are hypocritical? Why or why not?
3. How do you think I'll respond when I believe you have been drinking or using drugs?
4. How would you like me to respond? Why?
5. What would it be like for you if I ignored your use of alcohol or drugs?
6. What do you think it would be like for me?

7. Do you think I follow through with what I say I'm going to do? How does my follow-through or lack of follow-through make you feel?

8. Do you think I judge you or your friends? If so, in what way?

9. If you could make any choices you wanted with regard to drugs and alcohol, what choices would you want to make?

10. If I could make any choices I wanted with regard to your use of drugs or alcohol, what choices do you think I would want to make?

You may not like or agree with everything you hear from your daughter, but as you discuss each question let her know three things:

1. I am not going to look the other way, because I love you.

2. Your choices will result in specific choices (consequences) for me, because it is my responsibility to keep you safe.

3. I will follow through no matter how mean you are to me or how frightened or angry I am, because my commitment to loving you and keeping you safe is greater than any problem drugs or alcohol may bring into our lives.

Your daughter may roll her eyes, grit her teeth, and inwardly determine to go her own way, but she will know you are a resource of love and safety. If she continues to use drugs and alcohol, you are a resource she will most certainly need eventually.

RADICAL INTERVENTION

When you have tried everything listed in the preemptive intervention section and your daughter continues her behavior, a radical intervention will be necessary, unless a crisis such as jail or court-ordered treatment occurs first. Radical intervention requires that you go outside your normal scope of resources and get help from others who can step in and reach your daughter.

I have been privileged to work many times with Howie, an "interventionist" in the Denver area who works with families to formalize plans to confront their teenagers without shame. He also provides an escort for the teenager to a treatment facility. You can find an interventionist in your area by contacting inpatient treatment facilities and asking for recommendations.

Laurie was one of my seventeen-year-old clients who I believed needed a radical intervention. Laurie had been arrested twice for use and possession of alcohol and cocaine. I called Howie, and he met with all of the family members and me several times. He asked how drugs and alcohol were impacting Laurie and everyone else involved. Then he asked each of us to write a letter to Laurie telling her about the alcohol- or drug-related behaviors we knew about or had witnessed, how we felt about these behaviors, and what we wanted for her and from her. Howie also asked us to include all of the wonderful things we knew about Laurie and how drugs and alcohol were erasing these parts of her.

There were lots of tears at these meetings as well as agonizing choices for Laurie's parents to make. Because Laurie had been using drugs and alcohol repeatedly for over a year, had been in trouble with the law, and was failing the eleventh grade, it was clear that inpatient treatment would be best for her. (More about treatment options on the following pages.) Her parents researched treatment facilities and sought my advice as well as Howie's. My heart broke with sorrow and humility when I learned how Laurie's parents planned to pay for treatment for their daughter. Tena (Laurie's mom) had diamond earrings and a necklace that had been in the family for years. She put them up for sale on eBay and within two weeks had raised the money necessary for a good adolescent treatment program.

When Tena told me about selling the diamonds, I thought of the story in the New Testament about the man who stumbled upon treasure in the middle of a field. Matthew 13:44 says that "the kingdom of heaven is like a treasure." The man sold everything he had to buy the field. You see, he couldn't buy the treasure because it was priceless. But he bought the field that contained the treasure. Laurie's parents were willing to sell what they had so they could buy a context in which the kingdom of heaven could flourish within their daughter. That context was health and recovery from drug and alcohol addiction.

Howie helped set up the intervention. Laurie came home from school to find us all seated around her dining room table. She looked at me and, of course, felt a little angry and afraid. Howie asked her to sit down. He explained who he was and that he had learned from us that alcohol and drugs were causing problems in Laurie's life. He asked each of us to read his or her letter to Laurie aloud. We had all practiced reading our letters, but that didn't stop the tears from flowing. Laurie could not doubt that we were filled with compassion and concern.

After the letters were read, Howie asked Laurie what she thought. She was silent and refused to look at any of us. What she didn't know was that her parents had already decided that she would be escorted to treatment that afternoon. When she was told, at first Laurie was in shock and quietly gathered the few possessions that Howie told her she could take to the treatment facility. Two female escorts quietly entered the dining room and waited for Laurie. That's when her shock turned to anger, and she screamed at her mother, "I hate you! You have ruined my life! I never want to see you again."

Howie had prepared the family for the possibility of an angry response, but no mother is ready to hear these words from her daughter. Laurie's

TREATMENT OPTIONS

If an adolescent has a serious problem with drugs or alcohol, most insurance companies will recommend outpatient treatment first. Intensive outpatient therapy can involve up to eight hours of some sort of recovery program every day. Less intensive outpatient programs usually take place after school or on weekends. Outpatient counseling will include drug and alcohol education, group therapy, individual counseling, a medical evaluation, some family counseling, drug testing, and relapse prevention programs. Good outpatient programs will introduce your teenager to a Twelve Step group right away and will require participation in this group as part of the program.

When you research programs, you should get answers to the following questions:

1. Is this program specifically for adolescents?
2. Does this program address the unique realities of adolescent female addiction? How? Are there therapy groups just for girls? Are female therapists available?
3. Does this program involve the family at some point in the adolescent's therapy?

"braveheart" mom choked out the words she had practiced: "I have never loved you more."

Moms, be prepared to be the target of your daughter's anger. That instinctual, symbiotic connection that leads her to vent her rage and terror toward you can become the connection that bonds her with you in gratitude and health when she returns from treatment.

If you are considering radical intervention for your daughter, you may be wondering, *Where do I find help? How can I do this? What if it doesn't work? What if I never see my daughter again?* There are many excellent treatment facilities for teenagers. You are not alone.

I often think of my adolescent clients' parents when I am practicing my swimming. Because I am so new at this, I lose my sense of direction, and my coach must call out numerous times, "You're heading the wrong way. Adjust

4. Does this program facilitate Twelve Step groups and encourage participation in Twelve Step groups after treatment is completed?

You may want to send your daughter to a facility that is completely "Christian" in philosophy. Just make sure that it also incorporates the four components listed above. With most programs, you can request printed material or go to their Web site to find details about what will go on hour by hour in the program.

A word of caution: Experience has taught me that, unfortunately, local treatment programs can become a place for your adolescent to meet peers who are struggling with drug and alcohol use. Sometimes these teens bond and, after treatment, continue substance use. If your teenager is ensnared in addiction and it is financially possible for you to take drastic measures, I recommend a program that removes her from her local environment for a time. This will give her a better chance of becoming committed to her own recovery and staying away from familiar temptations and peers when she comes home. I add this word of caution not to discourage you from using resources that are available to you close to home, but to underscore that, whatever treatment you choose, there is no perfect, money-back guarantee. That is why the third type of intervention is so essential.

your direction." Your daughter's treatment counselors are skilled in helping her and you find the right path. Good treatment programs always involve the family and work to facilitate healing of the relationships as well as recovery from the addiction. Take heart from the following words of encouragement from addiction experts Katherine Ketcham and Nicholas Pace, who explain why intervention works:

> When intervention follows these simple rules, they work. They *always* work—even if the adolescent refuses to go into treatment or relapses soon after treatment. They work because, in the process of learning about drugs and the disease of addiction, family members are released from ignorance, confusion, guilt, shame, and fear. They learn how the drug user has affected their own lives, and they make a commitment to themselves and to each other to stop lying and hiding from the truth. Educated about the disease, they know what must be done to free themselves from its influence. They learn how to communicate with each other and how to talk about their feelings. They discover the importance of community and the need to reach out to others for help and support.[3]

GOD'S INTERVENTION

Preemptive intervention requires patience, consistency, and consequences. Radical intervention requires planning, support, and courage. God's intervention requires nothing from you.

Read that last sentence again. Aren't you a bit relieved to know that there is Someone stronger than your daughter, more in love with her than you are, and more committed to her recovery than you are? If you don't believe that, I think I might understand why.

Consider the story of the Canaanite mother in the New Testament. This desperate mom came to Jesus with a plea for help for her afflicted daughter. In doing so she took a tremendous risk. Even though she was a pagan (the Canaanites were pagans), she approached Jesus amid a group of religious people and pleaded for help for her daughter. Almost unbelievably, "Jesus did not answer a word" in response to her anguish (Matthew 15:23).

Sometimes God is silent when we are screaming most loudly for His answers and His presence. I'm not wise enough to explain God's silence in your crisis. But I can say from experience that you are right: Sometimes He is silent.

The desperate mother in Matthew's gospel did not stop begging and pleading for Jesus's intervention. When He finally replied, he said something that probably made no sense to the woman asking for His help: "I was sent only to the lost sheep of Israel... It is not right to take children's bread and toss it to their dogs" (verses 24,26).

What was Jesus saying here? Can this be true? Was Jesus so mean and heartless that He would call this mother a "dog" and let her suffer in fear and humiliation?

As I have studied this story, I have come to see that Jesus never called her a dog, but I believe He was setting a context for her faith to grow—a context of silence and suffering.

Are you there right now, in the midst of silence and suffering, wondering what kind of God allows such pain and humiliation? Consider that your daughter's struggle can be the context for your own growth and transformation as well as hers. We can learn much from this woman who apparently wasn't as pagan as the community she came from, for in the midst of silence and suffering, she humbly approached Jesus yet again. "Lord," she said, "even the dogs eat the crumbs that fall from their masters' table" (verse 27).

Martin Luther gave an explanation of this confusing text:

[The Canaanite mother] asks nothing more than that he let her be a dog. [Only desperate mothers understand why a woman would be willing to humiliate herself for the sake of her own daughter.] Therefore Christ now completely opens his heart to her and yields to her will, so that she is now no dog, but even a child of Israel. Now whoever understands here the actions of this poor woman...says, "Lord, it is true, I am a sinner and not worthy of thy grace; but still thou has promised sinners forgiveness, and thou art come not to call the righteous, but as St. Paul says in 1 Timothy...'to save sinners.'"[4]

Are you still feeling a bit dubious, even after Luther's explanation? I have not met a parent with a child in crisis who has not cried out to God, "How can You let this happen?! Why won't You answer? How long must we all suffer?"

I believe that what happens in the story of the Canaanite mother answers all of these questions. What must happen in our children who struggle and get ensnared by drugs and alcohol must happen in *us* as well. We are going to be far more powerful in our children's lives if we trust God's work in and around and through all of the problems. If we surrender *first,* then we can truly be allies in helping our daughters with their battles against drugs and alcohol.

Brennan Manning, one of my favorite writers, says it this way:

> Humble people are small in their own eyes, honest about their struggles, and open to constructive criticism.... They trust that they are loved, accepted, forgiven, and redeemed just as they are. Aware of their innate poverty, they throw themselves on the mercy of God with care-free abandon.[5]

And so we come to the conclusion (or new beginning) of the story of the Canaanite mother. "Then Jesus answered, 'Woman, you have great faith! Your request is granted.' And her daughter was healed from that very hour" (Matthew 15:28).

While I cannot promise that your daughter's drug and alcohol problems will be resolved quickly in response to intervention and treatment, I can promise that as you allow God to intervene through all means necessary, *you* will become a woman of great faith.

If this is not the final answer you were hoping for, hang on a little longer. I have more encouragement for you. Don't put this book down until you read the conclusion.

That is why, if we keep clamouring for things we want from God, we may often find ourselves disappointed.... We had thought of God as the dispenser of all the good things we would possibly desire; but in a very real sense, God has nothing to give at all except himself.

—SIMON TUGWELL, *Prayer: Living with God*

Hope and Healing

We don't yet see things clearly. We're squinting in a fog, peering through a mist. But it won't be long before the weather clears and the sun shines bright! We'll see it all then, see it all as clearly as God sees us, knowing him directly just as he knows us!

—1 Corinthians 13:12, *The Message*

I sat in my living room with a group of eight moms. These were "brave-heart" moms who had been or were in the midst of the heartache and horribleness of loving a child who is using drugs or alcohol. They each described their moments of hopefulness and hurt while trying to help a difficult daughter. It was two weeks before Easter, so my mind meandered to the Passion story. Thinking of that frightening, fear-filled night before the unfolding events of Christ's crucifixion and resurrection, I said, "It sounds like it has been 'Friday night' for you for a long time."

One thoughtful mother mused, "No, I think it's more like being in the tomb. You know something unthinkable has happened, but you're not sure what it means and if or how it's ever going to end."

I think of her words whenever I meet a mom who is shattered and scared because her daughter is using alcohol or drugs. I know she's been hurt, she's in shock, she may feel suffocated, and she has very little vision for the future—for herself or her daughter. Perhaps you're there, in the deafening silence and overwhelming emptiness of the tomb.

Part of the privilege of working with others is that, by now, I have a PhD in human suffering. I have listened to many stories and seen the ways children can hurt their parents and themselves and the ways parents, in turn, can help or hurt their children. I have learned vicariously what mistakes not to make, what mistakes are inevitable, and what can actually make a difference. I have witnessed the train wrecks that follow parents who refuse to acknowledge that their child might have a problem. I have seen exhausted and furious parents try to control their daughter and everything in her world. I have seen parents love their children wisely and unconditionally and watched their children hurt them deeply. And I have seen girls who were headed for certain destruction grab hold of their mother's worn and shaking hand and change directions.

I have acquired a tuition-free education in the consequences of various choices and in the possibility of true change when everything seems hopeless. Sometimes my mother or my friends will ask if it's depressing listening to people's struggles all day long. I tell them, "Quite the contrary. My work is a way of exploring pain and confusion to produce meaning and hope."

As you finish reading this book, I want you to walk forward with great hope. Since hope seems more real to me when it comes in the form of a story, I want to finish some of the stories I began in this book to encourage you to hang on, to try one more time, to keep praying, and to believe the wise and wonderful words of Frederick Buechner: that grace is what happens when "[it] can't possibly happen because it can only impossibly happen and happens in the dark that only just barely fails to swallow it up."[1]

REGRESSION

I ended up in therapy myself shortly after the events began unfolding that would lead to a divorce. I moaned to my therapist, "I can't think, can't pray, and can't believe that I will ever experience another good day."

She wisely answered, "Sharon, during stressful times people regress to their worst behaviors."

Something in her words gave me hope. I guess her words allowed me to acknowledge that I was under stress, that I was human, and that I was not alone.

If your daughter is using alcohol or drugs, you are under stress. Researchers have discovered that a home with a rebellious child has *75 percent* more stress than a home with a less difficult child.[2] I hope that offers you some relief. When your home is under the stress of a teenager using drugs or alcohol, you *are* more likely to yell, say things you don't mean, threaten ridiculous consequences, think about running away, and pretend that some things never happened. There's something about a struggling child that is intended to reveal our humanness—that we don't know exactly what to do all the time, and neither does anyone else. We all "labour and are heavy laden" under the yoke of being human (Matthew 11:28, KJV).

I hope that reading this book has not discouraged you. I hope, instead, that it has armed you with information, and I hope it has given you permission to tell the truth about yourself and your life. *Holding it all in and keeping it all secret are the biggest mistakes Christian parents make!* I understand your agony. I've experienced it, in part, and walked through it with many families. Please consider this next statement: *The bad news that your daughter is struggling and that you are struggling too makes way for the good news that you alone can't change her and that you don't have to be in this alone.* If you don't do anything else with this book, I urge you to take this one piece of advice: Tell someone else what is going on in your life. Acknowledge your mistakes and confusion, ask for prayer and support, inquire of others who have been through dark days with their children, and fill your life with positive people.

In chapter 4 I told you about Carol and her daughter Blair. Carol was the mom who threw all of her deck furniture into the backyard in frustration over her daughter's marijuana use. She also stalked the drug dealers and worked really hard on improving and changing her relationship with her daughter. As I mentioned earlier, Blair continued to be tempted to use marijuana. Even after Carol and her daughter started attending Twelve Step meetings, Blair made a huge mistake. She got arrested for smoking pot in the parking lot of a local mall. Once again Carol converted this moment of truth into a moment that mattered initially for her own well-being, but ultimately for Blair's as well.

When Blair was arrested, Carol threw all her caution to the wind and called five of her closest friends. She told them everything that had been going on over the past several months with Blair and asked them to form a "task force" to support her during the continuing storm. She asked one friend to be in charge of prayer and to organize and remind others to pray for her and Blair. She asked another friend, who was proficient on the computer, to research treatment options. She asked another friend to look out for her two younger children and remind her of their needs. She asked another friend to pray for her marriage, and she asked if she and her husband could get together occasionally with this friend and her husband, not just to talk about Blair, but to have fun and sometimes get their minds off Blair. She asked the fifth member of the task force to be her encourager—to send her notes, jokes, and anything else that would help her during these dark days.

Throughout the rest of high school, Blair continued in an off-again-on-again relationship with marijuana, and Carol continued in relationship with her five friends. She told me, "They wove a blanket that kept me from freezing." As Blair approached graduation, her interest in marijuana and her pot-smoking friends seemed to wane. And when Blair left for college in the fall, she and her mother had cemented a good relationship, and Blair seemed to be headed in a healthy direction.

"It's kind of a mystery to me what changed her," Carol explained to me, "but it's not a mystery what enabled me to survive: my task force of friends."

I believe that Carol's friends kept her afloat, and her steady presence in the midst of Blair's storm kept Blair from being swept out to sea. I love the poem by W. B. Yeats titled "A Prayer for My Daughter." Yeats describes the "mysterious connection" that remains even though (and sometimes *because*) we fail and falter but hang in there—together:

> Hearts are not had as a gift,
> But hearts are earned
> By those that are not entirely beautiful.[3]

I hope you know by now that I am not one to simplify and spiritualize complicated, tricky situations. I don't like spiritual platitudes, and carelessly flung scriptures discourage me as much as I suspect they do you. But I have learned that there is something about the awfulness and agony of a child in trouble that makes us cling to our faith, perhaps as never before.

During the days before Christ's death, His disciples certainly regressed and "re-regressed" to some of their worst behaviors: doubting, condemning, betraying, and hiding. Jesus wisely and compassionately understood that they were in turmoil. He watched the masses hail Him with palm leaves and adoration and then run from Him in fear and misunderstanding.

At one point in His ministry, Jesus turned to His closest followers and asked, "You do not want to leave too, do you?" (John 6:67). I love Peter's answer, and it reminds me of many mothers I have known who have been caught in the confusion and turmoil of their daughter's use of drugs. Peter turned to Jesus and said, "Lord, to whom shall we go?" (verse 68). I think it was the apostle's way of saying, "Lord, we don't have anyone but You, and if we let go of You, we will surely be lost."

So how do you turn to Jesus when your daughter's behavior shouts so loudly that you can't hear Him, when your own fear surpasses your love for your daughter, or when your guilt and shame about being a "bad mother" keep you from feeling the warmth of His presence?

Sadly, for many Christians the rich experience of forgiveness takes place only at salvation. No wonder our hearts grow cold, resentful, and eke out mere pittances of love. The gift of my addiction to alcohol was a radical experience of forgiveness and a heart open to a continual awareness of my foolishness and my need for God's mercy and grace.

—SHARON HERSH, *Bravehearts*

In chapter 3 I told you about Krista, who had been squeezed in the vise of peer pressure, had sex with her boyfriend, and then began drinking after her boyfriend broke up with her. Krista's mom learned not only about Krista's sexual behavior and alcohol use during counseling but also that Krista was still suffering from the effects of childhood sexual abuse. That's a lot for any mom to handle.

Krista's mom admitted to me that she was embarrassed, mad at Krista, and overwhelmed with helplessness regarding her daughter. After about two months of working primarily with Krista and sometimes with her mom, they came to see me together. They had been on a weeklong vacation, and they looked tan, relaxed, and comfortable in each other's presence. I couldn't help but comment on their apparent connection to each other.

"Wow, it looks like vacation agreed with you two!"

Krista explained to me, "The vacation was great, but something good is going on with Mom and me. I can't explain it, but we're friends again."

After our session I asked to speak with Krista's mom alone. I asked, more for my sake than hers, "What *did* happen between the two of you?"

I will never forget her answer: "I turned to my faith. I mean I *really* believed in the gospel story for *my* life. Every day I would pray to God and complain about Krista and her behavior and my pain. Slowly, I began to hear God say to me, 'Forgive her.' I didn't know what He meant. She wasn't asking for forgiveness, and she was still making bad choices. I would moan and cry and rage and complain, and He would still say, 'Forgive her.' One day I was reading in John 7 about the woman caught in adultery. That morning I had yelled at Krista and told her that I didn't believe a word out of her mouth and never would! As I read about this accused woman, I felt caught in my own anger and contempt. For once I read the words of Jesus as if they had to do with *me*, not my wayward daughter:

> " 'If any one of you is without sin, let him be the first to throw a stone
> at her....' At this, those who heard began to go away one at a time, the
> older ones first, until only Jesus was left, with the woman still standing
> there. Jesus straightened up and asked her, 'Woman, where are they?
> Has no one condemned you?... Then neither do I condemn you....
> Go now and leave your life of sin.' " (John 8:7,9-11)

Krista's mom read me the scriptures and finished her story of hope. "It's still kind of a mystery to me, but when I forgave Krista for embarrassing me, hurting me, and scaring me, it's almost as if she was released to come back to me. Forgiving her not only set me free, but it set her free too!"

Both Krista's mom and Blair's mom talked about the "mystery" of connection. After hearing hundreds of mothers' stories, I acknowledge that it is a mystery *how* it works, but there is no mystery that it *does* in fact work. We were made to be connected to one another and to God. When that connection is broken, we ourselves are broken. When connection is restored, healing begins.

In my book *Bravehearts,* I tell of my own encounter with God and my experience of His forgiveness *because* of my addiction to alcohol. Our failures—both in mothering and in life—can become the context for understanding God's forgiveness, offering our forgiveness to our children, and, in turn, inviting them to connect with God.

RELEASE

When the eight "braveheart" moms and I met to talk about mothering, we acknowledged that we had all regressed during stressful times with our children. We cried together and laughed at our foibles and failings. One mom talked about waking up in the middle of the night fearing that her daughter and her three houseguests had all been drinking. After all, her daughter had struggled with the temptation to drink and had not really "proven" herself with regard to this challenge. This mom woke everyone up at 3:00 a.m. and made them all take a Breathalyzer test. Both she and her daughter were embarrassed when everyone passed the test, proving that there had been no alcohol use. But this mom decided that rather than dissolving into guilt and apology, she would be matter-of-fact and make a quick exit. She said, "Well, thank you very much for passing our routine Breathalyzer check. There will be chocolate-chip pancakes in the morning. Good night!"

Acceptance does not mean we're giving our approval. It does not mean surrendering to the will and plans of another. It does not mean commitment. It is not forever. It is for the present moment. Acceptance does not make things hard, it makes things easier. Acceptance does not mean we accept abuse and mistreatment; it does not mean we forego ourselves, our boundaries, hopes, dreams, desires, or wants. It means we accept what is, so we know what to do to take care of ourselves and what boundaries we need to set. It means we accept what is and who we are at the moment, so we are free to change and grow.

—MELODY BEATTIE, *The Language of Letting Go*

The moms agreed that one of the hardest things about *waiting* for Sunday morning and resurrection was that change didn't always come in the ways they predicted or wanted. They all explained to me that there came a time when they just had to let go of their plans, their agendas, and their daughters.

In chapter 11 I told you about Lois, the mom who decided to send her daughter to inpatient treatment. Over the past ten months, I have watched Lois miss her daughter fiercely, doubt her own decision, and let go of Lindsey. She told me about seeing pictures, artwork, and "evidence" of Lindsey everywhere in their home. She recalled reaching for a glass in the cupboard and seeing a cup Lindsey had made in the second grade that had "I love my mom" scrawled in seven-year-old letters on the side. Lindsey is still struggling intensely, and the treatment facility has recommended that she stay another ten months. Lois tried to describe these dark days of deciding whether to let Lindsey stay ten more months and about the guilt she felt for not being "there" for her daughter.

"Woman," he said, "why are you crying? Who is it you are looking for?"
Thinking he was the gardener, she said, "Sir, if you have carried him away,
tell me where you have put him, and I will get him."
Jesus said to her, "Mary."
She turned toward him and cried out in Aramaic, "Rabboni!"

—John 20:15-16

We took a break from the agonizing conversation about Lindsey to talk about "lighter" matters. I told her about my swimming lessons and how difficult it was for me to resist panic while swimming in the open water. I finally surrendered and requested a "swim angel" for the upcoming triathlon. The swim angel would swim by my side throughout the race, encourage me, and keep me from going too far off course.

Lois began to cry. "That's what I need," she said. "A 'parent angel' to tell me what to do."

"Perhaps the counselors in this treatment program are your 'parent angels,'" I suggested gently. "Maybe you need to let go again."

I saw Lois just a few days ago. She is a woman of wisdom and compassion, which come from heartache and courageous living. She told me she and her husband had decided to keep Lindsey in treatment for ten more months. She said, "Every day I get up and let go and trust that there is Someone who knows more than I do to keep us from going too far off course."

I thought again of the story of Christ's Passion. Even after Sunday morning and the empty tomb, Jesus's followers were confused as to how this awful story would be redeemed. They had the strange words of Jesus echoing in their ears about destroying a temple and rebuilding it in three days. I imagine that they each had pictures in their minds—their own agendas—of what redemption would look like. Even Jesus's closest followers almost missed Him.

Can a mother forget the baby at her breast
and have no compassion on the child she has borne?
Though she may forget, I will not forget you!
See, I have engraved you on the palms
of my hands.

—ISAIAH 49:15-16

Letting go will look different for every mom. You may have to let go of your idea of who your daughter was going to be. Perhaps you need to let go of covering for her or trying to fix her life. Maybe you need to let go of trying to control everything. Or maybe, like Lois, you need to let go of having things work out in your way and your time.

I could not "let go" in swimming unless I knew someone was there beside me. Likewise, we can't let go in mothering unless we are convinced that Someone, who is wiser, more loving, more compassionate, and more committed to our daughters' well-being than we are, is there beside us.

REDEMPTION

These verses in Isaiah have special meaning to me. I have written before about my own mother's dark night of mothering when my brother, addicted to cocaine, stole thousands of dollars from her bank account. Even now I marvel at her faith in the midst of such terrible times.

I stood with my mom in the Jefferson County district attorney's office as she pressed charges against her own son. Her hand shook as she signed the paperwork, and then she did the strangest thing. She wrote on her hand.

I asked her, "Mom, what are you writing?"

She explained, "I am writing the number of your brother's arrest warrant. It's all I know about him right now."

It took me many years of living and mothering to understand her actions and see in them the image of the One who writes our name on His hands, even when we are making bad choices, heading away from Him, or harming ourselves and others.

In chapter 5 I told you about my own son, Graham, and his experimentation with marijuana. I have learned about regression firsthand as I've been sleepless with worry and ineffective in talking to him about drugs. I've learned about release as I've had to let go many times and trust Graham to the consequences we've put in place as well as to supernatural consequences that I'm not in control of at all. And I am learning about redemption. Oh, how I am learning. I could never have imagined on that day at the Jefferson County DA's office that fifteen years later, when my life fell apart and my teenage son desperately needed a man in his life, my brother, Jim—that once wayward prodigal—would be my prodigal's mentor, friend, and the one who is talking to him of faith and loving him during a hard and lonely time.

Redemption seldom happens exactly as we think it will. But it does happen. I remind myself often of Eugene Peterson's paraphrase of Galatians 3:3: "For only crazy people would think they could complete by their own efforts what was begun by God." I have been crazy, thinking it was all up to me. But in the midst of turmoil, sanity has come in the reminder that God *is always* working in and around and through our foolish schemes and shattered dreams.

RESURRECTION

Without the Crucifixion, there would have been no Easter morning. Without our failings and sinfulness, there would be no redemption. Without our children's waywardness, we might never seek direction. I encourage you, if you are in the dark of Friday night or in the tomb of in-between, that all is not lost. But redemption may not be found according to your plans or your schedule. Perhaps the best place to begin to find hope is in looking at your own heart, not your daughter's. I imagine that since you started on this journey to mother your difficult daughter, you have become wiser, more compassionate, fiercer, more loving, and more committed in your relationship to her than ever. Look inside and see that redemption is already taking place.

During my early adult years, we lived in Winston-Salem, North Carolina, the home to a Moravian village that provides a glimpse into a time and tradition long past. Our first year in Winston-Salem, we heard about the Easter service the Moravians hosted and, with some hesitations, decided to attend. We were not going to church at the time, and the thought of dragging ourselves out of bed before sunrise seemed dreadful. I also harbored suspicions that the Moravians might be a cult.

So we're not giving up. How could we! Even though on the outside it often looks like things are falling apart on us, on the inside, where God is making new life, not a day goes by without his unfolding grace.... There's far more here than meets the eye. The things we see now are here today, gone tomorrow. But the things we can't see now will last forever.

—2 CORINTHIANS 4:16-18, MSG

We arrived, however, just before the sun came up, along with what seemed like most of the people in town. I was stunned at the complete silence with which everyone stood in the dark. When the first rays of sun met the unlit morning, a trumpet fanfare filled the air. And then an echo of voices floated back and forth in the crowd as "He is risen! He is risen!" was repeated again and again.

Tears filled my eyes as I thought, *What if it's true? What if He really has risen?* I have asked that question in various forms so many times—when facing my own addiction, when my family fell apart, when my children questioned their faith, when my daughter left for college, and when my son smoked marijuana. And I've asked that question with others facing the agony of their own struggles. It is a way of asking, "Are we alone here? Can anyone save us?" The answer to the second question is, "Of course." Because at the most bloodthirsty moment in history, Someone saved us all by transforming an unspeakably horrible abyss into an empty tomb.

Hope rises anew every day in the midst of individual stories of redemption. The teenager tempted and tormented by drugs and yet open to change and recovery, and the mother wearied and worn by parenting and yet getting up another morning to love her child—both give resurrection a face.

Finding a Counselor

As you walk hand in hand with your daughter, encouraging her to resist the temptations of drugs and alcohol while she develops a healthy self-image, you and your daughter may need to talk with a counselor. The best counseling will not replace your relationship with your daughter but will enhance it by providing insight and guidance to strengthen your alliance. Listed below are some tips for finding the best counselor and some suggestions when insurance or income is not available to cover the costs of counseling.

- The best referrals come from those who have been through a similar struggle. If you don't know of anyone whose daughter has struggled with emotional development, depression, or substance abuse, contact youth pastors and/or school counselors and ask them if they can help you locate other parents who have sought counseling and help for their daughters.
- Contact your health-insurance carrier for a list of providers and information about how many therapy sessions they will pay for (both individual and family) and how much they will pay.
- Interview at least three therapists (with your daughter) before choosing a counselor. It is important that your daughter feel that she is part of the process for choosing who will help her.
- Choose a therapist whose work focuses primarily on adolescents.
- When you interview the counselor, explain that you want to be involved in your daughter's recovery, and ask the therapist how he or she will incorporate you into the process.
- If insurance is not available and money is tight, ask the counselor if you can pay on a sliding scale. Many therapists will slide their fees to correspond with your income.
- Ask your church about a counseling support fund. Sometimes a church will pay half of the counseling fee while you pay the other half.
- If counseling is out of the question due to your financial situation, look for a support group in your community. Even if you are in counseling, a good Twelve Step program like Alcoholics Anonymous,

Al-Anon, or Narcotics Anonymous can be an invaluable resource for
information and support.

- Contact the National Mental Health Association Information Center
  for referrals to local support groups and/or community resources:
  1-800-969-NMHA.
- Check with your local hospital regarding educational meetings about
  adolescent emotional development and/or substance abuse and
  recovery.
- To find a physician who specializes in addiction, contact the American
  Society of Addiction Medicine: *www.asam.org.*
- The Addiction Resource Guide provides detailed information about
  treatment programs: *www.addictionresourceguide.com.*
- The Substance Abuse Mental Health Services Administration provides
  a "treatment locator" on its Web site: *http://findtreatment.samhsa.gov.*
- The National Council on Alcoholism and Drug Dependence offers
  help lines for crisis counseling and information about intervention and
  treatment. Call 1-800-475-HOPE.

Resources

The following resources may not reflect all of your beliefs and values. I have listed them as a source of information, but they should be reviewed and evaluated before you decide to make them available to your daughter.

Addiction

Addiction and Grace: Love and Spirituality in the Healing of Addictions. Gerald G. May. New York: HarperCollins, 1988.

Change Your Brain Change Your Life: The Breakthrough Program for Conquering Anxiety, Depression, Obsessiveness, Anger, and Impulsiveness. Daniel G. Amen. New York: Three Rivers Press, 1998.

Other Resources

National Council on Alcoholism and Drug Dependence: 1-800-NCA-CALL; *www.ncadd.org.*

National Institute on Alcohol Abuse and Alcoholism: *www.niaaa.nih.gov.*

National Institute on Drug Abuse: *www.nida.nih.gov.*

Substance Abuse and Mental Health Services Administration: *www.samhsa.gov.*

Alcohol and Alcoholism

Alcohol and the Addictive Brain. Kenneth Blum. New York: Free Press, 1991.

Alcoholics Anonymous: The Story of How Many Thousands of Men and Women Have Recovered from Alcoholism. 4th ed. New York: Alcoholics Anonymous World Services, 2002.

Drinking: A Love Story. Caroline Knapp. New York: Dial Press, 1996.

Other Resources

Alcoholics Anonymous: *www.alcoholics-anonymous.org.*

Breath Alcohol Home Test Kits: Available online at *www.mrstest.com* and *www.homedrugtestingkit.com.*

The National Clearinghouse for Alcohol and Drug Information: *www.healthfinder.gov/.orgs/HR0027.htm.*

ANXIETY

The Hidden Face of Shyness: Understanding and Overcoming Social Anxiety.
    Franklin R. Schneier and Lawrence Welkowitz. New York: Avon Books,
    1996.
The Highly Sensitive Person: How to Thrive When the World Overwhelms You.
    Elaine N. Aron. New York: Broadway Books, 1996.
*The Shyness and Social Anxiety Workbook: Proven Techniques for Overcoming Your
    Fears.* Martin M. Antony and Richard P. Swinson. Oakland, CA: New Har-
    binger, 2000.
Thoughts and Feelings: Taking Control of Your Moods and Your Life. Matthew
    McKay, Martha Davis, and Patrick Fanning. Oakland, CA: New Harbinger,
    1997.

Other Resources
Anxiety Disorders Association of America: *www.adaa.org.*
Freedom From Fear: *ffnadsd@aol.com.*

DEPRESSION

Depression Is the Pits, but I'm Getting Better: A Guide for Adolescents. E. Jane
    Garland. Washington, DC: American Psychological Association,
    1998.
*"Help Me, I'm Sad": Recognizing, Treating, and Preventing Childhood and Adoles-
    cent Depression.* David G. Fassler. New York: Penguin, 1998.
More than Moody: Recognizing and Treating Adolescent Depression. Harold S.
    Koplewicz. New York: Penguin, 2002.
Moving Beyond Depression: A Whole-Person Approach to Healing. Gregory L.
    Jantz. Colorado Springs: Shaw, 2003.
Overcoming Teen Depression: A Guide for Parents. Miriam Kaufman. New York:
    Firefly Books, 2001.

DRUGS

*Buzzed: The Straight Facts About the Most Used and Abused Drugs from Alcohol to
    Ecstasy.* Cynthia Kuhn, Scott Swartzwelder, and Wilkie Wilson. New York:
    W. W. Norton, 1998.

Dangerous Drugs: An Easy-to-Use Reference for Parents and Professionals. Carol Falkowski. Center City, MN: Hazelden, 2003.

Dirty: A Search for Answers Inside America's Teenage Drug Epidemic. Meredith Maran. San Francisco: HarperCollins, 2003.

Ecstasy: The Complete Guide: A Comprehensive Look at the Risks and Benefits of MDMA. Julie Holland, ed. Rochester, VT: Inner Traditions, 2001.

More, Now Again, A Memoir of Addiction. Elizabeth Wurtzel. New York: Simon & Schuster, 2002.

Other Resources

Home Drug Testing Kits: Available online at *www.mrstest.com* and *www.homedrugtestingkit.com.*

Narcotics Anonymous: *www.na.org.*

PARENTING

Alcohol: What's a Parent to Believe. Stephen G. Biddulph. Center City, MN: Hazelden, 2003.

Another Chance: Hope and Health for the Alcoholic Family. Sharon Wegsheider-Cruse. Palo Alto, CA: Science and Behavior Books, 1989.

The Epidemic: The Rot of American Culture, Absentee and Permissive Parenting, and the Resultant Plague of Joyless, Selfish Children. Robert Shaw. New York: Regan Books, 2003.

Leadership and Self-Deception: Getting Out of the Box. Arbinger Institute. San Francisco: Berbett-Koehler, 2000.

The Language of Letting Go: Daily Meditations for Codependents. Melody Beattie. New York: Fine Communications, 1990.

"Mom, I Hate My Life!": Becoming Your Daughter's Ally Through the Emotional Ups and Downs of Adolescence. Sharon A. Hersh. Colorado Springs: Shaw, 2004.

The Second Family: Reckoning with Adolescent Power. Ron Taffel. New York: St. Martin's Press, 2001.

SMOKING

Smoking: The Artificial Passion. David Krogh. New York: W. H. Freeman, 1991.

SUBSTANCE ABUSE

Changing for Good: A Revolutionary Six-Stage Program for Overcoming Bad Habits and Moving Your Life Positively Forward. James O. Prochaska, John Norcross, and Carlo DiClemente. New York: Quill, 2002.

Educating Yourself About Alcohol and Drugs: A People's Primer. Marc A. Schuckit. New York: Plenum Press, 1995.

Teens Under the Influence: The Truth About Kids, Alcohol, and Other Drugs—How to Recognize the Problem and What to Do About It. Katherine Ketcham and Nicholas A. Pace. New York: Ballantine, 2003.

TREATMENT

Alcoholics Anonymous. New York: Alcoholics Anonymous World Services, 2001.

Getting Them Sober: You Can Help. Toby Rice Drews. Deerfield Beach, FL: Health Communications, 1998.

It Works How and Why: The Twelve Steps and the Twelve Traditions of Narcotics Anonymous. Chatsworth, CA: Narcotics Anonymous World Services, 1993.

Love First: A New Approach to Intervention for Alcoholism and Drug Addiction. Jeff Jay and Debra Jay. Center City, MN: Hazelden, 2000.

Narcotics Anonymous. Van Nuys, CA: World Service Office, 1988.

Other Resources

Addiction Resource Guide: *www.addictionresourceguide.com.*

American Medical Association "doctor finder": *www.amaassn.org/aps/amahg.html.*

American Society of Addiction Medicine, 4601 North Park Ave., Arcade Suite 101, Chevy Chase, MD, 20815; 301-656-3920; *www.asam.org.*

National Council on Alcoholism and Drug Dependence: 1-800-NCA-CALL

The Substance Abuse Mental Health Services Administration "treatment locator": *http://findtreatment.samhsa.gov.*

"Treating Teens: A Guide to Adolescent Drug Problems": 202-289-0970; *www.drugstrategies.org/teens/programs.html.*

www.daytop.org/adolescent.html.

www.familiesanonymous.org.

www.phoenixhouse.org/treatment/adolesc.asp.

www.teenchallenge.com/main/centers/adolescent.cfm.

Notes

Introduction

1. See Meredith Maran, *Dirty: A Search for Answers Inside America's Teenage Drug Epidemic* (San Francisco: HarperCollins, 2003), 8.
2. See Katherine Ketcham and Nicholas A. Pace, *Teens Under the Influence: The Truth About Kids, Alcohol, and Other Drugs—How to Recognize the Problem and What to Do About It* (New York: Ballantine, 2003), 70-71.

Chapter 1

1. See Christopher Collins, comp., "Girls and Substance Use," Girl's Incorporated Fact Sheet (2002): 2; www.girlsinc-alameda.org/facts/factsheet1.htm.
2. Greater Dallas Council on Alcohol & Drug Abuse, "Girls More Prone to Alcohol, Drug Abuse," (2002), www.gdcada.org/stories/girls.htm.
3. See Meredith Maran, *Dirty: A Search for Answers Inside America's Teenage Drug Epidemic* (San Francisco: HarperCollins, 2003), 289-90.
4. See Karen Springen and Barbara Kantrowitz, "Alcohol's Deadly Triple Threat," *Newsweek*, May 17, 2004, 2.
5. See Maran, *Dirty*, 9.
6. See Substance Abuse & Mental Health Services Administration, *2000 National Household Survey on Drug Abuse*, www.samhsa.gov.
7. Greater Dallas Council, "Girls More Prone."

Chapter 2

1. J. Bachman and P. O'Malley, "Monitoring the Future: National Results on Adolescent Drug Use," in The Office of National Drug Control Policy, *National Drug Control Strategy: 2000 Annual Report* (Washington, DC: US Government Printing Office, 2000), 97.
2. Mary Pipher, *The Shelter of Each Other: Rebuilding Our Families* (New York: Putnam, 1996), 130.

Chapter 3

1. Bruce Simons-Morton, National Institutes of Health 2001 study, quoted in Associated Press, "Girls Feel More Pressure to Drink," *CBSNews.com,* January 23, 2001, www.cbsnews.com/stories/2001/01/23/national/main266323.shtml.
2. Rosalind Wiseman, *Queen Bees and Wannabes: Helping Your Daughter Survive Cliques, Gossip, Boyfriends, and Other Realities of Adolescence* (New York: Crown, 2003), 280-81.
3. This phrase was coined by Ron Taffel, *The Second Family: Reckoning with Adolescent Power* (New York: St. Martin's Press, 2001).
4. Dean Borgman, *When Kumbaya Is Not Enough: A Practical Theology for Youth Ministry* (Peabody, MA: Hendrickson, 1997), 75.
5. Taffel, *Second Family,* 46.
6. Taffel, *Second Family,* 118.
7. U.S. Department of Health and Human Services, National Institute on Drug Abuse, "Alcohol Use and Alcohol Problems in Women: Epidemiological Trends," *Research Monograph* 132 (1993): 30, www.health.org/govpubs/ml011.

Chapter 4

1. Bruce Simons-Morton, National Institutes of Health 2001 study, quoted in Associated Press, "Girls Feel More Pressure to Drink," *CBSNews.com,* January 23, 2001, www.cbsnews.com/stories/2001/01/23/national/main266323.shtml.
2. See Substance Abuse and Mental Health Services Administration, *2001 National Household Survey on Drug Abuse* (Rockville, MD: U.S. Department of Health and Human Services, 2001).
3. Ron Taffel, *The Second Family: Reckoning with Adolescent Power* (New York: St. Martin's Press, 2001), 38.
4. See Cynthia Kuhn, Scott Swartzwelder, and Wilkie Wilson, *Buzzed: The Straight Facts About the Most Used and Abused Drugs from Alcohol to Ecstasy* (New York: W.W. Norton, 1998), 25.
5. See Substance Abuse and Mental Health Services Administration, *1999 National Household Survey on Drug Abuse,* Summary of Findings (Rockville, MD: U.S. Department of Health and Human Services, 1999).

6. Greater Dallas Council on Alcohol & Drug Abuse, "Girls More Prone to Alcohol, Drug Abuse," (2002), www.gdcada.org/stories/girls.htm.

7. See Terri Apter, *The Myth of Maturity: What Teenagers Need from Parents to Become Adults* (New York: W.W. Norton, 2001), 40-41.

CHAPTER 5

1. Katherine Ketcham and Nicholas A. Pace, *Teens Under the Influence: The Truth About Kids, Alcohol, and Other Drugs—How to Recognize the Problem and What to Do About It* (New York: Ballantine, 2003), xiii.

2. See Ketcham and Pace, *Teens Under the Influence,* 92.

3. Marcel Danesi, *Cool: The Signs and Meaning of Adolescence* (Toronto: University of Toronto Press, 1994), 118.

4. See Danesi, *Cool,* 90.

5. See Ketcham and Pace, *Teens Under the Influence,* 70-71.

6. See Rachel Simmons, *Odd Girl Out: The Hidden Culture of Agression in Girls* (San Diego, CA: Harcourt, 2002), 179-83.

7. See Ketcham and Pace, *Teens Under the Influence,* 71.

8. See Cynthia Kuhn, Scott Swartzwelder, and Wilkie Wilson, *Buzzed: The Straight Facts About the Most Used and Abused Drugs from Alcohol to Ecstasy* (New York: W. W. Norton, 1998), 123.

9. See Ron Taffel, *The Second Family: Reckoning with Adolescent Power* (New York: St. Martin's Press, 2001), 19.

10. Linkin Park, "In the End," *Frat Party at the Pankake Festival,* copyright © 2000, Warner Brothers Records.

11. Sharon Hersh, *Bravehearts: Unlocking the Courage to Love with Abandon* (Colorado Springs: WaterBrook, 2000), 174.

12. Statistics from Susan Flagler, "Teenage Girls and Smoking," The National Center for Tobacco-Free Kids, January 3, 2002, www.tobacco freekids.org/research/factsheets.

13. Peter Hiett, "Why Jesus Rose from the Dead" (sermon, Lookout Mountain Community Church, Golden, CO, May 2, 2004).

14. C. S. Lewis, *The Magician's Nephew* (New York: Collier Books, 1955), 171.

15. C. S. Lewis, *The Last Battle* (New York: Collier Books, 1956), 148.

16. Hiett, "Why Jesus Rose from the Dead."

CHAPTER 6

1. See Kira Vermond, "Where There's Smoke, There Are Teenage Girls," *National Post Online,* April 2004, 1.
2. See University of Washington Women's Health, "Teenage Girls and Smoking: Fact Sheet for Providers," April 2004.
3. Dr. Elinor Wilson, quoted in Vermond, "Where There's Smoke," 2.
4. See Kaori Honjo, PhD, Okayama University, in Jeanie Lerche Davis, "Girls May Smoke to Stay Thin," *WebMD Medical News,* April 24, 2003, http://my.webmd.com/content/article/64/72236?src=Inktomi &condition=Weight%20Control.
5. See Katherine Ketcham and Nicholas A. Pace, *Teens Under the Influence: The Truth About Kids, Alcohol, and Other Drugs—How to Recognize the Problem and What to Do About It* (New York: Ballantine, 2003), 100.
6. David Krogh, *Smoking: The Artificial Passion* (New York: W. H. Freeman and Company, 1992), 97.
7. See Krogh, *Smoking,* 94.
8. Krogh, *Smoking,* 93.
9. See Ketcham and Pace, *Teens Under the Influence,* 92-98.

CHAPTER 7

1. See Greater Dallas Council on Alcohol & Drug Abuse, "Girls More Prone to Alcohol, Drug Abuse," (2002), www.gdcada.org/stories/ girls.htm.
2. Karen Springen and Barbara Kantrowitz, "Alcohol's Deadly Triple Threat," *Newsweek,* May 17, 2004, 2.
3. See Springen and Kantrowitz, "Alcohol's Deadly Triple Threat," 2.
4. See Katherine Ketcham and Nicholas A. Pace, *Teens Under the Influence: The Truth About Kids, Alcohol, and Other Drugs—How to Recognize the Problem and What to Do About It* (New York: Ballantine, 2003), 65.
5. Caroline Knapp, *Drinking: A Love Story* (New York: Dial Press, 1996), 7.
6. See Greater Dallas Council on Alcohol & Drug Abuse, "Girls More Prone to Alcohol, Drug Abuse," (2002), www.gdcada.org/stories/girls.htm.
7. See Jodie Morse, "Women on a Binge," *Time* 13 (2002): 159, www.time.com/time/2002/wdrinking/story.html.

8. See The Youth Risk Behavior Survey is conducted by the Centers for Disease Control and Prevention, www.cdc.gov.

9. Daniel G. Amen, *Change Your Brain, Change Your Life: The Breakthrough Program for Conquering Anxiety, Depression, Obsessiveness, Anger, and Impulsiveness* (New York: Three Rivers Press, 1998), 55, 71.

10. Ketcham and Pace, *Teens Under the Influence,* 74.

CHAPTER 8

1. See Michael T. Lynskey et al., "Escalation of Drug Use in Early-Onset Cannabis Users vs. Co-Twin Controls," *Journal of American Medical Association* 289, no. 4 (2003): 427-33.

2. This information is based upon the author's experience and understanding of adolescent girls and substance use as well as her broad research on this topic.

3. Graham Hersh, used by permission.

4. See Lynskey, "Escalation of Drug Use," 427-33.

5. See The Office of National Drug Control Policy, "Kids and Marijuana: The Facts." See www.mediacampaign.com/marijuana/kids_and_marijuana.html.

CHAPTER 9

1. Amy Herdy, "Frat Rite Tied to Death," *Denver Post,* September 23, 2004.

CHAPTER 10

1. Sharon A. Hersh, *Bravehearts: Unlocking the Courage to Love with Abandon* (Colorado Springs: WaterBrook, 2000), 90.

2. Karen Conterio and Wendy Lader, *Bodily Harm: The Breakthrough Healing Program for Self-Injurers* (New York: Hyperion, 1998), 22.

3. Dominic Maruca, "A Reflection on Guilt," *Human Development* 3, no. 1 (Spring 1982): 42.

4. Frederick Buechner, *Telling Secrets* (San Francisco: HarperSanFrancisco, 1991), 92-93.

5. M. J. Hyland, *How the Light Gets In* (New York: Canongate, 2003), 307.

CHAPTER 11

1. Carol Kent, *When I Lay My Isaac Down: Unshakable Faith in Unthinkable Circumstances* (Colorado Springs: NavPress, 2004), 12-13.

2. James Prochaska, John Norcross, and Carlo DiClemente, *Changing for Good: A Revolutionary Six-Stage Program for Overcoming Bad Habits and Moving Your Life Positively Forward* (New York: Quill, 2002), 96-97.

3. Katherine Ketcham and Nicholas A. Pace, *Teens Under the Influence: The Truth About Kids, Alcohol, and Other Drugs—How to Recognize the Problem and What to Do About It* (New York: Ballantine, 2003), 268-69.

4. Martin Luther, quoted in Donald A. Hagner *Word Biblical Commentary: Matthew 14–28*, vol. 33b (Nashville: Nelson, 1993), 43.

5. Brennan Manning, *Ruthless Trust: The Ragamuffin's Path to God* (New York: HarperCollins, 2000), 124.

CONCLUSION

1. Frederick Buechner, *Telling the Truth: The Gospel as Tragedy, Comedy, and Fairy Tale* (New York: HarperCollins, 1977), 58.

2. See Patricia Evans, *Teen Torment: Overcoming Verbal Abuse at Home and at School* (Avon, MA: Adams Media, 2003), 7.

3. W. B. Yeats, "A Prayer for My Daughter," *The Collected Poems of W. B. Yeats,* ed. Richard J. Finneran (New York: Macmillan, 1989).

ABOUT THE AUTHOR

SHARON HERSH is a licensed professional counselor and the director of Women's Recovery & Renewal, a ministry of counseling, retreat, and support services for struggling women. She is an adjunct professor in Addictions Counseling at Reformed Theological Seminary, Mars Hill Graduate School, and Colorado Christian University. She is the author of several books including *Bravehearts*, *"Mom, I Feel Fat!"* and *"Mom, I Hate My Life!"* She is a sought-after speaker for conferences and retreats. Sharon lives with her family in Lone Tree, Colorado.

Be your daughter's greatest ally

"Mom, *I hate my life!*"

Becoming your daughter's ally through the
emotional ups and downs of adolescence

sharon a. hersh

"Sharon Hersh lives and writes with brilliance, wisdom, and winsome wit. This book will allow you to encounter the depth of your daughter's adolescence with greater confidence and joy."
—DAN ALLENDER, author of *How Children Raise Parents*

"Mom, *I feel fat!*"

Becoming your daughter's ally
in developing a healthy body image

sharon a. hersh

FOREWORD BY DEBBIE SMITH
AFTERWORD BY NATALIE LARUE

"Mom,
Everyone Else Does!"

Becoming Your Daughter's Ally in Responding
to Peer Pressure to Drink, Smoke, and Use Drugs

sharon a. hersh

Navigating an adolescent daughter's emotional life is one of a mom's toughest challenges. A teenage girl's volatile emotions can seemingly toss her—and you—like a hurricane. When a scary external world and a turbulent internal world collide, the-result is sometimes overwhelming and confusing. Allow the Hand-in-Hand books to help you guide your daughter through her emotions and assure her you are truly on her side.